ONE FAITH, ONE LAW, ONE KING

French Armies of the Wars of Religion 1562–1598

T. J. O'Brien de Clare

Helion & Company

Pour ma chérie; à la lune et aux étoiles.

Et mon ami de bataille;
un chevalier sans peur et sans reproche.

Helion & Company Limited
Unit 8 Amherst Business Centre
Budbrooke Road
Warwick
CV34 5WE
England
Tel. 01926 499 619
Email: info@helion.co.uk
Website: www.helion.co.uk
Twitter: @helionbooks
Visit our blog http://blog.helion.co.uk/

Published by Helion & Company 2021
Designed and typeset by Serena Jones
Cover designed by Paul Hewitt, Battlefield Design (www.battlefield-design.co.uk)

Text, colour artwork and maps © T. J. O'Brien de Clare 2021
Black and white illustrations © as individually credited

ISBN 978-1-914059-70-4

British Library Cataloguing-in-Publication Data.
A catalogue record for this book is available from the British Library.

For details of other military history titles published by Helion & Company Limited, contact the above address, or visit our website: http://www.helion.co.uk

We always welcome receiving book proposals from prospective authors.

Contents

Introduction

During the latter half of the sixteenth century, the Kingdom of France was wracked by religious and factional disturbances that engendered 37 years of endemic violence. This period was repeatedly punctuated by larger scale conflicts. History has dignified these struggles with the title of the French Wars of Religion. Although their brutal massacres and notorious personalities are well established in cultural memory, and they have been thoroughly explored from religious, economic, social and political points of view, the wars have been relatively poorly served from a military perspective. Indeed, the prolific (and controversial) historian, Major General Fuller, dismissively stated that: 'Militarily, little is to be learnt from the French Wars of Religion'.[1] The most notable exception to this general dearth of interest, at least in English, is Wood's *The King's Army*, a detailed study of the royalist forces to 1576.[2]

This present work focuses on the native French troops that fought these Wars. Its goal is to provide the reader with an introduction as to how these troops were led, raised, organised, equipped, dressed, deployed and fought, so they may better understand the conduct of warfare in this period. Despite the inclusion of a summary of the course of the wars and their principal actions, this work is not intended to be a detailed military history of the conflicts. For this, the reader is directed to Knecht's *The French Civil Wars*, supplemented for military analysis and accounts of individual battles by the venerable, but still relevant, *The Art of War in the Sixteenth Century* by Oman.[3] My own contribution is not even an adequate treatment of all the armies that took part in the wars, since it deliberately excludes the Spanish, German, Italian, Albanian, English, Swiss and Dutch troops that played a major role in these affairs.

This work has two inspirations. Whilst studying for my Masters in Military History, I encountered The Perfect Captain, a group of Canadian game designers who altruistically donate the fruits of their labours to any who are interested, and only ask in return that one considers making a

---

1   John F C Fuller, *Armament and History* (London: Eyre and Spottiswoode, 1946), p.98.
2   James B Wood, *The King's Army: warfare, soldiers and society during the Wars of Religion in France, 1562–1576* (Cambridge: Cambridge University Press, 1996).
3   Robert J Knecht., *The French Civil Wars, 1562–1598* (London: Routledge, 2000). Oman, Charles., *A History of the Art of War in the Sixteenth Century* (London: Greenhill Books 1987).

small donation to a worthy cause.[4] They have produced a whole range of simulations that allow one to experience the unique nature of warfare in this period. The second inspiration comes from Ian Heath's *Armies of the Sixteenth Century*.[5] This clearly summarises information relating to the military forces of England, Scotland, Ireland, the United Provinces and the Spanish Netherlands during this period; but alas, to my frustration, not those of France. If this work consciously imitates some elements of the style of that volume, I hope that this is accepted as sincere flattery rather than mere lack of originality. Heath's work deals with most of the wars' foreign contingents not covered herein, Swiss and Italians excepted.

Initially created to satisfy my own curiosity, this work makes but limited pretence to original research. It is simply a synthesis of material drawn from a variety of published sources summarised into an accessible format. As such, it is far from the last word on the subject. Its intent is to provide an introduction and to simulate further debate and discovery into this neglected corner of military history. It is my sincere wish that others, with a deeper knowledge of the period, will come forward with more information and extend our mutual understanding.

The title of this book derives from the alliterative medieval motto 'Une Foy, Une Loy, Ung Roy' readopted by the Catholic party subsequent to the Colloquy of Poissy in 1561, but also associated with Michel de l'Hospital, the moderate Chancelier de France during the minority of Charles IX. The Calvinist representatives at Poissy harangued the young king over points of theology. The Catholic clergy talked politics. They expressed the view that religious affiliation was inherently related to loyalty to the Crown.

---

4   'Spanish Fury', *The Perfect Captain*, <http://perfectcaptain.50megs.com/SpanishMain.html>, accessed 5 May 2020.

5   Ian Heath, *Armies of the Sixteenth Century* (Guernsey: Foundry Books, 1997).

Note on Terminology

The original (and inconsistent) Middle French spelling has been retained for most technical terms. There seems little value in using modern French equivalents or translating them into English words that may be equally unfamiliar to most readers. Thus, genoüllieres (knee guards) has been preferred to either genouillères or poleyns. A full glossary has been provided. However, a few exceptions are made in those instances where the contemporary French or English is assumed to be familiar to readers. Most proper nouns are also rendered in the same archaic language. There is less real justification for this, other than aesthetics. Non-French individuals are generally named in their native language rather than modern English or Middle French.

The terms Huguenot and Calvinist have been used more or less interchangeably to describe most Protestant communities in France and the armies they raised in defence of their religion. The origin of the term Huguenots (mangled by contemporary Englishmen as 'Howegenosys') is obscure. Even the Huguenot historian, Aubigné, was unsure, offering two implausible explanations.[1] More prosaically, it may derive from the local dialect of Geneva, a centre of Calvinism; 'eyguenot' meaning someone opposed to the influence of Savoye and seeing themselves as a Swiss confederate or 'eidgenoss'. It has also been suggested that it derives from Hugues, either the place in Bretaigne (Brittany) or the personal name, that is, Hugh. The Huguenots were also frequently referred to as the Reformed or belonging to the Reformed Religion. The Huguenots' German, Dutch and English allies were also Protestant, but Lutherans or Anglicans as well as Calvinists.

The terms royal and Catholic are generally synonymous until the accession of Henry III in 1574. After this point, Catholic is used only to refer to the various Catholic (or Holy) Ligue forces, while royal is reserved for those forces currently loyal to Henry III or his successor from 1589, Henry IV.

Until 1564 the new year was reckoned to start in France at Easter. Subsequently 1 January was adopted. All dates in this work assume the year starts on 1 January regardless of this change. In terms of military activity, this

---

1 Théadore-Agrippa D'Aubigné, *Histoire Universelle du Sieur d'Aubigné* (Geneva: 2nd Edition 1626), volume 1, pp.130–131: 'The King wanted to enter Tours, suspected for the number of Reformed or, as some would have it, Huguenots, who have taken their name because of the Tower of Hugon, where they gather, or a lutin (sprite) of the same name, with whom one threatens children in this city.'

only relates to the Siege of Orleans, Coligny's campaign in Normandie and the assassination of the Duc de Guise. The Gregorian (New Style) Calendar was first introduced in October 1582. It was adopted in France in December of that year. All dates are given in the calendar style in use at the time the events took place.

1

The Wars

Providing even a basic summary of the French Wars of Religion is not straightforward. Firstly, although most of the military action took place within the then boundaries of the French kingdom, the conflicts saw Spanish and English monarchs, Popes, Dutch stadtholders, German princes and all their various armies involving themselves in these events. Secondly, the period was marked by widespread localised conflict beyond the somewhat arbitrary start and end dates for the individual 'Wars' presented below. There is not even unanimity over the number of these wars, as they increasingly tended to merge into one another. The end date adopted is also somewhat arbitrary since violence continued into the reign of Louis XIII. Finally, although religion was one of the key motivating factors during the early Wars, it became less so, at least for many of those involved, during those that followed.

France exited from the Great Italian Wars (1494–1559) with little to show for its considerable efforts except a nobility addicted to the rewards that flowed from military service. The untimely death of King Henry II as a result of a jousting accident left his 15-year-old son to be crowned François II in 1559. Noble factions vied for influence over the young monarch. Pre-eminent among them was François Duc de Guise and his relatives. King François was married to the Duc's niece, Mary Queen of Scots. The Guise dominance led to the alienation of other noble houses, some of which provided leadership to the discontented Protestant minority. The sickly François' 18-month reign ended with his death in 1560, leading to a rather undignified scramble for control over his 10-year-old brother, Charles IX.

Faith became the cause célèbre around which factions manoeuvred for power. Protestants had been steadily growing in numbers in France. And while always a minority, they were vocal and counted many artisans, bourgeoisie and country nobles in their ranks. The years up to 1562 had seen steadily escalating persecutions of Protestants by both the Crown and local authorities. To protect themselves from this violence, Huguenot communities had begun to organise for their own defence and placed themselves under the authority of noble 'protectors'. Paradoxically, just prior to the outbreak of the wars, the intimate royal councils began to be dominated by factions led by these Huguenot nobles.

Map of France During the Wars of Religion

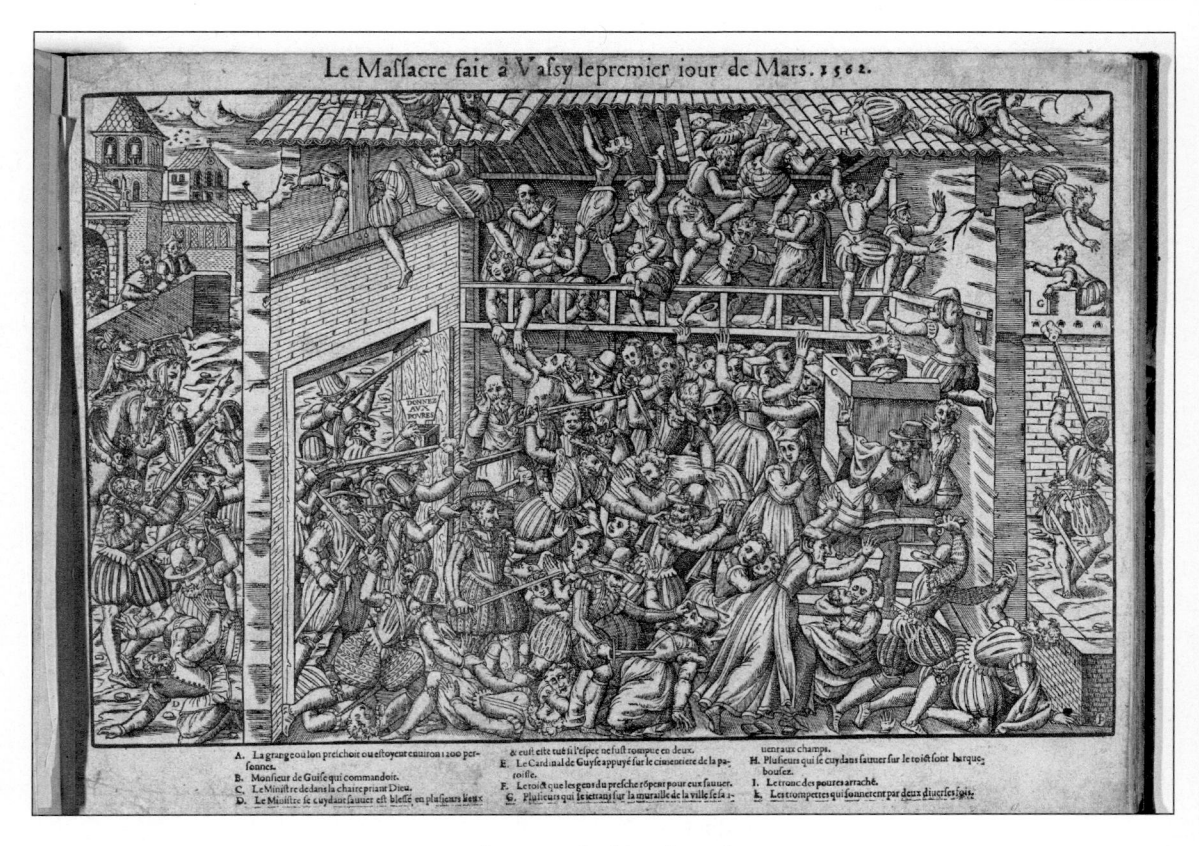

Le Maſſacre fait à Vaſsy le premier iour de Mars. 1562.

A. La grange ou l'on preichoit ou eſtoyent environ 1200 perſonnes.
B. Monſieur de Guiſe qui commandoit.
C. Le Miniſtre de dans la chaire priant Dieu.
D. Le Miniſtre ſe cuydant ſauuer eſt bleſſé en pluſieurs lieux

& euſt eſté tué ſi l'eſpee ne fuſt rompue en deux.
E. Le Cardinal de Guyſe appuyé ſur le cimetiere de la paroiſſe.
F. Le toiſt que les gens du preſche ſ'apent pour eux ſauuer.
G. Pluſieurs qui ſe ietrans ſur la muraille de la ville ſe ſa-

tienraux champs.
H. Pluſieurs qui ſe cuydans ſauuer ſur le toiſt ſont harquebouſez.
I. Le tronc des poures arraché.
K. Les trompettes qui ſonnerent par deux diuerſes fois.

Huguenot communities were scattered across the kingdom, but were most numerous in an arc extending along the Loire valley, the Atlantic coast past La Rochelle, the north side of the Gironde, then west across Quercy and the Cévennes uplands to the Rhosne (Rhône) and the lower slopes of the Alps. There were two outlying bastions as well: in the north, Normandie and in the far south-west, Navarre and Béarn. They were found in far fewer numbers along France's eastern frontiers from Lion (Lyon) to Calais and in staunchly Catholic Bretaigne. Apart from Normandie, Huguenot strongholds were generally located in regions distant from the Crown's concentrations of military power, which lay in Picardie, Piemont (Piedmont) and Paris.

Tortorel and Perrissin print of the Massacre of Vassy. (Rijksmuseum, Amsterdam)

The First War (April 1562 to March 1563)

The event that ignited the first sustained period of open conflict between the Huguenots and Catholics in France was the Massacre of Vassy, on 1 March 1562. The Duc de Guise and his followers, returning to court from self-imposed exile, attacked a Huguenot service being held in a barn. As a result of this action, he was greeted as a hero by the staunchly Catholic population of Paris. Seizing the moment, Guise and his allies took control of the court, then at Fontainebleau, and forced the young king and the Queen Mother to return with them to the capital. In response, Huguenot communities, led by nobles opposed to the Guise faction, seized control of cities across France.

On 2 April, their most prestigious leader, Louis Prince de Condé, and his followers took Orleans. This was quickly followed by the capture of Rouen, Bloys (Blois), Tours and Lion. In other cities, such as Thoulouze (Toulouse), they were countered by resistance from local Catholics and royal forces.

Neither side acted decisively. The Royalists, taken aback by the speed and initial success of the revolt, took time to assemble their scattered garrisons and raise new units, while the Huguenot rebels, still protesting their loyalty to the Crown, awaited reinforcements from friendly Protestant powers in Germany and England. What fighting there was generally favoured the Royalists, who inflicted defeats on small Huguenot forces in the south of the country and recaptured Bloys, Tours, Poictiers (Poitiers) and Bourges (though here one of the King's two colonels general of infantry, Charles Comte de Randan, was mortally wounded). An English force supporting the Huguenots occupied Havre de Grace with 4,000 men.

The first major engagement occurred at the Siege of Rouen (28 May to 26 October 1562). The main royal army retook the city from a garrison based around 700–800 men of the vieille bandes (or vieux bandes, both meaning veteran infantry) that defected along with their commander, François Seigneur d'Andelot;[1] though he himself was absent, having been sent to Germany to recruit mercenaries. It also included a small contingent of 200 Scottish and, later, 300–500 English, troops. Gabriel Comte de Montgomery (the man who accidentally killed Henry II) led the defence. Despite their success, one of the senior Royalist commanders, Antoine de Bourbon Roy de Navarre,[2] was mortally wounded by arquebus fire whilst getting caught up in an assault.

In the south, Blaise Seigneur de Monluc was able to prevent the majority of a force of 5,000 or 8,000 southern Huguenots under Symphorien Sieur de Duras from marching north by defeating them at the Combat of Vergt (9 October 1562) with his Gascons reinforced by Spaniards.[3] A portion of Monluc's army, including the Spanish, were then able to join the main royal force.

The Huguenot army, now with the substantial force of German mercenaries recruited by Andelot in tow, advanced from Orleans and threatened Paris, but its leaders recognised the impossibility of taking the capital. They moved instead in the direction of Chartres. Despairing of taking even this more modest goal, they focused their attention on the smaller city of Dreux and opening a route into Normandie to join forces with their English allies. The main Catholic force moved to intercept their line of march, deploying in a strong position without being detected. So occurred the only full-scale battle of the war.

---

1   Aubigné, *Histoire Universelle*, vol. 1, p.219 and Wood, *The King's Army*, p.107. François de La Noue, *Discours politiques et militaires du Seigneur de La Noue* (Basle: François Forest, 1587), p.581, mentions two English enseignes under Sir Henry Killigrew.

2   The Kingdom of Navarre, and the associated Principality of Béarn, was a small independent state north of the Pyrenees. It was the rump of a much larger kingdom that once extended on both sides of the mountains, but Spain conquered the southern portion in 1512.

3   La Noue, *Discours politiques*, p.583.

Battle of Dreux (19 December 1562) – 'Avec infini regret'

The Huguenot main army was marching with little discipline and failed to detect the proximity of the Catholic force, whereas the latter were better informed. On the night of the 18th, the Catholic commander, Connestable Anne Duc de Montmorency, moved his troops across the River Eure to block the direct road to Dreux. He arranged his men in a defensible, if a little cramped, position between Bois de la Marmousse and the Bois de la Place. He took command of the 'corps de bataille' (the main or largest contingent in a field army) on the left wing. This consisted of 18 compagnies of gens d'armes (heavy cavalry) directly under himself,[4] in front of the village of Blainville, with eight compagnies of chevaux legers (literally 'light horse' but in fact only slightly less heavily armed and armoured than the gens d'armes) under their Colonel General, Louis Seigneur de Sansac, on his flank,[5] a block of 20 enseignes (companies) of legion foot from Picardie and Bretaigne,[6] and then, in the centre of the line, 28 enseignes of Swiss.[7] Eight guns were placed in front of the latter. The 'avant-garde' (normally the second, smaller division into which a field army was organised) was commanded by Mareschal Jacques Seigneur de Sainct-André and was on the right. Next to the Swiss were three compagnies of gens d'armes under Montmorency's son, Henry Seigneur de Damville, and Claude Duc d'Aumale,[8] then 10 enseignes of landsknechts (mercenary German infantry),[9] and then a further 12 compagnies of gens d'armes under the Mareschal himself.[10] Because of the woods, the 20 enseignes of vieille bandes of Piemont and 14 of Spanish infantry had to be deployed somewhat behind these horsemen.[11] Guise, who had refused a more senior command, led his own double compagnie of gens d'armes and a band of gentlemen volunteers located behind this infantry. His force is sometimes described as an 'arriére-garde' (prior to these wars, this would have been the third division of the army, but it was no longer regularly employed) but was, in reality, too small to function as such, as it amounted to no more than 200–300 horsemen. There were 14 more guns in front of the village of Epinay, which were protected by a body of enfans perdus (detached arquebusiers in open order). The whole Catholic force probably amounted to 2,500 horse and 16–20,000 foot.

The battle began when the leading cavalry units of the Huguenot army appeared and were fired on by the Catholic guns, causing them to fall back. Upon reviewing the Catholic position, Admiral Gaspard de Coligny

---

4   Charles Oman, *War in the Sixteenth Century*, pp.412–413, summarises the strengths given by d'Aubigné, Castelnau and d'Avila. Only 12 compagnies are noted in the key to a print by Tortorel & Perrissin: see Philip Bendict, *Commentaire des gravures des Quarante tableaux de Tortorel et Perrissin source principale des commentaires* (Geneva: 2007), p.17.

5   Or only three according to Raymond de Coynart, *L'Année 1562 et la Bataille de Dreux* (Paris: Firmin Didot, 1894), p.17. Which flank also varies in contemporary accounts.

6   According to D'Aubigné and 16 by Castelnau, quoted by Oman, see above. Tortorel & Perrissin (hereafter: T&P) give their number as 17 enseignes.

7   Or 22 in T&P.

8   Or five in T&P.

9   Or 11 in T&P.

10 Or 13 compagnies in Castelnau. Only six compagnies are listed in T&P. Coynart also suggests six but specifies these troops as chevaux legers.

11 Or 22 enseignes of vieille bandes in T&P.

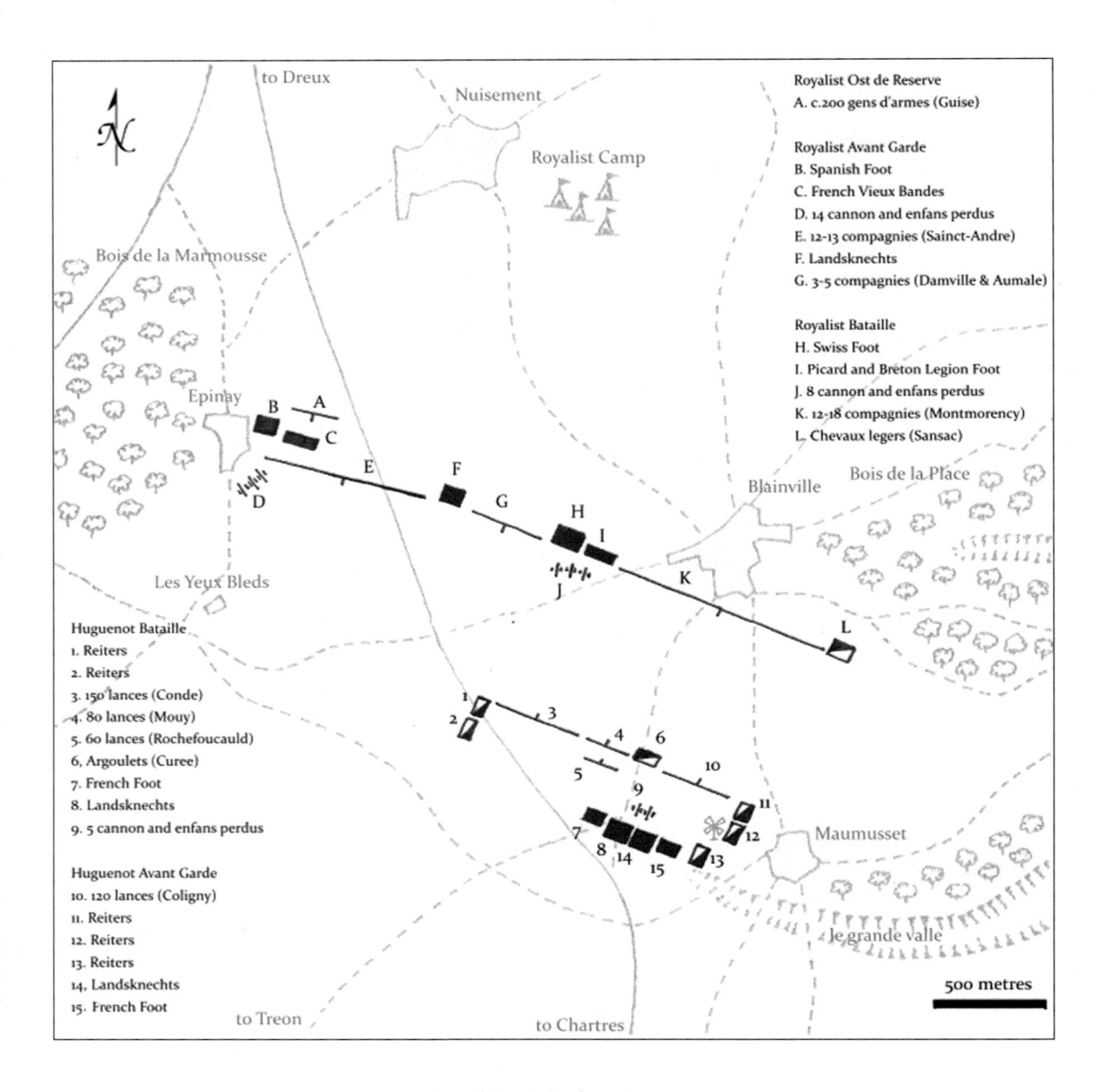

Map of the Battle of Dreux. 1562

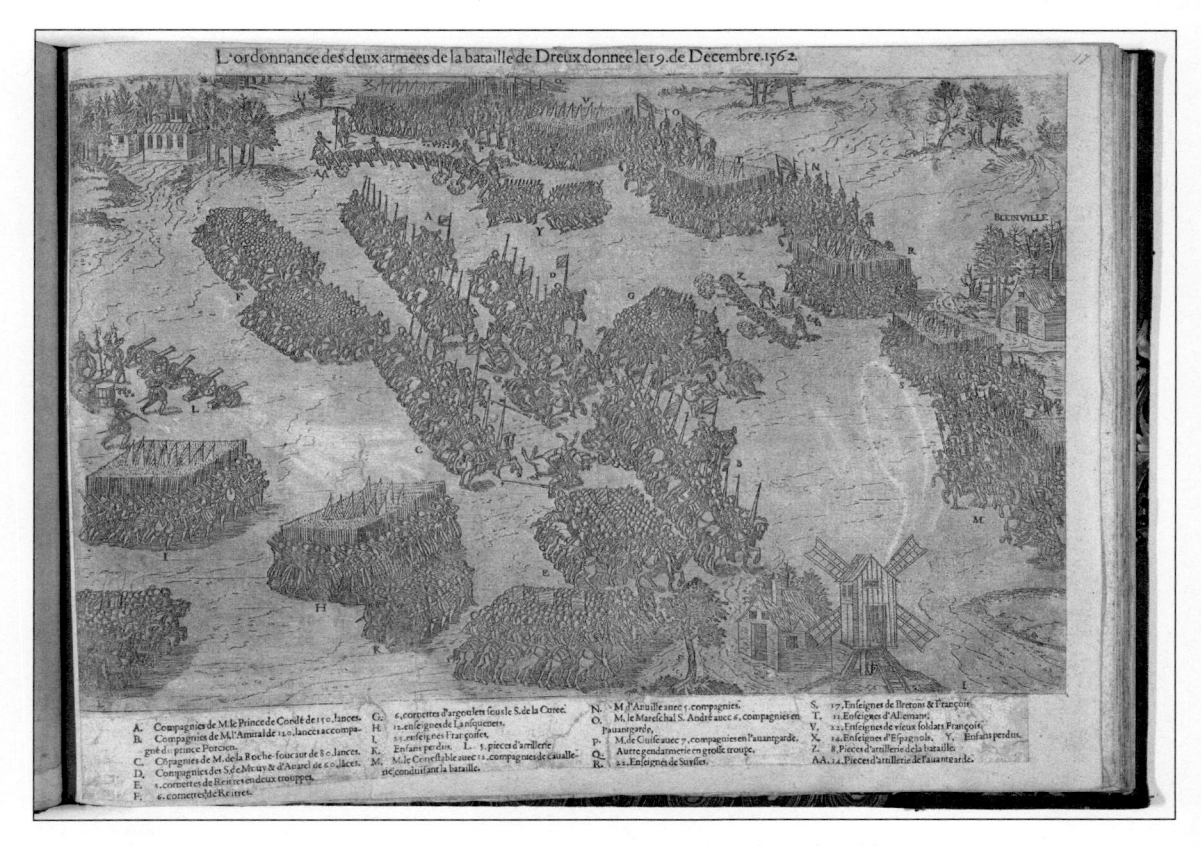

L'ordonnance des deux armees de la bataille de Dreux donnee le 19.de Décembre.1562.

suggested to Condé that they were unlikely to attack, and that they should bypass it, by crossing the River Blaise at Treon. As a result, their baggage and all the artillery except five light guns moved off in that direction. The army deployed to cover their march. Like their enemies, they also formed into a an avant-garde and bataille. Coligny's avant-garde faced Montmorency on the right of the Huguenot line. His open flank was covered by four large cornettes of German reiters (mercenary cavalry primarily armed with pistols) in two deep columns,[12] next to them were his own 120 lances (about 300 men) of gens d'armes. His second line consisted of another regiment of German reiters, a regiment of six enseignes of landsknechts and then a regiment of 11 southern French foot enseignes. The few Huguenot guns were deployed in front of the French foot. Condé's forces where deployed to the left of Coligny, facing the centre of the Catholic line. His open flank was composed of six cornettes of reiters in two units, followed by three units of gens d'armes (of 150, 80 and 60 lances) and then six cornettes of mounted arquebusiers (argoulets) linking up with Coligny's cavalry. His infantry consisted of a unit of landsknechts in six enseignes and 12 enseignes of French.[13] The entire Huguenot force consisted of 4,000 horse and 8,000–9,000 foot.

---

12 Or 5 in T&P.

13 The French infantry included the bandes de Guienne, sometimes referred to as the Gardes du Roi de Navarre, which ultimately became the Regiment of Navarre.

From about 10:00 a.m. to noon the two armies faced each other in battle array. The delay has been attributed to either the unwillingness of both sides to shed the blood of their kinsmen in the first battle of the wars or, more likely, neither commander wishing to sacrifice a tactical advantage by making the first move. At length, Condé decided the Catholics would not interfere with his march and issued orders to move off. As they did so, the Catholic line began to move forward. Quickly countermanding his instructions, Condé ordered a general attack.

On his own wing, two compagnies of reiters, his landsknechts and 60 lances of gens d'armes under François Comte de La Rochefoucault masked the bulk of Sainct-André forces while the rest of cavalry, gens d'armes to the fore, advanced. His target was the Swiss pike block. Meanwhile, the Admiral's charge quickly routed Montmorency's gens d'armes and Sansac's chevaux legers. He then went on to cut up the legionnaires and take the guns before them. The 69-year-old connestable was unhorsed, lightly wounded and captured during this phase of the battle. The exultant Huguenot cavaliers pursued the retreating Catholic forces towards their camp.

The Condé's initial attack on the Swiss was rebuffed, but once the Connestable's wing collapsed they found their flank open. Having few arquebusiers, they could do little but endure the short-range pistol fire of the reiters, and charges by the Huguenot gens d'armes cut into their formation. Damville tried to support them, but his own gens d'armes were heavily outnumbered by the reiters Condé threw against them. They retreated as far as Guise's reserve. Amazingly, despite the punishment they received, the Swiss did not break, but steadily pulled back to Sainct-André's as-yet-unbloodied infantry. Their steadfast resistance probably saved the royal army from defeat.

Condé ordered forward his landsknechts towards the Swiss, but the latter saw off this attack with contemptuous ease. The chastened Germans retreated into Blainville and barricaded themselves in this village. In disgust, Condé then threw in La Rochefoucault's reserve, but such small numbers of men could do little despite their heroism.

With the last of his cavalry used up, Condé was now attacked by Guise's reserve and the rest of Sainct-André's wing. This fresh force had little difficulty in defeating the jaded Protestant horse, the raw Huguenot foot and their rather faint-hearted German mercenaries. Condé was captured trying to rally his men. By this time dusk was falling and the battle seemed to be over. Coligny, however, had other ideas. He had rallied numbers of his victorious cavalry and now returned to the fray. As darkness fell, there was a period of confused fighting as the Catholic forces tried to reform against this new threat. Their cavalry was driven off, but the infantry stood firm. Sainct-André was captured and quickly murdered by those holding a grudge against him. But, sensing the inevitable, the Admiral eventually sounded the retreat and his cavalry covered the withdrawal of what remained of the infantry.

Coligny claimed to have lost 140 horse and 2,200 foot, in addition to the 1,500 landsknechts who surrendered. Catholic sources put his losses at 6,000 in total. Their own losses amounted to at least 3,000 foot and 1,000 horse. The foot casualties included 1,000 Swiss alongside their Colonel, Gebhard

Tamman. Many of the surviving Royalist cavalry were scattered as far as Paris, carrying false reports of a Protestant victory.

With the Connestable captured and both Antoine de Navarre and Sainct-André dead, François de Guise assumed overall command of the Royalist forces. It took a little while to re-organise after such a pyrrhic victory, but he eventually moved to invest the Huguenot 'capital', opening the Siege of Orleans (5 February to 12 March 1563). While Andelot organised the city's defence, the Admiral struck north with a view to rekindling the Huguenot cause in Normandie and linking up with his English allies. At the height of his power and prestige, Guise was felled by an assassin, thereby removing one of the principal impediments to a negotiated peace. The Queen Mother, Caterina de' Medici, mediated a truce, resulting in the Edict of Amboise granting limited toleration to the Huguenot minority on 19 March 1563. The opposing factions took the opportunity to bond while jointly ejecting the Huguenot's erstwhile English allies from Havre de Grace, though the Admiral was sufficiently circumspect to avoid direct participation.

The Second War (September 1567 to April 1568)

In the summer of 1567, a large Spanish force moved up from Italy along the 'Spanish Road' close to the French border to reinforce the Netherlands, where their Protestant subjects were beginning their epic struggle for independence. Nervous of their proximity, the French monarchy hired Swiss mercenaries to counter any possible aggression. However, the Huguenot leadership suspected a secret alliance between the Catholic powers, and so planned a pre-emptive strike to capture the King and his court at Meaux: this failed. Having shown their hand, Condé and Admiral Coligny felt they had no alternative but to initiate a new revolt. Their gathered forces blockaded Paris while other towns such as Orleans, Auxerre, Vienne, Valence, Nysmes (Nîmes), Montpellier, Montauban and La Rochelle fell to their supporters. Once again, this was followed by something of a hiatus as both parties built up their strength and numerous sporadic local fights broke out across France. Catholic provincial troops converged on the capital, whilst Friedrich III Kurfürst von der Pfalz, agreed to the recruitment of 6,500 reiters and 3,000 landsknechts. Pending their arrival, the Huguenot forces were stretched in a thin cordon around a larger enemy. After some skirmishing, the Connestable led his forces out of the capital against Condé's headquarters at Sainct Denys (Saint Denis).

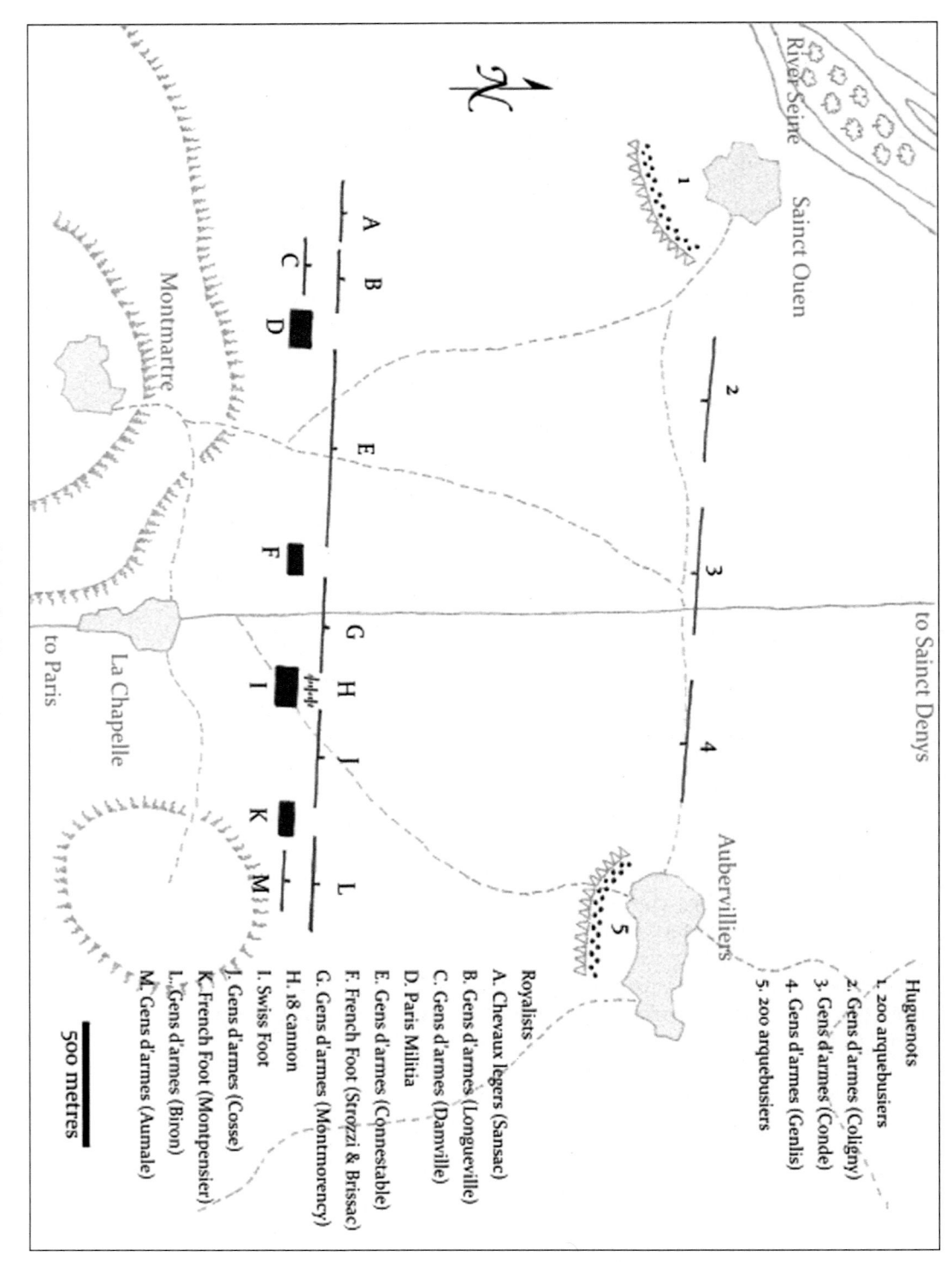

Map of the Battle of Sainct Denys 1567

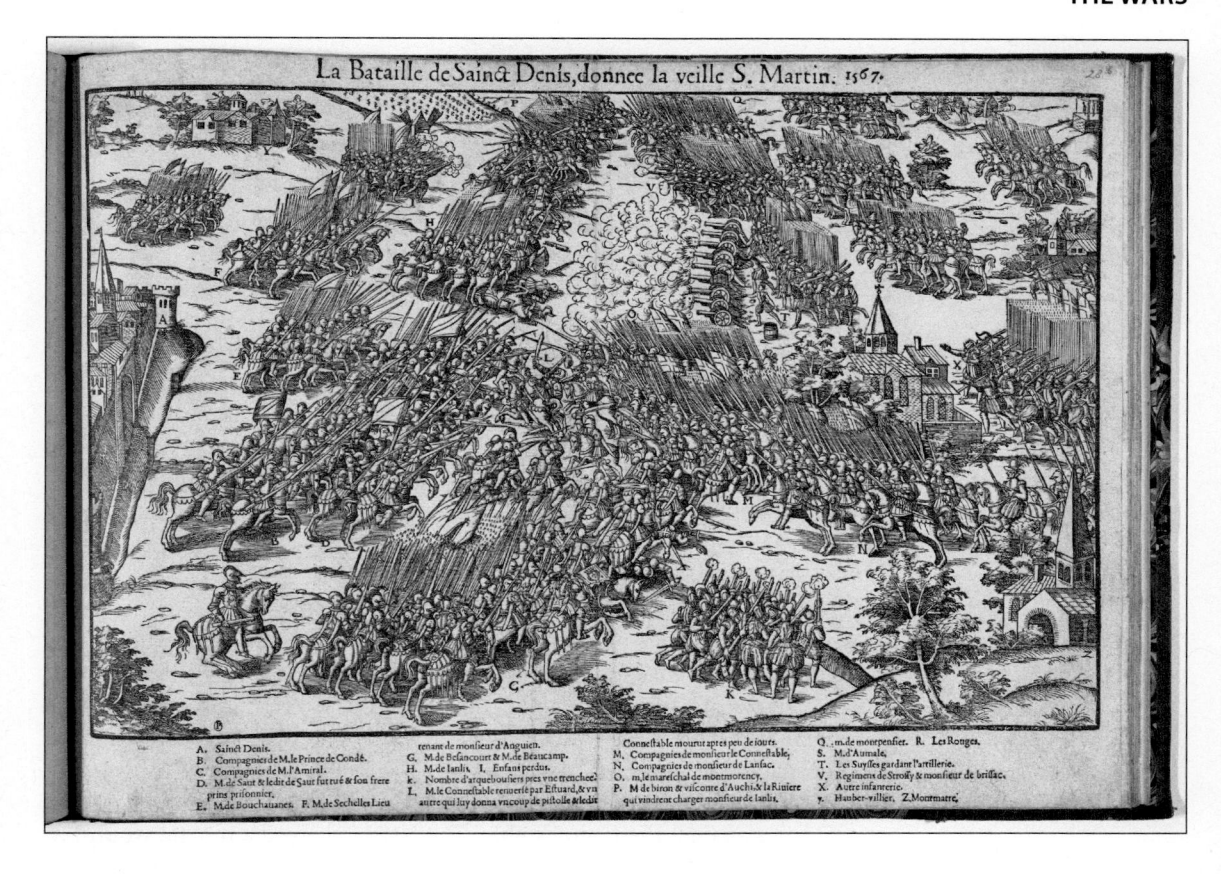

La Bataille de Sainct Denis, donnee la veille S. Martin. 1567.

A. Sainct Denis.
B. Compagnies de M. le Prince de Condé.
C. Compagnies de M. l'Amiral.
D. M. de Saut & ledit de Saut fut tué & son frere prins prisonnier.
E. M. de Bouchavannes.
F. M. de Sechelles Lieutenant de monsieur d'Anguien.
G. M. de Besancourt & M. de Beaucamp.
H. M. de Ianlis.
I. Enfant perdus.
k. Nombre d'arquebousiers pres vne trenchee.
L. M. le Connestable remené par Estuard, & vn autre qui luy donna vn coup de pistolle & ledit Connestable mourut apres peu de iours.
M. Compagnies de monsieur le Connestable.
N. Compagnies de monsieur de Lansac.
O. m. le marechal de montmorency.
P. M. de biron & visconte d'Auchi, & la Riuiere qui vindrent charger monsieur de Ianlis.
Q. m. de montpensier.
R. Les Rouges.
S. Md'Aumale.
T. Les Suysses gardant l'artillerie.
V. Regiment de Stroisly & monsieur de brissac.
X. Autre infanterie.
y. Hunber-villier.
Z. Montmartre.

Tortorel and Perrissin print of the Battle of Sainct Denys. (Rijksmuseum, Amsterdam)

Battle of Sainct Denys (10 November 1567) – 'La beauté et la gloire de la mort'

The Connestable's advance caught Condé ill-prepared. Although he had plenty of opportunity to draw up the troops he had on hand, he was unable to recall either Andelot's or Montgomery's more distant forces. It would have been more sensible for the prince to fall back before the Catholic army, which would have been unlikely to stray far from Paris. Instead, he chose to stand and fight.

Condé took up a position between the villages of Sainct Ouen on his right and Aubervilliers on his left. In front of each of these settlements, he dug a trench and lined both with approximately 400 arquebusiers. The remainder of his infantry, perhaps 1,000 pikemen and 200 arquebusiers, were held in reserve in front of Sainct Denys. Between the entrenched villages, he strung all of his available cavalry: no more than 1,500 horsemen (and only 1,000 according to La Noue).[14] These were deployed in a long, thin line (en haye), as they had been at Dreux. Coligny commanded the body of horsemen on the right, Condé himself in the centre and François Seigneur de Genlis on the left.

---

14 La Noue, *Discours politiques* (Basle: François Forest, 1587), p.618.

Connestable Montmorency's army took much longer to debouche from the city and take up its positions. This was in part due to the size of his force, and in part due to the unprofessional nature of some of the militia. The rightmost unit was gens d'armes under Armand Baron de Biron, then a block of French infantry under Louis Duc de Montpensier, then more gens d'armes under Artus de Cossé and then the formidable Swiss, some 5,000 strong. In front of the Swiss were placed the army's 18 guns. Next to the Swiss were gens d'armes under François de Montmorency, the Connestable's son, then two regiments of more French foot under the Colonels General, Filippo di Strozzi and Timoléon Comte de Brissac. The Connestable himself, though now 74 years old, commanded the next body of gens d'armes. On his left were the Paris militia, and then more gens d'armes as well as chevaux legers under Sansac and Léonor Duc de Longueville. A small cavalry reserve was placed behind each wing, under Aumale on the right and Damville on the left. Apart from these reserves, the cavalry was placed a little in advance of the infantry. The whole Catholic army numbered some 16,000 men, including 3,000 cavalry.

The battle began, sometime in the afternoon, with long range artillery fire against Genlis' cavalry in front of Aubervilliers. This was followed by an attempt by Royalist cavalry to flank both ends of the shorter Huguenot line. Unaware of the trenches, they fell victim to short range fire from the arquebusiers Condé had positioned there. Coligny and Genlis then charged the disordered horsemen, pushing them back on the main Royalist line. The Paris militia gave way as they closed. Condé now launched his own compagnies against the Connestable. The latter received a mortal wound in the melee that followed. Although the cavalry of his son, François, galloped to the rescue, they were unable to do much beyond stabilising the situation, and the cavalry became locked in a general melee. During this time Condé was unhorsed and briefly captured. Meanwhile, Genlis was unable to make much impression on Montpensier's infantry.

Freed and remounted, Condé recalled his horsemen, who reformed on the Huguenot pikemen in front of Sainct Denys. The Royalists, now leaderless, showed little inclination to pursue in the failing light. They remained on the battlefield overnight and then drifted back to Paris. Deaths on both sides of the battle were relatively few, probably a few hundred in total.

Although the result of the battle was inconclusive and the royal forces declined to resume the action the following morning, partly because Andelot's Huguenot force of 500 horse and 700 foot had arrived, Condé realised he had too few forces to continue the blockade. He made instead for the eastern border, with a view to joining up with the German mercenaries under the command of Friedrich's son, Johan Casimir, and picking up levies from Poictou and Orleans on the way. Now under the nominal command of the King's brother, Henry Duc d'Anjou, a large royal army, some 37,000 men strong, pursued them. The sheer size of this force slowed them down and they failed to catch their enemies before they managed to unite on 11 January. Confronting them, Anjou was joined by additional forces under Aumale and Louis Duc de Nevers, bringing his total to some 60,000 men. But he remained reluctant to engage until 8,500 Catholic reiters had also arrived.

Condé took the initiative and side-stepped the royal forces, marching west and looting villages along the way to keep his troops fed during the winter season. They eventually reached Orleans, lifting the feeble blockade mounted by the Royalists. As he was doing so, a Huguenot column of 4,000 men moving to join him defeated a Royalist blocking force of 5,000 at the Combat of Cognac (Cognat) (6 January 1568). From Orleans Condé launched the Siege of Chartres (24 February to 13 March 1568), as much to entice his mercenaries with the promise of plunder as for any strategic reason. However, the garrison was reinforced by 4,000 men just prior to the commencement. Although of only two weeks duration, this was a hard-fought affair, but was broken off after mutual financial exhaustion caused both sides to seek a negotiated settlement. The Peace of Longjumeau, signed on 23 March, restored the status quo antebellum and obliged the Crown to pay off the Protestant mercenaries.

The Third War (September 1568 to August 1570)[15]

The settlement satisfied no one. Widespread inter-confessional violence continued throughout the spring and summer of 1568, and both Condé and Coligny left court for Bourgógne (Burgundy). Receiving warnings that they were about to be arrested, they fled with their families and a handful of followers to the Huguenot stronghold of La Rochelle. Here they were joined by Andelot with Bretons, Montgomery with Normans and Antoine's Protestant widow, Jeanne Royne (Queen) de Navarre, with Gascons. They were able to establish control over most of Poictou and Xanctoing (Saintonge) and were successful in their Siege of Angoulême (28 September to 14 October) which gave them control of the Charente valley.

A large force of reportedly 25,000 Huguenots (but more likely 18,000–19,000 infantry and 700–800 chevaux legers and arquebusiers à cheval) from the Daulphine (Dauphine), Prouvence (Provence) and Languedoc under Jacques Seigneur d'Acier, rose in defence of their leaders and made for the fortress. They were opposed by Montpensier commanding a smaller force, though one superior in cavalry. A Huguenot flank guard under Paulon Seigneur de Mouvans, became somewhat detached from the main force. While Montpensier demonstrated against the latter at Sainct Astier, 2,000 infantry and 1,200 horsemen under Colonel General Timoléon de Brissac and François Prince de Dombes, attacked Mouvan's 2,500 arquebusiers who lacked supporting pikemen. Brissac's initial assault on their strong position was repulsed, but he feigned a retreat and set up an ambush. At the Combat of Mensignac (or Riberac, 26 October) he killed Mouvans and 1,200 of his men. Local peasants reputedly accounted for a further 600–700 in the following days. Despite this setback, the remainder of Acier's army linked up with Condé's cavalry. Against this united host, Montpensier was forced to fall back

---

15 The most detailed military history of the Third War is to be found in Stéphan C Gigon, *La troisième guerre de religion. Jarnac-Moncontour (1568–1569)* (Paris: Charles Lavauzelle, 1911). This is based on primary sources and a careful examination of the actual terrain crossed by the armies involved.

to rendezvous with the main royal army forming under Anjou and Gaspard Seigneur de Tavannes. A sharp encounter occurred between the main armies at the Combat of Jazeneuil (17 November) where the Condé failed to defeat Anjou's now heavily outnumbered, but well positioned, force. There was a stand-off outside Loudon between 16 and 18 December, but the snow and ice made fighting a battle impractical. The hard winter put an end to active campaigning. Both ill-supplied armies suffered losses during this period. Meanwhile, on the eastern frontier, Aumale's army destroyed a Huguenot force of 1,500 men moving from the Daulphine to join the Protestant reiters massing in Germany at the Combat of Neuberg (5 November 1568).

In the spring, the main Huguenot army moved south, aiming to join forces being raised in Quercy (see below).

Battle of Jarnac (13 March 1569) – 'Tuez … Mordiou … Tuez!'

In March, Tavannes and Anjou took the royal army south over the River Charente, getting ahead of the Huguenots and cutting them off from their principal power base in the south-west of the country. Condé and Admiral Coligny responded by spreading out their army along the north bank of the river, defending the various crossing points. Condé's forces held the western end of this line, towards Cognac, while Coligny deployed to the east.

The town of Châteauneuf lies at the southernmost tip of a bend of the Charente, and here Tavannes planned to make a crossing. He made a feint west-ward and then doubled back to the town, managing to both repair the existing bridge and construct a pontoon. The Huguenot forces left by the Admiral to defend this point were negligent in their duties and did not detect the Catholic forces until the majority had passed over.

Coligny now had to concentrate his dispersed forces in the face of this unexpected thrust. He brought as many of these as he could find to the villages of Bassac and Triac, which lay to the west of the marshy Guirlande stream. This position offered at least some defensive possibilities. Initially, he did not feel his position was unduly compromised and was slow to send to Condé for reinforcements.

Around 11:00 a.m., the Catholic avant-garde under Montpensier, consisting in total of 4,000 horse and 7,000 foot, attacked Coligny's position along the Guirlande. This was defended by five or six enseignes of Poictevine (Potevin) arquebusiers under their Colonel, Christophe Seigneur de Puyviaud. He had been loaned 40 argoulets of Acier's own guard as initially he had no other cavalry in support. Brissac engaged these with 1,200 arquebusiers drawn from his own veteran infantry regiments while the energetic Sébastian Vicomte de Martigues and the young Henry Duc de Guise (son of the assassinated François) sought a crossing for their 400–500 cavalry further upstream. The Royalist infantry pushed Puyviaud back from his position and he was forced to retreat to the village of Bassac. To cover this movement, Huguenot small cavalry unit under François Seigneur de La Noue and Louis Seigneur de La Loue were dispatched. Meanwhile, the Royalist avant-garde cavalry had found a crossing and wheeled down against their left flank. The Huguenot horse were scattered towards Triac and their commanders taken.

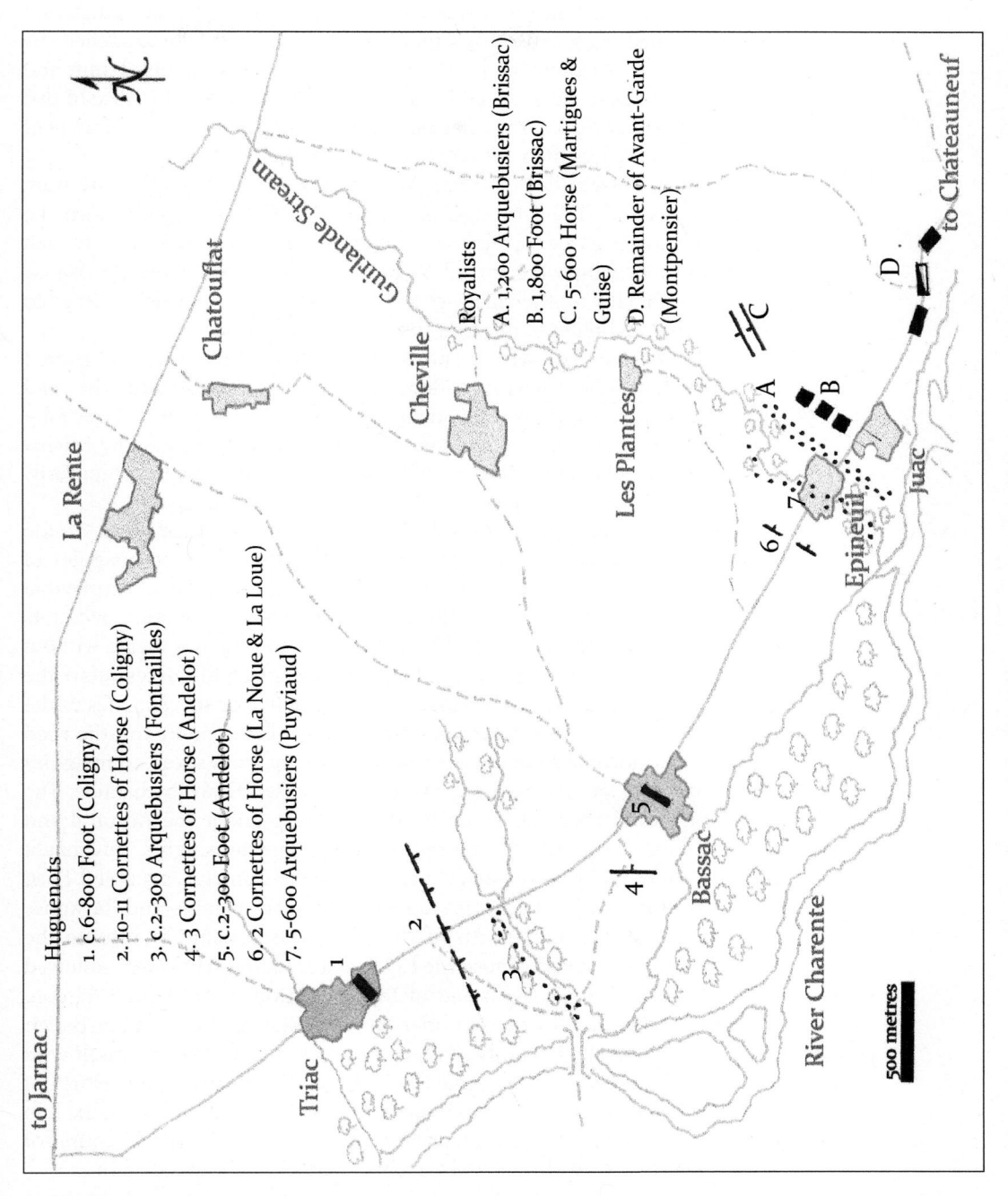

Map of the Battle of Jarnac 1569, c. 11:00 a.m.

Coligny had left his brother, Andelot, to command the defence of Bassac with three cornettes and a few infantry, but he had done little to improve the village. Puyviaud made it safely to this point but realised that it was poorly suited to defence and was too advanced from the main Huguenot line. He pulled back as Brissac's infantry advanced. Andelot launched his fresh cavalry at Martigues and Guise's now somewhat disorganised units and drove them back to the Guirlande. Growing more confident because of this success, Puyviaud reoccupied Bassac. Coligny still had 10–11 small units of horse and a little less than 1,000 foot around Triac.

Tavannes sensed that the forward elements of the Royalist army were becoming extended and brought forward 2,500 Catholic reiters from the remaining avant-garde cavalry to support them. They were able to halt Andelot's men, who were forced to retreat. When the Comte de Brissac resumed his attack on the village of Bassac, Puyviaud was likewise forced to fall back to the Huguenot position forming around Triac.

The southern end of the Triac position, next to the Charente, was covered by a large pond and a narrow valley carved by a marshy stream. The road from Bassac to Triac crosses this ravine which was some 1,500 metres long. It was covered by a force of Coligny's arquebusiers commanded by Michel Baron de Fontrailles. The difficulty of negotiating these obstacles temporarily deterred the Catholic advance.

Having received the Admiral's tardy request for assistance, Condé marched immediately towards the battle. He gathered up compagnies of cavalry as he did so. He arrived by Triac at 1:00 p.m., about the same time that Andelot's cavalry were forced to retire to this same point. Romantic accounts of the action have him charging headlong into an ongoing melee without thought of his own safety. In fact, he had time to draw up his forces before the next Royalist attack. His right wing, consisting of five or six cornettes under Montgomery and La Rochefoucauld, faced towards the pond and the road to Bassac. Condé commanded the centre, made up from seven compagnies of gens d'armes and chevaux legers he had collected from the bataille. The remaining seven cornettes made up the left wing under the Admiral and Andelot. These horsemen were tired from their previous fights. Puyviaud's infantry, supported by some detachments of other regiments, occupied Triac.

By this time Anjou had come up with the main bataille and Tavannes realised that the ground north of the pond was suitable to resume the advance. Montpensier's avant-garde cavalry moved first. They were followed by the bataille. The southern end of this formation, nearest the Charente, consisted of the Catholic reiters under Philibert Markgraf von Baden-Baden, adjacent to them came a body of French foot, and then Anjou himself with the bulk of his cavalry. Next came the Swiss, and the army's guns. North of the Swiss stood another body of French foot and finally, at the end of the line, chevaux legers under Jean Seigneur De La Valette. The guns fired a couple of salvoes before the cavalry moved forward to attack at about 2:00 p.m.

The Huguenots countered by attacking with both the left and right wings of cavalry, but these jaded horsemen gave way before Montpensier's more numerous host, despite the help of 200 of Puyviaud's arquebusiers who had moved up to support them. At this point the prince threw himself and

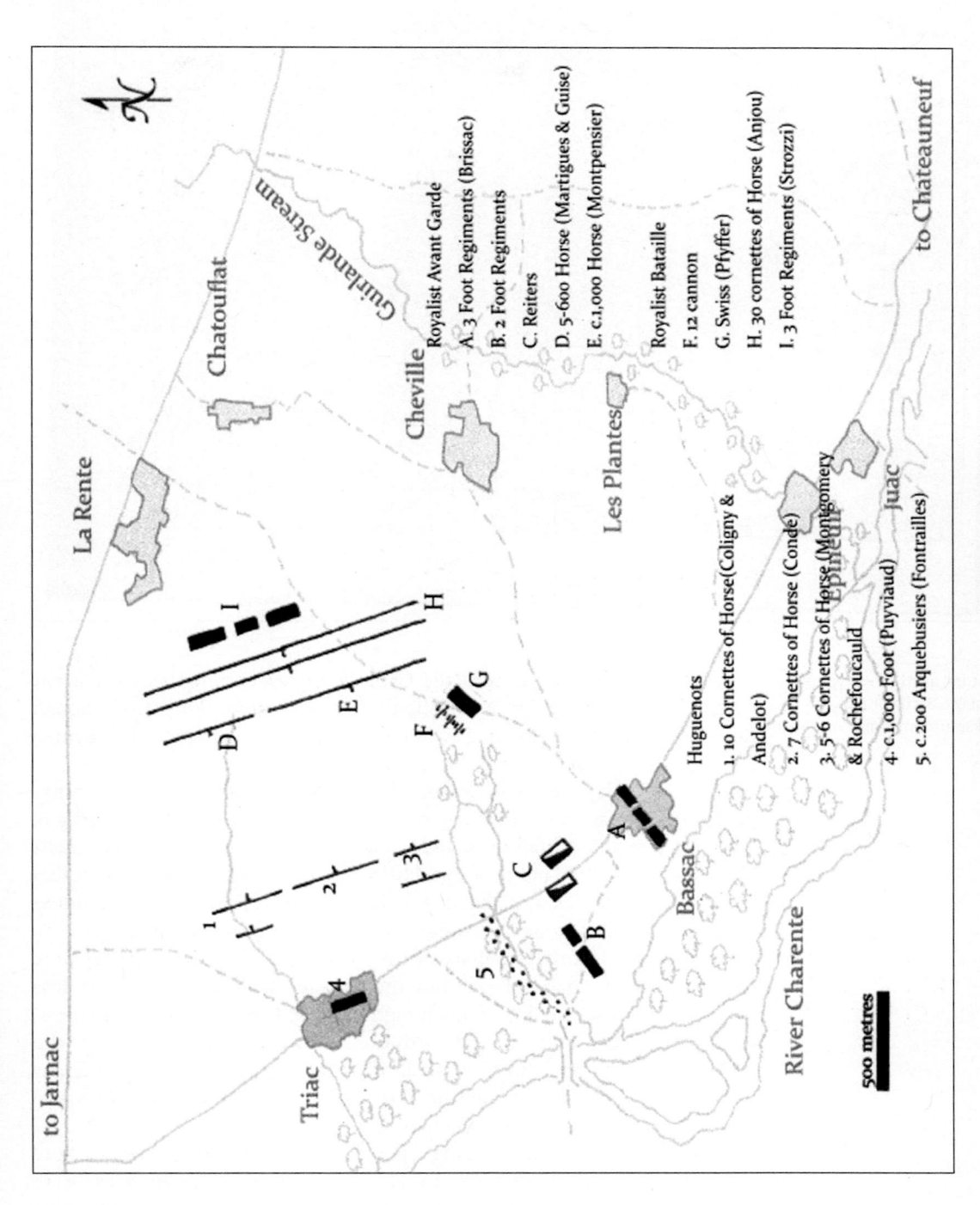

Map of the Battle of Jarnac 1569, c. 1:00 p.m.

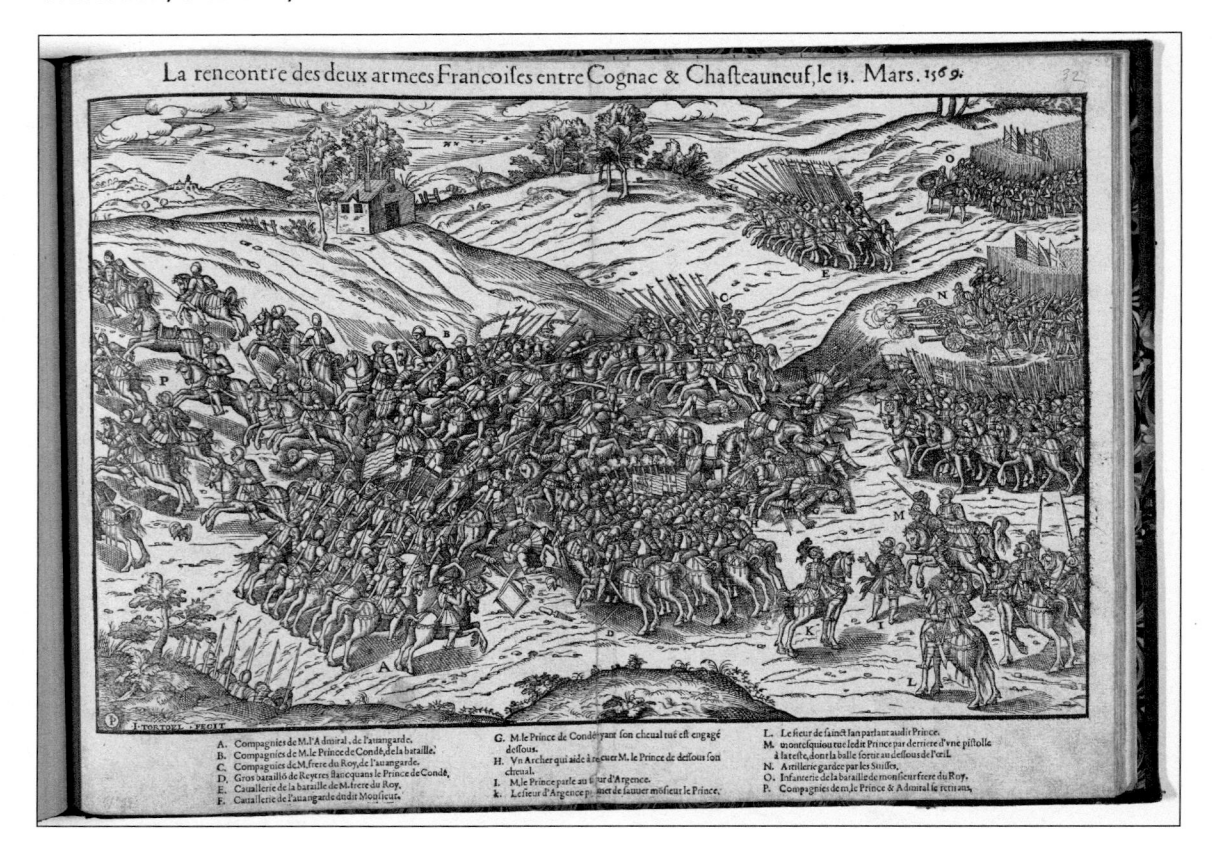

Tortorel and Perrissin print of the Battle of Jarnac. (Rijksmuseum, Amsterdam)

his followers into the midst of the Catholic forces, turning back the avant-garde cavalry and driving into Anjou's own horsemen. But gallant though the charge was, it was doomed to failure. The scattered Huguenot horsemen could make no impression on the Catholic foot.

The Catholic reiters had managed to force their way past the infantry guarding the road that linked Brassac to Triac. From this position, Markgraf Philibert was able to fall on Condé's flank. Condé was dismounted, many Huguenot gentlemen falling around him. Despite being unarmed and under guard, the prince was dispatched, possibly by a Gascon named Montesquiou. His body was later paraded through the streets of Jarnac tied to an ass.

Despite the recorded ferocity of the fighting, the Huguenot forces were able to extricate themselves from the disaster with relatively little loss, perhaps no more than 400 men (though many of these high-born cavaliers) but possibly as many as 800. The Admiral retreated on his own forces who had not had the opportunity to reach the battlefield. Condé's intact infantry, and his remaining cavalry fell back to La Fère. Catholic losses were also slight, possibly only 200–300 men.

Despite their defeat, The Huguenot army remained largely intact, and Coligny, now in sole command, was able to retreat west. The Royalists were detained at La Fère by the lack of siege guns. Meanwhile, a 14,000-strong German mercenary army, led by Wolfgang von Pfalz Zweibrücken and accompanied by the Dutch princes, Willem and Lodewijk van Nassouwe,

Tortorel and Perrissin print of the Battle of La Roche l'Abeille. (Rijksmuseum, Amsterdam)

invaded from the east. Jacques Duc de Nemours and Aumale attempted to prevent it moving further into France, but they failed to co-operate and were bypassed. Fighting numerous small actions, the Germans met their Huguenot allies on 11 June. However, Wolfgang had died the previous day. His successor was Wolfrad Graf von Mansfeldt. Nemours and Aumale joined Tavannes and Anjou.

Having a slight numerical advantage, Cologny manoeuvred his army against Anjou. The latter occupied a strong position while he awaited the arrival of 4,000 foot and 1,000 horse sent by the Pope and France's Italian allies. At the Combat of Roche l'Abeille (25 June) the detachment of Colonel General Strozzi was routed with loss when they ventured too close to the enemy lines. They lost 500 veteran troops and Strozzi was captured. Meanwhile, a strong Catholic column undertook the Siege of Niort (20 June to 3 July) but the imminent arrival of a relief column allowed the energetic Puyviaud, who had forced his men through the encircling Royalists and into the town, to repulse several assaults despite being wounded in one of these. Coligny then set about the Siege of Poictiers (24 July to 7 September 1569), a stronghold that threatened his intended march north. The Duc de Guise, seemingly disregarding his orders, managed to get inside before it was invested. His presence inspired the defenders and they were able to hold off the Huguenot assaults.

In September, Tavannes took the offensive and forced Coligny to abandon the siege. The two armies manoeuvred, and fought several sharp actions, before Tavannes caught up with his opponent.

Battle of Moncontour (3 October 1569) – 'Des victorieux … enivrés de leur bonheur'

As at Jarnac, Tavannes chose to make an operational flank march to unhinge the strong position chosen by the Admiral for his army along the River Dive. Coligny attempted to rectify the situation by moving to a better location across the River Thouet by way of Ervault but was delayed by a strike by his German mercenaries, who demanded their pay before moving. By the time he was able to get underway, the Royalist army had formed a line of battle and were advancing on his flank.[16] With no choice now but to fight, Coligny formed up to meet them.

The royal army is reckoned to have numbered 7,000–8,000 horse, 16,000–18,000 foot and 11–15 guns. It included 6,000 Swiss and 3,000–4,000 Italian infantry, 400–500 Italian cavalry, 3,000 reiters and a few hundred Spanish-supplied Walloon cavalry under Ernst von Mansfeld (brother of the Wolfram who fought on the Huguenot side). They were deployed as an avant-garde on the right and the bataille on the left.

The former, as at Jarnac, was commanded by Montpensier. He deployed the Italian horse on the extreme right, followed by French horse under Martigues. A little to their rear, he placed two Italian foot regiments on the right, a large Swiss regiment in the centre and five French regiments on his left. La Vallette's chevaux legers and a small body of gens d'armes under Guise guarded their left flank. Finally, he placed another line of cavalry behind his infantry: 12 cornettes of reiters behind the Italians and his own compagnies behind the Swiss. To the rear of this whole body was a small cavalry reserve under Biron. The avant-garde numbered some 3,500 horse and 8,000 foot.

Anjou commanded the bataille in person. On the right of his line, next to the avant-garde, was the mass of French cavalry under himself, including his guard of 50 chevaliers on barded horses. On his left were deployed four French regiments and the main body of the Swiss under Ludwig von Pfyffer. To their left were the Walloons. Behind this main line, reiters under the Markgraf von Baden formed behind Anjou and the Guillaume Seigneur de Thoré (another of Montmorency's sons) commanded another substantial body of French cavalry behind the infantry. And finally, another small cavalry reserve under Mareschal Cossé. It was of a similar size to the avant-garde, at 4,000 horse and 9,000 foot.

---

16 The exact location of the battlefield is debateable. This account generally follows the analysis of Gigon, *La troisième guerre*, pp.377–380. However, given the relatively deep formations adopted by both sides, the line of battle he describes probably extends too far to the west. Also, his concept of both army's western wings being bent at a right angle to the rest of the line does not seem to be supported by the primary accounts.

On this occasion the Royalist gens d'armes seem to have formed up in deeper formations than was normal.[17] Whether this was a deliberate tactical choice, or an expedient forced upon them by the terrain is unknown.

The royal artillery was deployed in two batteries, one in front of each body of Swiss. Each was flanked by units of enfans perdus.

The total size of the Huguenot army is less certain, but was somewhat smaller, perhaps 18,000–20,000 men and 11 guns. This included 4,500 reiters and 4,000 landsknechts. Although Coligny had plenty of cavalry available, Tavannes was of the opinion that they were not as good as previously.[18] Their losses suffered at Jarnac had been made good from elements drawn from the bourgeoise, who lacked the same level of equipment, experience and élan.

The Huguenot army was also divided into an avant-garde and bataille. The Admiral commanded the former on the left of the line, while Lodewijk van Nassouwe was given command of the bataille on the right. The Admiral's avant-garde was possibly the larger of the two wings. The left of his line consisted of two bodies of gens d'armes, each drawn up en haye, but in successive lines; the first under Louis Seigneur de Mouy and La Loue, the second under François Seigneur de Bricquemont, Antoine Marquis de Resnel, Charles-Louis Seigneur de Teligny and La Noue. These were supported by a

Tortorel and Perrissin print of the Battle of Moncontour. (Rijksmuseum, Amsterdam)

17 This is clearly shown in Bendict, *Tortorel et Perrissin*, p.35. and described by La Noue, *Discours politiques*, p.409.

18 Quoted in Oman, *War in the Sixteenth Century*, p.449.

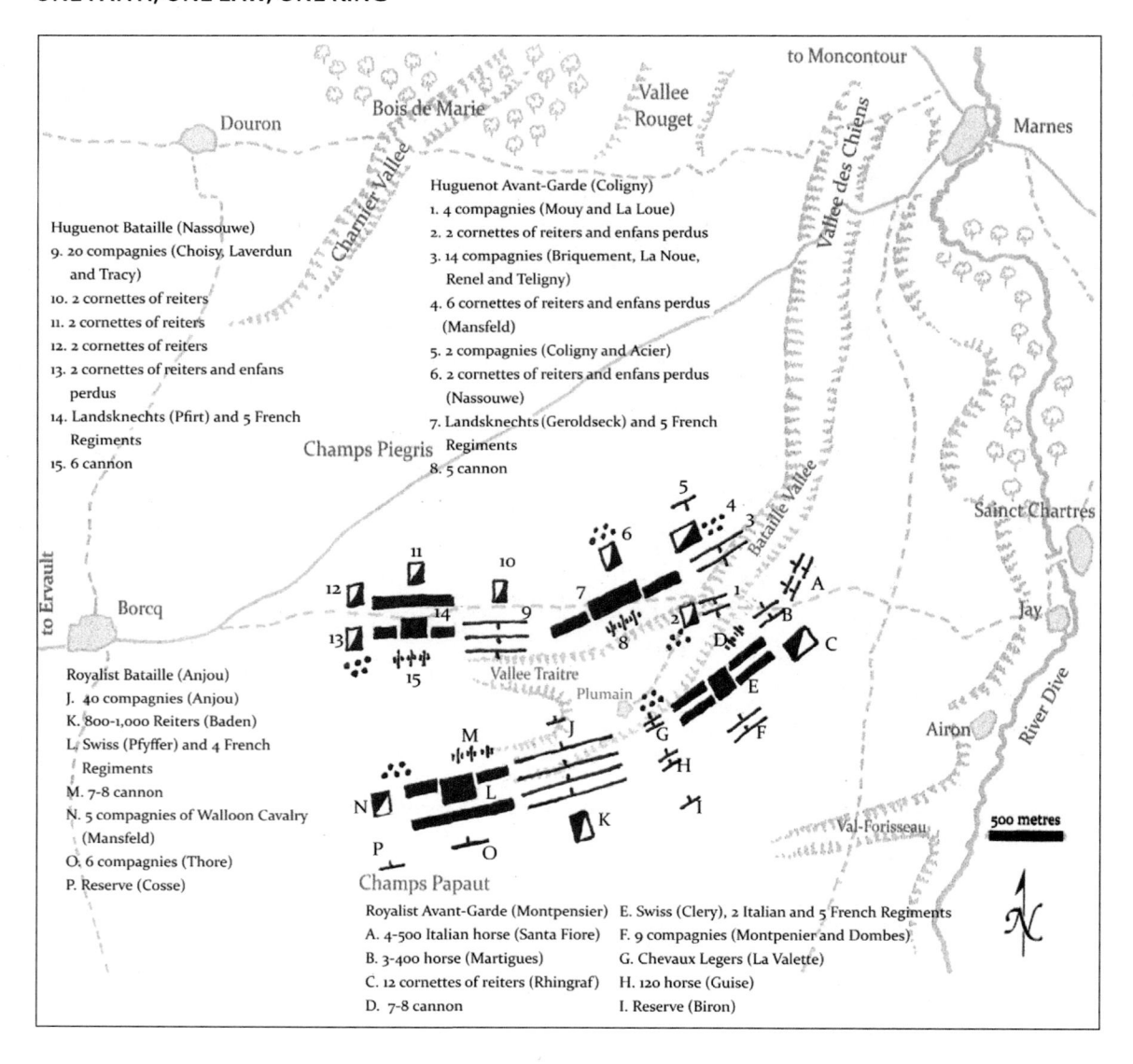

Huguenot Bataille (Nassouwe)
9. 20 compagnies (Choisy, Laverdun and Tracy)
10. 2 cornettes of reiters
11. 2 cornettes of reiters
12. 2 cornettes of reiters
13. 2 cornettes of reiters and enfans perdus
14. Landsknechts (Pfirt) and 5 French Regiments
15. 6 cannon

Huguenot Avant-Garde (Coligny)
1. 4 compagnies (Mouy and La Loue)
2. 2 cornettes of reiters and enfans perdus
3. 14 compagnies (Briquement, La Noue, Renel and Teligny)
4. 6 cornettes of reiters and enfans perdus (Mansfeld)
5. 2 compagnies (Coligny and Acier)
6. 2 cornettes of reiters and enfans perdus (Nassouwe)
7. Landsknechts (Geroldseck) and 5 French Regiments
8. 5 cannon

Royalist Bataille (Anjou)
J. 40 compagnies (Anjou)
K. 800–1,000 Reiters (Baden)
L. Swiss (Pfyffer) and 4 French Regiments
M. 7-8 cannon
N. 5 compagnies of Walloon Cavalry (Mansfeld)
O. 6 compagnies (Thore)
P. Reserve (Cosse)

Royalist Avant-Garde (Montpensier)
A. 4-500 Italian horse (Santa Fiore)
B. 3-400 horse (Martigues)
C. 12 cornettes of reiters (Rhingraf)
D. 7-8 cannon
E. Swiss (Clery), 2 Italian and 5 French Regiments
F. 9 compagnies (Montpenier and Dombes)
G. Chevaux Legers (La Valette)
H. 120 horse (Guise)
I. Reserve (Biron)

Map of the Battle of Moncontour 1569

body of reiters under Wolfram von Mansfeld to which a body of arquebusiers was attached. Behind these were the Admiral's and Acier's compagnies in a single body. To the right of the gens d'armes was another body of reiters and then one of the army's two batteries of guns supported by enfans perdus. The avant-garde infantry consisted of landsknechts supported by five regiments of French foot. Some accounts have all the landsknechts placed here, others only half,[19] under the command of von Geroldseck. However, towards the end of the battle they seem to have all been formed together in one body. To their rear was another body of reiters, again with attached arquebusiers.

---

19 Aubigné, *Histoire universelle*, vol. 1, p.432 only mentions one body and the Tottorel and Perrissin print also shows a single group, but Gigon, *La troisième guerre, p.332*, relying on Henri de La Popelinière, *La vraye et entière*

The bataille consisted of three successive lines of gendarmes under Jacques Comte de Choisy, Jean Seigneur de Lavardin and the Seigneur de Tracy,[20] supported by a body of reiters on the left, then another battery of six guns supported by enfans perdus and, on the right of the line, a body of reiters. The remaining landsknechts under the Graf von Pfirt and five French infantry regiments, who had 'no polearms except the halberds and javelins (spontoons) in the hands of the captains and sergeants',[21] formed behind the guns and there where further units of reiters supporting their right and rear.

Before the start of the battle, Coligny sent the young Huguenot princes, Henry de Navarre and Henry de Condé, to the rear with an escort of 150 lances, an act which was subsequently blamed for lowering the army's morale.

The battle began with an advance by the Catholic avant-garde. Somewhat reluctantly, as Montpensier had no wish to engage unaided by the main bataille. Martigues' cavalry saw off the enfans perdus skirmishing before the Huguenot line around the Plumain Grange and then drove back Mouy's gens d'armes and reiters who advanced to support them.

Seeing the strength of the Catholic right, the Admiral ordered Nassouwe to send him some cornettes of reiters as reinforcements. The Dutch prince complied but also, disastrously, decided to accompany them himself, leaving the bataille leaderless.

Coligny sent his remaining cavalry against Martigues, who, in turn, was supported by Montpensier's own reserves. There followed a confused melee in which the Admiral, uncharacteristically, exposed himself somewhat recklessly. Legend has it that a Catholic reiter commander, Johann Philip II, Graf von Salm-Neufville,[22] was mortally wounded by Coligny himself. But in response, the Huguenot commander received a pistol shot to the face, which forced him to quit the field.

Now the royal bataille attacked. The Huguenots enjoyed some initial success against them: Anjou was unhorsed and had to be rescued by his guard and the Markgraf von Baden was killed. But there was no one to co-ordinate the Huguenot efforts. Tavannes committed his Swiss infantry, who entered the swirling cavalry melee 'at the trot' as well as Biron and Cossé's reserves. The latter saw off the Protestant reiters who attempted to shoot down the Swiss pikemen. This settled the matter and the Huguenot cavalry retreated from the field, covered by a resolute rearguard formed by Nassouwe from those reiters who had maintained their cohesion. The infantry was not so lucky. Many were slaughtered by the exultant Catholic cavalry. The landsknechts formed a defensive square and would probably have surrendered if they had been allowed to do so, but the Swiss were in no mood for mercy.

---

20 Which Seigneur de Tracy is puzzling. Richard de Pellevé, brother of Henry de Pellevé Seigneur de Tracy, is known to have served at Moncontour as a capitaine of gens d'armes, but on the Royalist side.

21 Aubigné, *Histoire universelle*, vol. 1, p.432.

22 Not to be confused with his uncle and namesake who served in a similar capacity against the English at Havre de Grace during the First War and who died in 1566. Both men are often referred to as the Wald-und Rheingraf zu Salm or, in English sources, the Rhinegrave.

Perhaps half the Huguenot infantry were lost, but only 400 cavalry. The Graf von Pfirt was killed and both La Noue and Acier captured. On the Royalist side, cavalry losses were slightly higher, at around 500, but their infantry emerged largely unscathed.

Jealous of his brother's success, King Charles IX decided to take control of the royal army in person. This did not sit well with Anjou or his mentor, Tavannes, who pleaded ill-health and retired home. For seven weeks the King largely squandered the benefits of victory by setting about the Siege of Sainct Jean d'Angely (10 October to 3 December 1569) on the approaches to La Rochelle, where many of the defeated enemy foot had taken refuge. Their tenacious defence was recognised, and these troops were eventually allowed to leave with their weapons and equipment. The delay brought the campaigning season to a close and once more allowed Coligny to rebuild his forces. He turned south.

Whilst the main armies were engaged with one another, a parallel campaign was being fought by substantial local forces in the south of the country. A group of Calvinist nobles known as the 'seven vicomtes de Quercy' raised forces in this part of Guienne (Aquitaine) and in 1569 attempted to link up with the Huguenots east of the Rhosne. In the Ariège (9 June) they were defeated by Roger Seigneur de Bellegarde.

Subsequently, they were joined by Montgomery with a detachment from the main army dispatched to protect Navarre from the Royalists, who were at that time successfully reducing the towns of that region. In a well-executed manoeuvre, Montgomery forced them first to retreat and then, on 13 August, to surrender. This gave him a solid base from which he was eventually able to link up with Coligny in January 1570.

In April of that year, Coligny with 3,000 cavalry, mainly reiters, and 3,000 arquebusiers mounted on nags made a long march northwards through Languedoc to Bourgógne. At the Combat of Arnay-le-Duc (26 June) he defeated a Royalist force under Mareschal Cossé. He then moved on to Champaigne (Champagne), picking up scattered garrisons and Huguenot bands on the way, to the point where Paris felt itself threatened. Simultaneously, the garrison of La Rochelle had some success in recapturing towns in Poictou. This convinced the court that the conflict had to end, and the Peace of Sainct Germain was signed on 8 August.

To add yet another dimension to this confusing war, a Dutch-Huguenot force also crossed the north-eastern frontier. François de Genlis, who had commanded one wing of Condé's forces at Sainct Denys, took a force of Protestants over the border to help their co-religionists against Spain after the Peace of Longjumeau. He joined Willem the Silent's force made up largely of German mercenaries. These were out-manoeuvred by the Spanish general, Alva, and forced into France in November 1568. However, they accomplished little here before Willem ran out of money and his mutinous German mercenaries returned home. Their activities did, however, prevent the Spanish from supporting the royal army. In 1572 Genlis' brother, Jean, returned to the Netherlands with 7,000 men. They were heavily defeated at the Battle of Sainct Ghislain (17 July 1572) before they could reach their allies.

The Fourth War (August 1572 to August 1573)

After the Peace of Sainct Germain, Coligny was able to reintegrate himself at court, and even gained a measure of influence over King Charles. He pushed for France to join the Dutch rebels in expelling the Spanish from the Netherlands. Meanwhile, Henry de Navarre was betrothed to the King's sister, and Huguenot nobles from throughout the kingdom gathered to celebrate the nuptials. But the Guise faction had not forgotten the assassination of Duc François before Orleans and they held Coligny responsible. The Queen Mother and her close supporters seem to have also come to the conclusion that the Admiral's power over King Charles could not be tolerated. There was a botched attempt on his life. This event seems to have panicked the King and led to the Sainct-Barthélemy's Day Massacre (24 August 1572), initially the targeted liquidation of the upper echelons of Huguenot leadership that spread out of control and resulted in the wholesale slaughter of Huguenots, first in Paris and then in many provincial cities. More abjured and returned to the Catholic faith, including their natural leaders, Henry Roy de Navarre and Henry Prince de Condé, who were effectively imprisoned at court.

However, the movement remained strong in the south of the country where they controlled a string of towns, including the bastion of La Rochelle. The Crown initially tried to negotiate a peaceful surrender, but it soon became clear that force would be necessary. Slowly an army, once more under the command of Anjou, and a train of siege guns was drawn together.

The Siege of La Rochelle (11 February to 6 July 1573) – 'Plus a me frapper on s'amuse, tant plus de marteaux on y use'

La Rochelle is a port located on the Atlantic coast of France in the tiny province of Aunis, between Xainctonge and Poictou. It is shaped somewhat like a rectangle, with its shorter sides facing south-west, out to sea, and north-east. As the longer sides of this rectangle faced towards low-lying marshes cut by many streams and pools, only the landward north-eastern face was susceptible to direct assault. It was protected by a dry moat and two large bastions, one on each corner. The whole city was enclosed by a curtain wall with some features of up-to-date bastion (trace Italienne) fortification, but its principle strength lay in its position. The Île de Ré, a flat marshy island, lies off the coast, and this contained several forts. Additional forts were established on the seaward approaches to the harbour.

La Rochelle had served as a Huguenot stronghold since the beginning of the wars and provided a useful base for both Huguenot and Dutch privateers to raid Spanish shipping in the Bay of Biscay. Survivors naturally gravitated to the city in the wake of the massacre. Both natives and refugees were enlisted to form a cornette of chevaux legers and 16 enseignes of infantry for its defence.

The initial royal response to the city's defiance was a blockade organised by Mareschal Biron during the winter of 1572/3. His efforts were hampered by the season, poor supply and the efforts of the Rochelais to disrupt his arrangements. La Noue was sent to negotiate a peace. The defenders were receptive and invited him to take over as governor, which he did with King

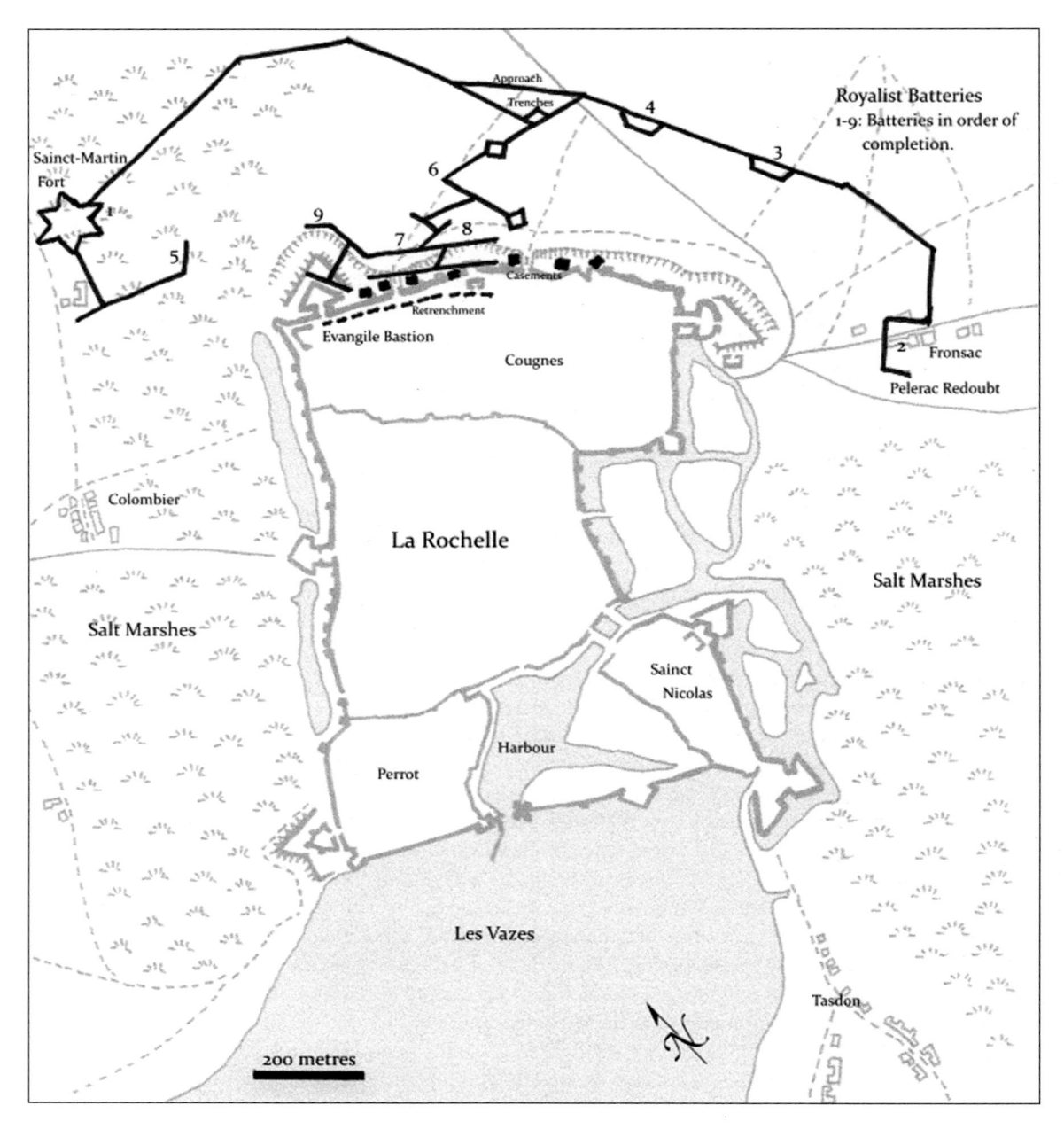

Map of the Siege of La Rochelle, 1573

Charles' blessing. However, they remained obdurate and it was obvious they were not about to submit to the King's will.

A formal siege did not commence until 11 February with the arrival of an army of 25,000 men under the command of Anjou. In addition, a small fleet had been assembled to interdict the city's supply by sea. Anjou was also accompanied by many of the kingdom's nobles, including both Navarre and Condé. Initially, the siege had an almost festive character, as gentlemen volunteers from across the kingdom assembled under the eyes of princes to win renown. Anjou's siege train consisted of 42 cannons and culverins, the largest number of heavy guns assembled by any army during the wars.

Contemporary wisdom stressed the importance of establishing and prosecuting a siege as quickly as possible, both to demoralise the defenders and to prevent them improving their defences. The Rochelais already had plenty of notice of royal intentions towards their city, but even at this stage it took until 26 February for the besieger's trenches to be opened and the battery site started. The latter took until 9 March before the guns were in position to fire. The delay was due to the shortage of locally available materials, poor weather and the vigorous sniping and skirmishing undertaken by the determined Huguenot defenders. These preparations were supplemented by sinking hulks in the city's harbour, but these efforts were not totally effective.

On 12 March La Noue left the city, as it became obvious that he could no longer serve both its residents and his king. He joined Anjou's camp. From this point, the defence was managed by a council of bourgeoisie rather than a member of the nobility.

The royal artillery concentrated its fire against the northern bastion, named Évangile. The guns pounded this fortification as the trenches crept closer to the counterscarp and moat. Despite this steady progress, the Royalists suffered mounting casualties, especially amongst their pionniers. This was not only due to enemy action, but also due to the disease and desertion that inevitably resulted from a large army being stationary for too long.

On 20 March, the trenches reached the counterscarp, but on 29 March it was discovered that the moat was studded with small fortified casements that could direct fire against anyone entering it. Nevertheless, on 7 April, Anjou launched the first assault against the city. The infantry was proceeded by 200 nobles eager for glory. It was beaten back with the loss of hundreds of men. When renewed the following day, the royal troops were notably less enthusiastic, and it petered out shortly after it began. On 10 April, Anjou varied his tactics. He launched a secondary attack to the south at the same time as the main assault, but neither were any more effective. Realising the futility of these actions, Anjou then ordered his pionniers to dig under the defences, so a mine could be placed. This was accomplished by 14 April and his troops stood ready in the trenches awaiting its detonation. Unfortunately, the blast, which turned a section of the walls into rubble, caused far more casualties to the Royalists, who were positioned too close. The attack went in as planned, but the heart had gone out of the men. The Huguenots were able to put up enough resistance to see them off.

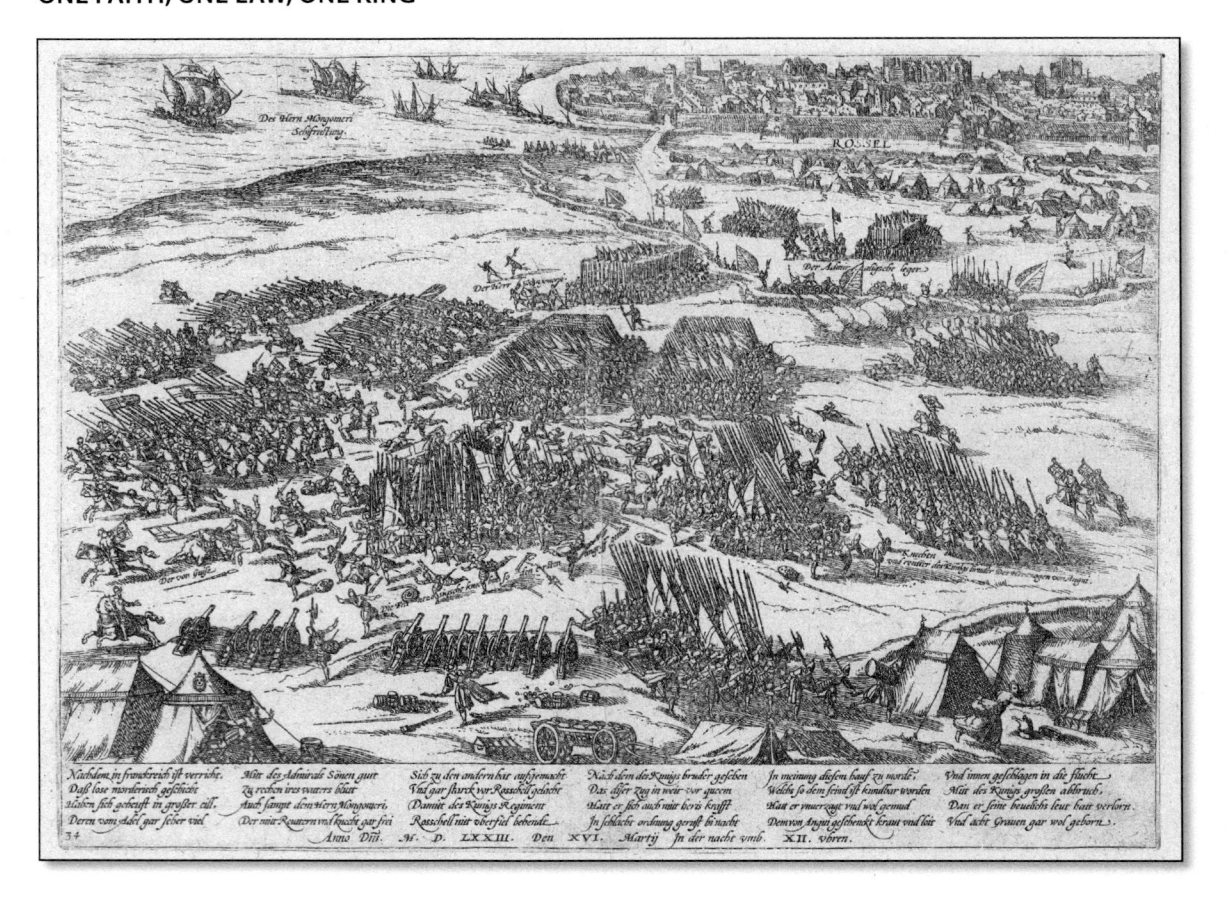

Hogenberg print of the Siege of La Rochelle. (Rijksmuseum, Amsterdam)

The Rochelais had also had plenty of opportunity to prepare their defences. They built a secondary wall behind the Évangile bastion, so even if it was taken, the defenders could fall back to a new position.

Montgomery tried to run the royal blockade on 20 April, but the latter were forewarned and were able to deter his attack with little difficulty, though it diverted their energies away from the city for a time.

New mines were blown under the bastion on 29 April, but despite the extensive damage, morale in the royal camp had reached such a low that their much-depleted regiments were extremely unwilling to assault the breach, and little was achieved. Therefore, extensive sapping of a wider section of the walls was begun and had some success. An assault on 16 May was pressed with renewed confidence, but the Huguenots were equal to the threat. The hard contest saw them secure their increasingly precarious fortifications. But by now, their own resources were running low. The shortage of powder prevented them from harassing the Royalists with sniper fire as they had been wont to do. Had it not been for the providential arrival on 20 May of a ship carrying powder, that managed to force its way into the harbour, their cause might have been lost. The Duc d'Aumale was killed in one of the almost continuous minor actions on 21 May.

On 23 May 6,000 Swiss infantry arrived as reinforcements. The Royalist troops flocked to greet their allies, but in so doing abandoned their watch on the city. A great sortie was launched which caused extensive damage and many casualties. After some days spent setting things aright, Anjou launched his seventh major assault on 26 May. This effort was hampered by his unwillingness to commit the dwindling number of gentlemen to the fray and the consequential unwillingness of the Swiss to be sacrificed in their stead. The result was a sporadic series of half-hearted attacks by the French infantry.

The next day, Anjou received news that he had been elected King of Poland. With some relief, he determined to bring the matter to a close and re-opened negotiations with the defenders, though it took another assault on 13 June to convince them that the royal army was still a capable force. A generous peace that guaranteed freedom of worship and the right to self-defence was agreed on 26 June and Biron was at last able to enter as the new governor. Total Royalist losses at the siege, from all causes, may have exceeded 12,000 men.

Huguenots also resisted the Catholic onslaught elsewhere in France. The Siege of Sancerre (9 November 1572 to 25 August 1573) was a smaller, though equally hard fought, conflict that saw the last use of medieval trebuchets employed against the defenders.

Henry de Damville was granted wide powers in not only his own province of Languedoc, but also Lionnois, the Daulphine and Prouvence, to re-establish royal control over the towns and communities that had taken up arms. He was hampered, however, by a lack of manpower and the King's urgings for moderation. The rebellious towns refused to accept the terms of the Edict of Boulogne and continued their resistance beyond the imposition of a general peace. In the spring of 1574, Damville fell under suspicion of plotting against the court and was replaced by the young François, Prince de Dombes. To ensure his own survival, Damville now allied with the local Huguenot rebels.

The Fifth War (February 1574 to May 1576)

Whilst local conflicts in the south of the country were far from extinguished by the Peace of La Rochelle, a more general conflagration did not break out until the following year. Huguenots, with the possible connivance of a court faction associated with Alençon tried, and failed, to capture the King at Sainct-Germain-en-Laye whilst simultaneously seizing towns in Normandie and along the River Rhosne. The Royalists formed three armies, under Jacques Seigneur de Matignon, Montpensier and the Prince de Dombes.

Matignon conducted the Siege of Domfront (9 to 27 May) in Normandie, defended by Montgomery, and captured that place. Montgomery was sent to Paris where finally the queen had her revenge on him. Matignon then went on to recapture Sainct-Lo before his unpaid army was disbanded.

In Poictou, Montpensier successfully undertook the Siege of Fontenaÿ (7 to 22 September) and then the more desperate Siege of Lusigná (24 September to 26 January 1575), after which his army, unpaid and reduced by desertion, was also largely disbanded. Troops roamed the countryside causing widespread destruction.

The Prince de Dombes began his campaign in the Daulphine with the short First Siege of Livron (23 June), but his force was repulsed by a sortie from the town. He had more success at the Siege of Pouzin (5 to 18 October) which fell once he had gathered a larger force.

On 4 May Mareschal François de Montmorency (Damville's brother) and Mareschal Cossé were arrested on suspicion of an involvement in a plot to release the Duc d'Alençon and Navarre from their detention at court. Damville reacted angrily to this development, which drove him further into alliance with the Huguenots.

On 30 May, Charles IX died, and Anjou was recalled from Poland to take up the crown as Henry III. He took his time doing so, however, not returning until September. He tried to patch up relations with Alençon, Navarre and Damville. The latter, however, resisted his heavy-handed approach and joined a group of disaffected Catholic nobles known as the Malcontents.

The newly minted Mareschal Bellegarde, returning with his king from Poland, began the 2nd Siege of Livron (17 December 1574 to 24 January 1575) with no more success than the first endeavour, despite the presence of the monarch. Montpensier had better luck. He captured a number of small towns covering the approaches to La Rochelle, but failed to take the Île de Ré. The war became bogged down in a series of small actions and raids, often with captains more interested in their own profit than serving any higher power.

In September, Alençon fled from court and raised his standard at Dreux. The Malcontents flocked to him and soon he had gathered a large following. In October, 2,000 reiters under Johann Casimir von Pfalz-Simmern and Guillaume de Montmorency Seigneur de Thoré (another of the late Connestable's sons) invaded. Although the Duc de Guise defeated a portion of their strength at the Combat of Dormans (10 October), they remained a threat. Between these forces and the rebels holding out in the south, the King found himself surrounded and opened negotiations. A truce was agreed, but Alençon found himself unable to control either the Huguenots or Germans. A larger force of the latter crossed the Meuse in January 1576 and marched into Bourgógne. The royal army was too weak to resist. Huguenot revolts were reignited in Normandie. In February, Navarre also escaped the court and began raising an army in his own lands in the south-west. Left with no choice, Henry III had to comply with the demands of his enemies: granting rights to the kingdom's Protestants under the terms of the Edict of Beaulieu, paying off Johann Casimir's mercenaries and reinstating the Malcontent nobility to positions of power. The settlement was widely derided as the Peace of Monsieur (the courtesy title of Alençon, as the King's younger brother).

The Sixth War (December 1576 to September 1577)

The Edict of Beaulieu was seen as a betrayal by many Catholics, especially those aligned to the house of Guise. There began the first stirrings of direct opposition to the Crown from this quarter. The meeting of the Estates General at Bloys was packed with Catholic representatives who pressured the King into repudiating the agreement and imposing a single faith on the kingdom. The Huguenots did not wait to see the outcome of this decision, but took to arms once again, rising in Poictou and Guienne.

Despite their enthusiasm for suppressing the Protestant rebels, the estates were less inclined to pay for this endeavour. A royal army, at least nominally under Alençon's command, of significant size was raised, but lacked the necessary funds for a long campaign. Their first action was the Siege of La Charité-sur-Loire (25 April to 2 May 1577). It then moved on to the Siege of Issoire (28 May to 12 June 1577), which suffered greatly when it fell. But the army itself was in an increasingly parlous state due to the lack of supplies and money. In contrast, the Huguenots began to receive support from England through their strongholds on the Atlantic coast. Henry III sent the Duc de Montpensier to negotiate the Peace of Bergerac, which was signed on 14 September 1577. It was followed by the Edict of Poictiers that once again restored a limited set of rights to the Huguenots.

The Seventh War, 'The Lover's War' (November 1579 to November 1580)

Following the Sixth War, Henry III set about establishing his position more securely. He surrounded himself with noblemen loyal to himself rather than any of the existing factions. These Mignons ('cuties'), as they became known, included Anne de Joyeuse and Jean-Louis Duc d'Espernon. Their stranglehold over royal offices further alienated the Guise faction at court and stimulated the creation of hardline Catholic ligues (leagues) in response.

In the meantime, Alençon was still a fractious presence at court. He eventually took himself off to the fight in the Netherlands with a force that included Frenchmen from both sides of the religious divide.

Despite the peace agreed between the King and the main Huguenot leaders the country, especially in the south, had fallen into a state of lawlessness, where tyrants ruled their own petty domains with little concern for any other authority. Low-level warfare between these warlords was endemic. The Seventh War can hardly be distinguished from these local affairs. Its romantic sobriquet derives from stories that it was instigated by the romantic intrigues of Margaret de Valois, the King's sister and estranged wife of Henry de Navarre. In fact, it was initiated by Henry de Condé's seizure of La Fère, in an attempt to consolidate his power in Picardie. Later, in May 1580, Henry de Navarre was successful in the short Siege of Cahors (28 May to 1 June 1580) in a similar quest for local control. But in the Daulphine, Charles Duc de Mayenne responded with the Siege of La Mure (31 September to 6 November 1580), a fortress held by the Huguenots that fell after 37 days. In the north, Mareschal Matignon successfully undertook the 1st Siege of La Fère (September 1580) recapturing it from Condé. Despite the activities of Coligny's son, François de Chastillon, in Languedoc, large-scale violence was contained to a few regions.

Concerned for the impact on his own mixed-confessional force in the Netherlands, Alençon was able to broker a cessation of hostilities by the Peace of Fleix in November. But little good it did him. His adventures here alienated the Dutch and his failed attempt on Antwerp in January 1583 lost him most of his army. He died of a fever the following year.

The Eighth War, 'War of the Three Henrys' (August 1587 to August 1589)

Discontent with Henry III's continued reliance on his Mignons and the toleration granted to the Huguenots was exacerbated by the death of the childless king's younger brother, as this left as his successor none other than the Huguenot, Henry of Navarre.

This was unacceptable to both the Guise faction and many of the urban bourgeoisie, especially those of the capital. The various Catholic or holy ligues coalesced into a more focused opposition and Henry Duc de Guise set about raising troops to support his cause. With these men he was able to take control of several regions and defy the King's authority. In the face of this threat, the latter capitulated and agreed not only to revoke the edicts of toleration, but also to deprive Henry de Navarre of his right of succession.

By this time, Navarre was widely recognised as leader of the Huguenot party. He was also allied to the moderate Catholic faction headed by Henry de Damville, so was not without resources. Both sides engaged in a war of propaganda as they sought to gain influence over those not yet committed to either party. Once again, the Huguenots looked to England for support, while the Ligue turned to Spain. The kingdom slipped into a state of violence as the King's armies sought to impose his authority on recalcitrant Protestant towns and a force under Guise moved to protect the eastern frontier.

It was here that the war began in earnest in August 1587. Fabian von Dohna commanded a force of 4,000 reiters, 3,000 landsknechts, 12,000 Swiss and 2,300 French under Guillaume-Robert Duc de Bouillon, raised by Johann Casimir and paid for by England and Denmark. The army moved from Lorraine into Champaigne, where it was joined by southern Huguenots and Swiss mercenaries under Chastillon.

The latter were refugees from the Combat of Jarrie (or Uriage, 19 August 1587). François Seigneur de Lesdiguières and Chastillon led a force of 3,000 arquebusiers and 600 chevaux legers to link up with Protestant Swiss consisting of 400 chevaux legers and 3,600 pikemen, supported by 500 French arquebusiers, advancing into the Daulphine. They were blocked on the River Isère by Bernard de La Valette (the Duc d'Espernon's brother) commanding 300 gens d'armes, 450 chevaux legers, 150 mounted arquebusiers and 2,000 on foot. Of these, 150 chevaux legers and 300 arquebusiers were Corsican mercenaries under the command of Alphonso d'Ornano. As the Swiss moved through the narrow, forested trails leading down to the river, they were ambushed by Ornano, leading 600–700 men. Unable to deploy properly, many were shot down as they stood. Others forced their way lower down, where they were met by Valette's main body and suffered a similar fate. They lost some 1,800 men compared to the Royalists' 50 dead and 100 wounded. Later, Chastillon was able to link up with the survivors and march north.

Even as these events were unfolding in the east of the kingdom, King Henry sent his mignon, Joyeuse, with a force of 6,000 foot and 2,000 horse to confront Henry de Navarre. Lacking men, the latter withdrew into La Rochelle while Joyeuse ravaged Poictou. Royalist control over the area was short-lived. Navarre reasserted himself as soon as they withdrew.

In September, Espernon, accompanied by Henry III, led a sizable army to the Loire, with a view to preventing Dohna's Germans from linking up with Navarre's Huguenots. Meanwhile, Joyeuse returned to Poictou. Although Navarre's force had grown somewhat because of an alliance with moderate Catholic magnates, and his own recruitment efforts, he still felt himself too weak to challenge the Royalist forces. He initially fell back south; with Joyeuse in pursuit, but eventually accepted a challenge to turn and fight.

Battle of Coutras (20 October 1587) – 'Rends-toi, Philistin!'

Joyeuse aimed at linking his own force up with a smaller army under Matignon coming up from Bordeaux. Aware of this, Henry decided to slip between these converging opponents by crossing the River Dronne at Coutras, ultimately with a view to striking east and joining his German allies. He succeeded in reaching the town before Joyeuse, his own avant-garde under Claude de Tremouille driving away Joyeuse's stradiots (light cavalry from the Balkans) who were ranging far ahead of his main body. While he still had the option of crossing the Dronne unmolested, Henry instead took up a defensive position between this river and one of its tributaries, the Isle. He also took the precaution of despatching 200 chevaux legers and 80 gens d'armes to observe the approach road along which Joyeuse must travel. His concerns were well founded, because the latter had decided to begin his march at midnight to catch Henry unawares. The stradiots, supported by 400 gens d'armes, were able to drive back Henry's pickets, but not before the latter had given ample warning of the Royalist's advance.

Joyeuse's initial force consisted of 6,000 foot in four regiments (including the veteran Picardie) and 2,000 horse made up from 24 compagnies of gens d'armes, six of chevaux legers and two (or four) of stradiots.[23] The latter were under the command of an Italian named Mercurio Bua. Joyeuse's gens d'armes were splendidly arrayed, but inexperienced. By the time they came to battle, these numbers had diminished somewhat, to not much more than 5,000 foot and scarcely 2,000 horse. He also had two cannon.

Despite, or perhaps because of, their early start, the royal army was slow in forming up from their column. On their far right, against the marshy banks of the Dronne, was a small body of argoulets. Next came two bodies of infantry: regiment Cluseau and a number of independent compagnies drawn together under the Seigneur de Verduissant. They numbered some 2,500 men in total. The centre was formed from cavalry: 1,200 horse, drawn up en haye, with Joyeuse himself in the centre, and then Mercurio's stradiots, 500 gens d'armes under François de Montigny and the chevaux legers all under

---

23 Aubigné rejected Sully's self-glorifying figure of 8,000 foot as too high according to Oman, *War in the Sixteenth Century*, p.471.

Die Kron Franckreich in dieser zeit
Stunt widrum auß ein schweren streit
Der Guiser mit gwalt greiff nach der Kron
Nauarra diselb auch wolt hon.

Der Bahst schlug zu ther jn den Ban
Den Nauarra, der keyrt sich nit dran
Griff wacker drauff, den Gwisen nahm
Waß er an Volck vnd gude bekam.

Dem Joyeusen solchs brach verdrieß
Ein Feltschlacht im ankunden ließ
Deß freugt sich der Nauarrisch helt
Bei Momgon seins feinds waert jm felt.

Schlug jm bei vier tausent Man
Der Joyeus starb auch auff dem plan
An 20 Octob: 1587.

Hogenberg print of
the Battle of Coutras.
(Rijksmuseum, Amsterdam)

Jean Marquis de Lavardin (converted Catholic son of the late Huguenot commander). The left wing consisted of the remaining infantry, numbering 2,800 men of the regiments Picardie and Charles(?) de Tiercelin (the army's Mareschal de Camp).

The Huguenots had no more than 5,000 foot, organised into eight small regiments, each with many more arquebusiers than pikemen. The cavalry was made up of 1,300 horsemen, probably mainly if not all pistoliers by this stage, reinforced by 200 more under the Condé's Catholic brother, Charles Comte de Saissons. Clermont d'Amboise commanded the modest artillery train of three guns. The right of their line rested on, or rather in, a 'warren' of scrubby parkland surrounded by a ditch. Four regiments of foot, perhaps 2,000 men, occupied this position. Like his opponent, Henry placed his cavalry in the centre, in five bodies. Those on the right, under Henry Vicomte de Turenne and Tremouille, were those who had been skirmishing before dawn. The centre, under himself and Condé, was two compact bodies of pistoliers. The left-hand body of horse were Soisson's men. Between each body of horse were groups of enfans perdus. Towards the left of the line, on a low mound, were deployed the army's guns and 300 arquebusiers. The remaining three infantry regiments were still marching behind the army's front line to reinforce the left wing when the battle began. Henry's position was a strong one but contained

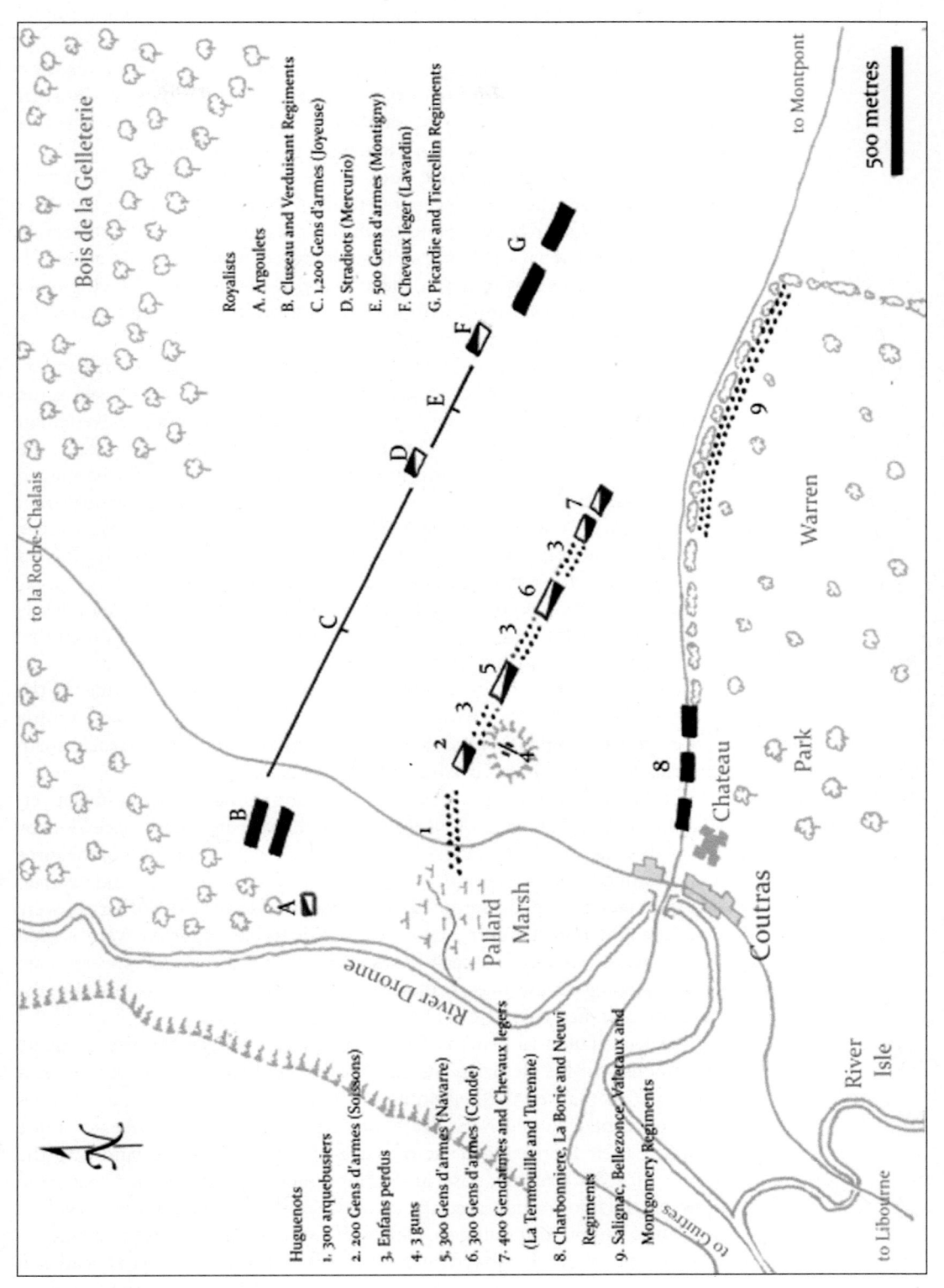

Map of the Battle of Coutras, 1587.

Huguenots
1. 300 arquebusiers
2. 200 Gens d'armes (Soissons)
3. Enfans perdus
4. 3 guns
5. 300 Gens d'armes (Navarre)
6. 300 Gens d'armes (Conde)
7. 400 Gendarmes and Chevaux legers (La Termfouille and Turenne)
8. Charbonniere, La Borie and Neuvi Regiments
9. Salignac, Bellezonce, Vateaux and Montgomery Regiments

Royalists
A. Angoulets
B. Cluseau and Verduisant Regiments
C. 1,200 Gens d'armes (Joyeuse)
D. Stradiots (Mercurio)
E. 500 Gens d'armes (Montigny)
F. Chevaux leger (Lavardin)
G. Picardie and Tiercellin Regiments

500 metres

a potentially fatal flaw. In the event of a defeat, the two rivers would funnel routing units through Coutras and over narrow fords.

The battle began at 9:00 a.m. Though few in number, Henry's guns were effective in galling the Royalist forces. The latter's artillery was badly sited and offered little in return. To escape the effects of this fire, the Royalist line moved forward. At this point the Huguenots recited Psalm 118.

In the warren, the Royalist foot came to grips with the Protestant arquebusiers, but the fight degenerated into a confused melee in the thick undergrowth. Lavardin was able to throw back Turenne and Tremouille, whose cavalry fled back to Coutras, though their commanders and a handful of men rallied on Navarre. On the other end of the line, the Huguenot infantry ordered to skirmish with the Royalist foot threw themselves on the enemy, despite being outnumbered by almost seven to one!

The battle was decided in the centre, where both army commanders fought. Joyeuse's inexperienced gens d'armes launched their charge some distance away from Henry's waiting pistoliers. By the time they arrived, their thin line was rather disordered, and their horses blown. At short rage, the enfans perdus opened fire, causing further mayhem, and into this ragged line charged Henry's men. Their compact formations cut through their opponents with comparative ease. The Royalist cavalry gave way. Joyeuse was killed as he attempted to surrender. Then the Huguenot cavalry turned on the wings of the royal army, causing them to retreat also.

The Royalists lost over 3,000 dead, including 400 gentlemen, while Henry's own losses were no more than 200. Henry famously exclaimed that never again would anyone say the Huguenots had never won a battle.

Despite the unequivocal nature of his victory, Navarre squandered the opportunity to follow it up with a more substantial move. Instead of marching east as he had originally intended, his army broke up. Condé struck north towards the Loire whilst Turenne moved against Matignon.

On the eastern frontier, the isolated and (though they did not know it yet) abandoned force under Dohna was defeated twice in quick succession by Henry de Guise. At the Combat of Vimory (26 October 1587) part of the force was encamped with poor security at the village of the same name and overrun in a swift attack. The disillusioned Swiss troops (the survivors of Jarrie) were persuaded to return home after their considerable expenses were settled. Then at the Combat of Auneau (24 November 1587) the reiters were again caught napping during an early morning assault. Now open to negotiation, the Germans accepted terms from Henry III on 8 December.

The King failed to provide Guise with what he believed was adequate recompense for his victories. Instead he showered Espernon with titles and favours. This marked the beginning of the end as far as the Ligue notables were concerned. Not even the death, through illness, of the Prince de Condé mollified their increasing sense of betrayal. Over the winter and into the spring of 1588 tensions rose and minor incidents of violence occurred between the two parties at court. In May, Guise entered Paris in breach of the King's ban on him doing so. Henry III's subsequent attempt to round up Guise's supporters were foiled by the Parisian mob who erected barricades in the streets. Fearing for his own safety in the hostile city, the King retired to

Chartres. With his own capital in arms against him, he had little option but to adopt a more conciliatory tone and accepted the Ligue's various demands.

Henry III was far from resigned to the situation, however. After failing to re-establish control by calling the Estates General at Bloys, he took the drastic step on 23 December 1588 of having the Duc de Guise assassinated by his bodyguard. The Cardinal de Guise followed his brother the following day. This act infuriated members of the Ligue, and across France towns and cities fell under their control, joining Paris in rebellion against the Crown. Henry's cousin, Charles Duc de Mayenne, assumed command of their forces.

The Picard town of Senlis had declared for Henry III and a force of 10,000 Ligueurs, including 6,000 Paris militia was dispatched against it. They were led by Charles Duc d'Aumale. A force of only 2,500 Royalists under the command of Henry Duc de Longueville, La Noue and Charles de Humières moved to relieve the town. At the subsequent Combat of Senlis (17 May 1589) they put the disorderly Ligue force to flight.

Having alienated the hardline Catholic faction, Henry III was left with little alternative but to ally himself with Navarre. The two kings marched on the capital and set about the 1st Siege of Paris (30 July to 5 August 1589). On 1 August Henry II was himself assassinated by a friar in revenge for his own killings. Before he expired, he recognised Henry de Navarre as his successor.

Ninth War, 'Henry IV's Conquest of the Kingdom' (August 1589 to April 1598)

Although many of the nobles present in the royal army besieging Paris accepted the succession of Navarre as Henry IV, many others refused to serve a heretic. The army rapidly dwindled in numbers and could no longer maintain the siege. Few towns in the north of the country supported his claim.

Rather than making for the safety of the south, Henry IV chose instead to march into Normandie and impose his will on the kingdom's richest province. He threatened Rouen, which brought Charles de Mayenne and a large Ligue army to confront him.

Battle of Arques (21 September 1589) – '… pour mourir avec leur roi?'

Arques was the largest and most hard-fought of a series of assaults led by Mayenne against Henry IV's forces based in the Normandie port of Dieppe between the middle of September and early October. His initial attacks were directed at the Dieppe suburbs, but were beaten off. So, he sought alternative means of completing his blockade of the city.

Two roads linked the village of Arques with the city of Dieppe. The roads are separated by the River Bethune, which being both tidal and marshy was an impediment to Mayenne's attempt to trap Henry. The bridge at Arques was, therefore, of vital importance. The eastern road, by which Mayenne advanced, ran between a thickly wooded hill known as the Foret d'Arques and marshes bordering the river. A relatively narrow cultivated area, bounded by thick hedges, lay between these two features on either side of the road. Henry reckoned it to be the best defensive position in the vicinity and set about improving it still further. Ditches were dug on either side of the road, one set where the gap between the woods and marsh was narrowest, near a small chapel known as the Maladerie de Sainct Etienne, and another 500 paces to the rear, closer to Arques itself.

The exact number and disposition of the Royalists are uncertain as contemporary accounts are difficult to reconcile.[24] According to Sully,[25] of the 8,000 men available to him, Henry deployed only 3,000 foot and 600 horse in this position, the balance remaining in Dieppe. This is probably an underestimate. Sully states that Henry's infantry was placed as follows: 600 arquebusiers in the forward trenches, the 1,200 Swiss on both sides of the road next to them or a little to the rear, and 1,200 French arquebusiers in reserve. He divided his cavalry into two groups. One, under his own command, was between the two lines of infantry between the wooded hill and the road. The other, under the young illegitimate son of Charles IX, Charles Comte d'Auvergne, was between the road and the marsh.

Avila gives a different arrangement.[26] In the days before the battle, he indicates that Biron deployed the forces he had on hand at the time: the trench about the Maladerie was occupied by 12 compagnies of Swiss and 300 French arqubusiers. The remaining Swiss, the so-called guard regiment under Colonel Galatti, were in a trench 500 paces *forward* of this position.[27] He also had with him a further 700 French foot and 600 cavalry.[28] Biron was then later joined by Henry with additional forces, including d'Auvergne's cavalry, chevaux legers supported by two compagnies of gens d'armes, who were initially positioned well forward. Avila has the Duc de Montpensier commanding the cavalry on the left wing, gentlemen volunteers and three compagnies of gens d'armes.

In some accounts, a regiment of 600 landsknechts is also mentioned as having been stationed at the first trench.[29] Henry placed guns in the Chateau d'Arques, but some accounts indicate four more were placed behind the first trench.[30] His troops spent the night under arms, expecting the Catholic attack at any time.

Mayenne's Ligue army reputedly numbered 24,000–35,000 men. When he left Paris he was recorded as leading 6,000 Swiss, 4,000 landsknechts paid for by Spain, 12,000 French and Lorrainer infantry and 4,500 cavalry.

---

24 Sully took part in the battle, but is not a careful chronicler and prone to self-aggrandisement. Avila is more considered, but also more removed from events. Aubigné, on this occasion, is rather light on detail.

25 Oman, *War in the Sixteenth Century*, p.488 summarises the different strength estimates for Henry's forces given by Sully, Aubigné and Avila.

26 Enrico Caterino D'Avila, *History of the Civil Wars in France* (London: Henry Herringman, 1678), translator Roger L'Estrange, pp.419–420.

27 He specifically says that they had their backs to the Maladerie and facing the oncoming Ligue forces. All other accounts have the second trench behind the Maladerie, closer to the town of Arques.

28 This probably amounts to around 3,600 men, which is Sully's total for the royal forces involved, but it is clear that the King brought substantial reinforcements with him from Dieppe.

29 Oman, *War in the Sixteenth Century*, p.488. D'Avila, *History of the Civil Wars*, p.420, says there were soldiers 'of the same nation' as the enemy Landsknechts in this position, but he may be referring to German-speaking Swiss.

30 Oman, *War in the Sixteenth Century*, p.488.

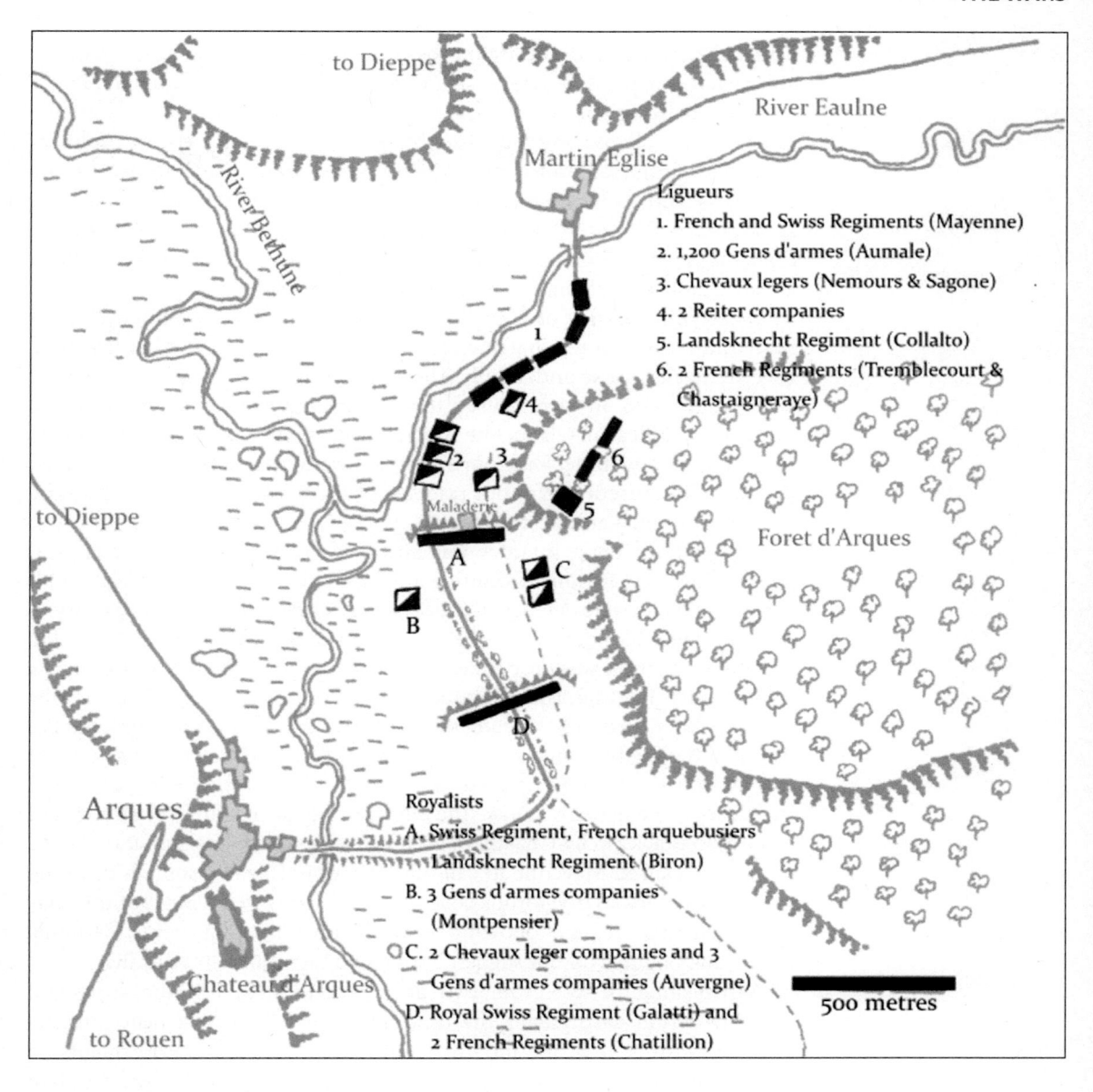

Ligueurs
1. French and Swiss Regiments (Mayenne)
2. 1,200 Gens d'armes (Aumale)
3. Chevaux legers (Nemours & Sagone)
4. 2 Reiter companies
5. Landsknecht Regiment (Collalto)
6. 2 French Regiments (Tremblecourt & Chastaigneraye)

Royalists
A. Swiss Regiment, French arquebusiers Landsknecht Regiment (Biron)
B. 3 Gens d'armes companies (Montpensier)
C. 2 Chevaux leger companies and 3 Gens d'armes companies (Auvergne)
D. Royal Swiss Regiment (Galatti) and 2 French Regiments (Chatillion)

500 metres

Map of the Battle of Arques, 1589.#

The Lorrainers were led by the son of their Duc: Henry Marquis de Pons. Mayenne's half-brother, the Duc de Nemours, led the Ligue troops from Lionnois. Mayenne was joined in Normandie by his cousin, Charles Duc d'Aumale, with additional forces. They spent the night before the battle at the village of Martin Eglise and began their attack in the early morning. The battlefield was covered by an early mist that prevented either side from fully seeing each other's dispositions. Mayenne must have had some inkling of the strength of the position, since he sent a body of landsknechts through the wood to outflank its main strength. They were followed by two French Regiments. This force was disordered by their march and upon reaching the Royalist trenches, claimed that they were unpaid deserters and wished to surrender (a common enough occurrence). Their brethren lining the trench were deceived and did not fire on them. Thus, the Ligue landsknechts were able to take the position with ease, unhinging the first defensive line.

Both the King and Biron moved forward independently to discover the cause of the collapse and were caught up in the rout of their foot soldiers. Biron was unhorsed and almost killed. Whilst Henry, surrounded by the enemy, is said to have cried out: 'What, are there not in all France fifty gentlemen with the resolution to die with their King!'[31] But help was at hand, François de Chastillon at the head of 500 arquebusiers delayed the Catholic advance sufficiently long for the King to be extricated.

Meanwhile, a body of 800–900 Catholic cavalry advanced between the road and marsh. In this narrow area, they were defeated and pushed back by 150 Royalist horse under Sully. They retreated onto four more supporting compagnies who, in turn, caused the Royalists to retire. Auvergne led the remaining 150 cavalry from the Royalist left wing to push back the Ligue cavalry a second time. But, once again, they were reinforced and forced the Royalists to retire. Without reserves of their own, they fell back to the infantry stationed around the chapel.

The Catholic Ligue infantry was now free to advance down the road. It engaged the new Royalist front line and would have overwhelmed it had it not been for the stoic defence of the Swiss. An attempt by Catholic cavalry to outflank them blundered into the marsh and came to nothing. Even so, the Royalists' situation was desperate, as they had no more fresh units to throw into the bitter fighting. The rising sun burnt off the fog and the whole Catholic force could be seen ranged along the road. This was a daunting sight, but the lifting of the fog benefited the Royalists more. Their artillery, firing from an elevated position in the chateau, was able to plough salvo after salvo into the close-packed enemy ranks. The effectiveness of this fire, the strength of a counter-attack led by Chastillon and the unexpected determination of the resistance, caused Mayenne to call off the action. Royalist sources claim he was thrown back by a vigorous counter-attack led by the King, but this may have been no more than following up an already retreating enemy. Certainly, the casualty figures do not suggest a rout: 600 Ligue and 200 Royalist.

Skirmishing between the two armies continued, but the successful delaying action gave Henry the time he needed for first a fleet carrying 5,000 English and Scots and then additional French reinforcements to arrive. Mayenne recognised that the opportunity of capturing the Protestant pretender or driving him into exile had passed, and he eventually withdrew to Picardie.

Henry's forces were bolstered by the arrival of English money as well as troops. With this he was able to recruit from the provinces. He made a second attempt on Paris but was able to achieve little beyond plundering its suburbs due to the lack of a siege train. By the end of November, he had set up his court in Tours.

He began his next campaign after only a few days, in December, marching once more on Normandie and its principal city, Rouen. He seized towns

---

31   Avila, *History of the Civil Wars*, p.421, is amongst others who report this incident.

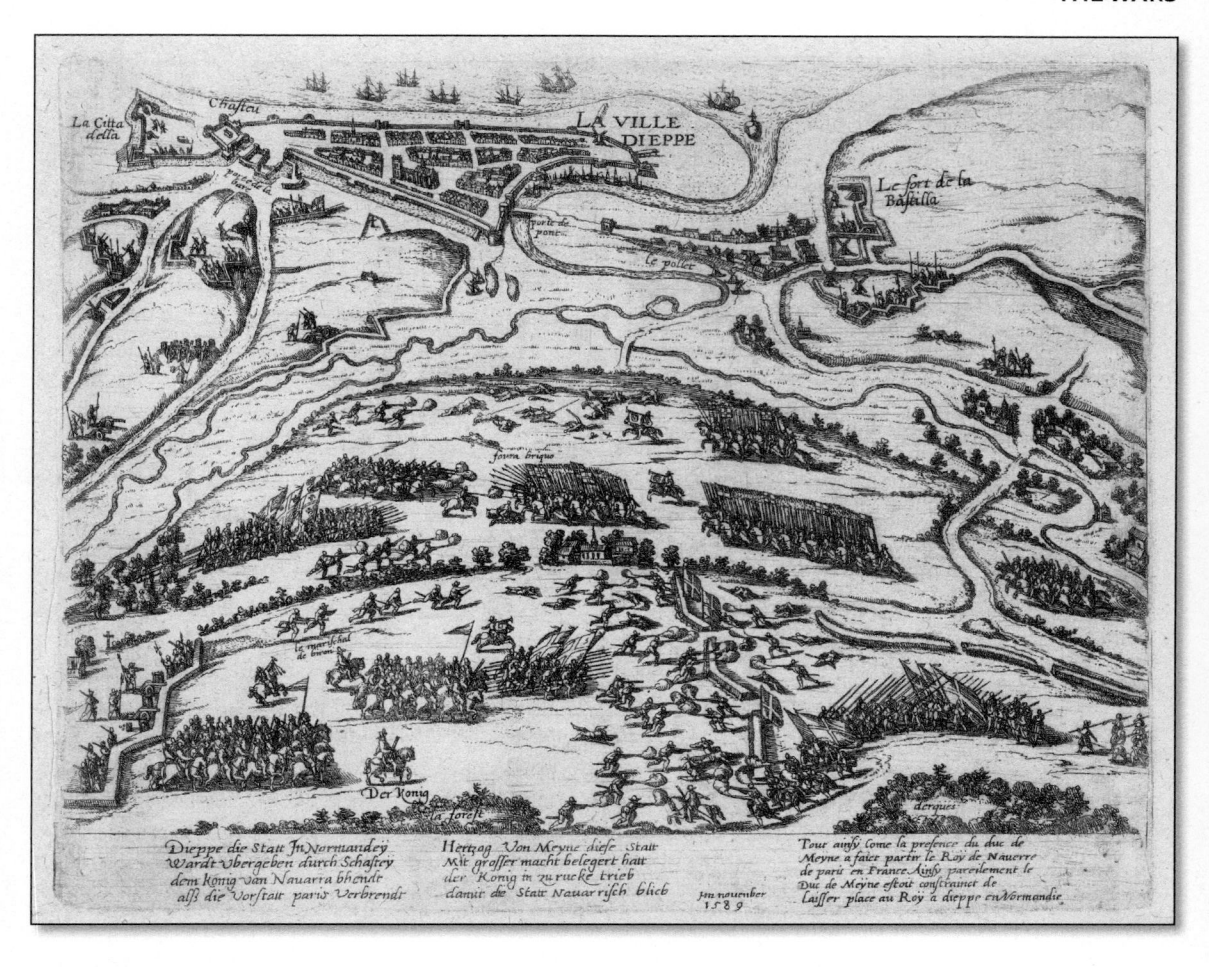

along the way and others opened their gates to him. In this way, he reduced the Ligue's control to only Rouen and Havre de Grace.

But Mayenne had not been idle. King Felipe II of Spain sent him 500 arquebusiers and 1,200 cavalry from the Netherlands under Filips, Graaf van Egmond.[32] With these, and his own Ligue forces, he was able to recapture a number of towns in Henry's wake. Interrupting his campaign in Normandie, Henry moved south and besieged Dreux with part of his army. Mayenne marched to its relief and then followed the royal army as it retreated northwards, where Henry turned on him.

Battle of Ivry (14 March 1590) – 'Ne perdez point de vue mon panache'
On 13 March, Henry deployed the Royalist force on the open ground of the Plaine de Sainct André, between Nonancourt and Ivry, taking great care with his dispositions. There was some skirmishing, but no general action was fought. The King feared that Mayenne might slip away despite having

---

32 Avila, *History of the Civil Wars*, p.441 has 1,500 lancers and 400 carabines [mounted arquebusiers] 'armoured for the most part in back, breast and pot'.

the advantage of numbers. The Royalist army had perhaps 3,000 horse and 8,000–9,000 foot, though chroniclers vary in their estimates, while the Ligue forces numbered 4,000 horse and 15,000 foot. On 14 March, Henry deployed in exactly the same manner as the day before, but, due to the reluctance of the Ligueurs to advance, he was obliged to manoeuvre his line some distance until he came within cannon shot.[33]

The Royalists were drawn up in two bodies, with a small reserve under Biron. Henry deployed the avant-garde on the left, starting with a body of 300 cavalry under the Mareschal d'Aumont on the far left of his line with a regiment of infantry on each of his flanks. Next was another body of cavalry under François Duc de Montpensier, who also commanded the avant-garde, with Swiss pikemen and half a regiment of French arquebusiers on his left and 400 landsknechts on his right. Beyond these were the army's five guns. Two groups of chevaux legers, totalling 400 horse, under Auvergne and Anne Seigneur de Givry formed the right flank of the avant-garde. The bataille was ranged to the right of this position. First came a regiment of 300 cavalry under the Charles de Gontaut, son of Mareschal Biron. These men were supported by a regiment of 800 infantry. Henry's own cavalry came next. This was the largest body of horse and supported by the cream of the infantry: four regiments of his Swiss and four of French, including the guards. On the right wing was Dietrich von Schomberg's regiment of reiters and more foot. The small reserve consisted of 150 cavalry and two regiments of infantry under the command of Mareschal Biron. A group of enfans perdus skirmished in front of the main line. By this date, all the royal cavalry were using pistols rather than lance. A body of horse under Charles de Humières and other nobles may have arrived only as the battle was starting (though it may have been on the previous day).[34]

Mayenne's army had a somewhat longer front as it was both larger and contained many lance-armed gens d'armes. He may have deployed in a crescent formation that was intended to envelop the Royalists' flanks.[35] He drew his army up with a right wing under Nemours and a smaller left wing under Aumale. The centre, under his own immediate command, seems to have belonged to neither. On the right wing, chevaux legers and gens d'armes

---

33 Many recent authors, following Oman, *War in the Sixteenth Century*, pp.499–501, place the battle in the position occupied by the Royalist army on 13 March, but it is clear that Henry advanced some distance towards the River Eure before engaging. This location is marked by the obelisk raised by Napoleon in 1802 to commemorate the event. Oman, taking his lead from Avila's and Aubigné's accounts, suggests that Henry's manoeuvres were small adjustments to 'gain some advantage of sun and wind'. However, Aubigné, *Histoire Universelle*, vol. 2, pp.318–319, makes it clear that Mayenne's army awaited his attack from its position close to the Eure.

34 Avila, *History of the Civil Wars*, p.444, has them arriving on the 13th. The English translation says four score horsemen from Picardie, but notes the French version has 400, plus 200 from Poictou. Aubigné, *Histoire Universelle*, vol. 2, p.317, suggests it was the 14th. One near-contemporary print of the dispositions on 14 March (Frans Hogenberg, 'Bataille d'Ivry', BNF Gallica Digital Library <https://gallica.bnf.fr/ark:/12148/btv1b8400933j.item>, accessed 2 May 2020) shows this body of horsemen behind the right of the main Royalist line while another (Anon., 'Bataille d'Ivry', BNF Gallica Digital Library, < https://gallica.bnf.fr/ark:/12148/btv1b8400936s.item>, accessed 2 May 2020) has them deployed within the line, on the far left.

35 Aubigné, *Histoire Universelle*, vol. 2, p.316.

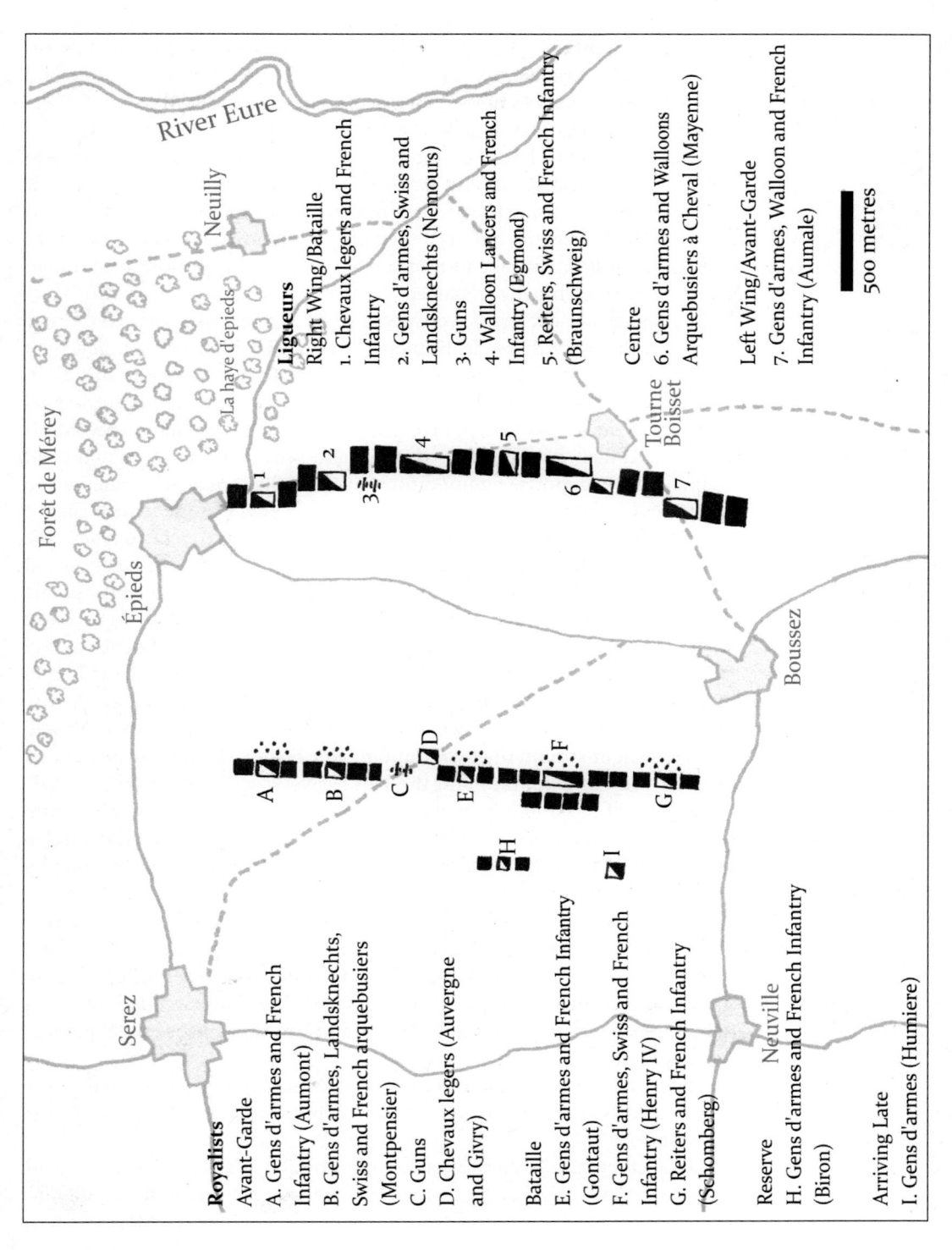

Map of the Battle of Ivry, 1590

were reinforced by landsknechts and Swiss foot under Nemours himself. Walloon lancers under Egmond came next, supported by some French foot. Beside these was the Ligue artillery. Next to the guns was a regiment of reiters commanded by Eric von Braunschweig. These were backed up by Swiss and French infantry. Next to the reiters were 700 lancers under Mayenne's direct command, and beside them, 400 mounted Spanish arquebusiers. Forming the left of the Ligue's line was a body of French cavalry under Aumale, also supported by landsknechts and Walloon infantry.

The battle took some time to begin. During this pause the Royalist guns caused several casualties amongst the Ligue Walloons and reiters. Their own guns inflicted little damage in return. Unwilling to stand motionless under fire, both sides eventually advanced.

The Ligue chevaux legers were defeated by Aumont's cavalry, who drove them into the Haye d'Épieds. Nemours closed with Montpensier, and their men were soon locked in a furious melee. The Catholics had more success in the centre, as Egmond beat the Royalist chevaux legers and then turned his attention to the guns and supporting arquebusiers. But Gontaut wheeled his cavalry into their now disordered ranks and sent them flying back behind their infantry supports. Egmond himself was killed. Mayenne intended to catch the King's own cavalry between the fire of the Spanish arquebusiers à cheval and the reiters while charging them with his own gens d'armes. The reiters began shooting and wheeling away in their 'caracole' fashion but were shaken by the return fire of the Royalist enfans perdus and became disordered. Their commander was killed, and they retired in some haste, disordering some of Mayenne's horsemen in the process. The Spaniards had more success, killing the King's standard bearer with their fire, but failing to halt the impetus of his charge. Henry crashed into Mayenne's gens d'armes, still sorting themselves out after colliding with the reiters, and there followed an intense fight around the two commanders. Eventually, the Royalists burst through the Catholic lines and the latter gave way. On their left, Aumale found himself in a tough fight with the Royalist reiters, who closed with him rather than trying to caracole. The matter was only decided when Mareschal Biron arrived with the reserve to tip the scales against them. Schomberg himself was killed, however.

Thus far, few of the infantry had taken any part in the battle. On seeing their cavalry defeated, most abandoned any idea of resistance. The Ligueur Swiss, staring down their Royalist brethren, signalled their willingness to surrender if granted quarter. This was granted. The King extended the terms to the French infantry, but the Walloons and landsknechts were slaughtered without mercy.

The Ligue lost 800 horse and 3,000 foot killed and many thousands more captured. It was effectively the end of their independent field army. The Royalists lost 500.

His victory gave Henry another opportunity to take Paris, though he was slow to take it. After capturing several smaller towns in its vicinity, he established a blockade of the city and began the 2nd Siege of Paris (7 May to 30 August 1590). The defenders of Paris numbered 1,500 landsknechts, a similar number of Swiss and other infantry, and some 48,000 militia, under

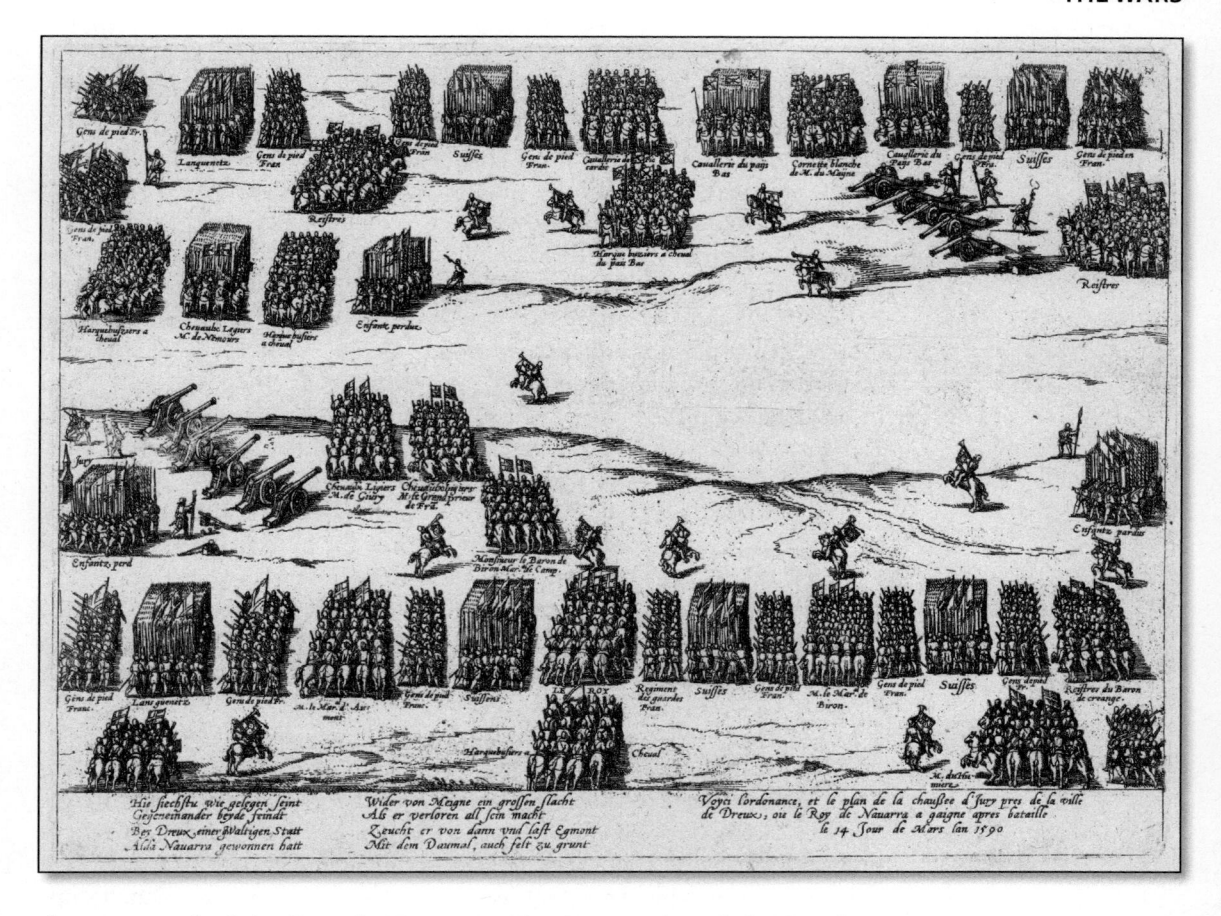

the command of the Duc de Nemours. They outnumbered the Royalists but lacked quality and cohesion. Consequently, the blockade succeeded in reducing the city to dire straits. The Ligue leadership tried to encourage the citizens by appealing to their faith: the clerics of the city even mustered an armed procession that marched through its streets. Still, the enthusiasm of many began to fade.

Filipe II responded to the Ligue's appeals by sending Alessandro Farnese, Duca di Parma, perhaps the most renowned general of his age, with 14,000 Spanish troops into France from the Netherlands. He was joined by 12,000 Frenchmen under Mayenne. They marched to the relief of Paris. Reasoning that he had to defeat this new threat quickly if he had any chance of continuing the siege, Henry took 27,000 men to meet them at Chelles. Parma recognised the effectiveness of the Royalist cavalry and entrenched his position, from which Henry was unable to draw him. Meanwhile, Parma sent a detachment around the Royalist flank and opened a route to Paris. Henry was forced to retreat and, after making an ill-considered assault against its walls, he broke off the siege, though he maintained a loose blockade until 1592. His mission complete, Parma returned to the Netherlands in November 1590, shadowed by Henry's forces.

Spanish intervention alarmed Elizabeth I of England. Having just seen off the Great Armada, she had no wish to see a Spanish-dominated France on

Hogenberg print of the Battle of Ivry. (Rijksmuseum, Amsterdam)

the other side of the channel. Thus, she was more willing to support Henry IV, providing money to raise German mercenaries and also sending English troops into Normandie, though initially Bretaigne was their destination, as 4,000 Spanish troops had been sent to bolster the Ligue in this province. They fought alongside Henry Prince de Dombes at the inconclusive Combat of Marc'hallac'h (22 June 1591). However, co-ordination between the Protestant monarchs was poor and instead of joining the English forces in Normandie, Henry chose to prosecute the successful Sieges of Chartes (19 February to 19 April 1591) and of Noyons (25 July to 19 August 1591). Even after these events, Henry did not initially go himself, as the Queen expected, but sent Mareschal Biron to co-operate with the 4,000 English troops under the Earl of Essex to begin the Siege of Rouen (11 November 1591 to 20 April 1592). The garrison contained 6,000 men under the André Seigneur de Villars. Henry IV arrived 23 November.

While Rouen held out, Parma was ordered by Filipe II back into France. Moving through Picardie, he marched towards the besieged city. Faced with a similar situation to that before Paris in 1590, Henry chose an alternative strategy. Leaving his infantry in the siege lines, he took 7,000 cavalry to harass Parma's march. The latter adopted a tight defensive formation that Henry was unable to disrupt, but such an expedient reduced the speed of the Spanish advance. On 5 February 1593, Henry was wounded while fighting in a cavalry skirmish, narrowly avoiding capture. He retired on Dieppe to recover.

Meanwhile Villars led a sortie from Rouen on 24 February and wreaked havoc among the siege lines. The Ligue would only allow a token force of Spanish inside the stronghold, fearing they would take control of one of France's largest cities. So, Parma withdrew to Picardie and the Royalists were able to maintain a blockade that reduced the morale of the city. Dutch ships carrying 3,000 men cut any hope of resupply from the sea. Villars begged Parma to return. He did so with 17,000 men. The Royalists abandoned the siege and Parma and Mayenne entered Rouen on 21 April.

Parma failed to engage Henry's depleted force, allowing him to rebuild its numbers. Instead he took the town of Caudebec, to secure the route to Havre de Grace, but was wounded during the assault. Henry, now with a larger force, moved to trap the Spanish and Ligue troops against the Seine, but in a brilliant manoeuvre, Parma built a bridge of boats under the noses of the Royalists and escaped on 21 May. He reinforced the garrison of Paris and then returned to the Low Countries. He never fully recovered from his wound and died on 2 December.

Henry's force was based on various Protestant and moderate Catholic factions rather than a royal army. After the exertions of the winter and spring many of these drifted away to their homes, leaving their king too weak to conduct large-scale operations during the summer. With a force of 3,000 horse and 6,000 foot he tried first to relieve and then re-capture Espernay in Champaigne. He succeeded on 8 August, but at the cost of the much-valued Mareschal Biron, who was killed in the action.

Meanwhile, warfare continued in the provinces. In Bretaigne, a Royalist force under Montpensier and another of the King's Catholic cousins, François Prince de Conti, conducted the Siege of Craon (14 April to 24 May 1592). They were assisted by English troops commanded by Sir John Norreys. but were attacked in the entrenchments by the Phillipe-Emmanuel Duc de Mercoeur and Spaniards under Don Juan del Águilia. Caught between this relief force and a sally by the town's defenders, the Royalists suffered a heavy defeat. Elsewhere the Ligue was less successful. In Guienne, Antoine Scipion Duc de Joyeuse, again supported by Spanish troops, was defeated by Espernon at the Combat of Villemur (19 October 1592). The young Joyeuse was drowned in the rout of his army. Lesdiguieres successfully defended Prouvence and the Daulphine from the predatory Duc de Savoye and the allied Ligue force commanded by the Duc de Nemours at the Combats of Esparron (15/16 April 1591) and Pontacharra (17 September 1591). He even carried the war into Piemont, fighting the Combat of Salbertrand (7 June 1593).

As the new year dawned, efforts to find common ground between the more moderate elements gained traction. France was in a parlous state. Foreign powers were seen as increasingly dangerous to the unity of the state. Military activity petered out. Henry then took the one step that undermined the central Ligue objection to his succession: he abjured his Huguenot faith on 25 July 1593.[36] He was formally crowned in a Catholic rite in Chartes on 27 February 1594. Many towns now rallied to his support, but Paris remained obstinate. Henry entered the city in force on 22 March via a coup de main, but there was little resistance. 3,000 Spaniards of the garrison were expelled. Other Ligue nobles and towns held out longer and with more determination.

Mayenne still held Bourgógne, Nemours Lionnois and Mercoeur Bretaigne. Espernon's position in Prouvence was ambiguous but hostile and Henry, the new Duc de Joyeuse, was resisting Montmorency in Languedoc. These factions were supported by Spain and, in Lionnois, by Savoye. To instil a sense of unity and brand the Ligue commanders as traitors to France, Henry formally declared war on Spain on 17 January 1595. In May, the King marched to Digion (Dijon). At the furious Combat of Fontaine-Française (5 June 1595) he was involved in a cavalry skirmish that evolved into a larger encounter. Their defeat led to disagreements between the Spanish commander, Don Luis de Velasco, and Mayenne. The former withdrew and Mayenne retreated. Digion's citadel surrendered and most of the province followed. Henry was liberal in rewarding those who accepted his clemency. Mayenne surrendered in January 1596. Espernon and Joyeuse quickly followed.

However, Henry's conversion meant the loss of support from his allies in England and Germany, though the Dutch continued to provide succour. When a Spanish force led by Pedro Enriquez Condé de Fuentes marched into Picardie in the summer of 1595, the King had limited resources to call upon. The Spanish took Le Catelet, Doullens and Cambrai before he could move against them. He established the 2nd Siege of La Fère (8 November 1595 to 16 May 1596) when he arrived. By the time it fell, the Spaniards had launched another offensive and, by means of a ruse, seized Amiens in March followed by Calais in April. Charles Duc de Biron initiated a Siege of Amiens

---

36 Unfortunately, it is unlikely he uttered the famous words 'Paris vaut bien une mess' (Paris is well worth a mass). It has been suggested that if the words are contemporaneous rather than apocryphal, they were spoken by Sully to the King.

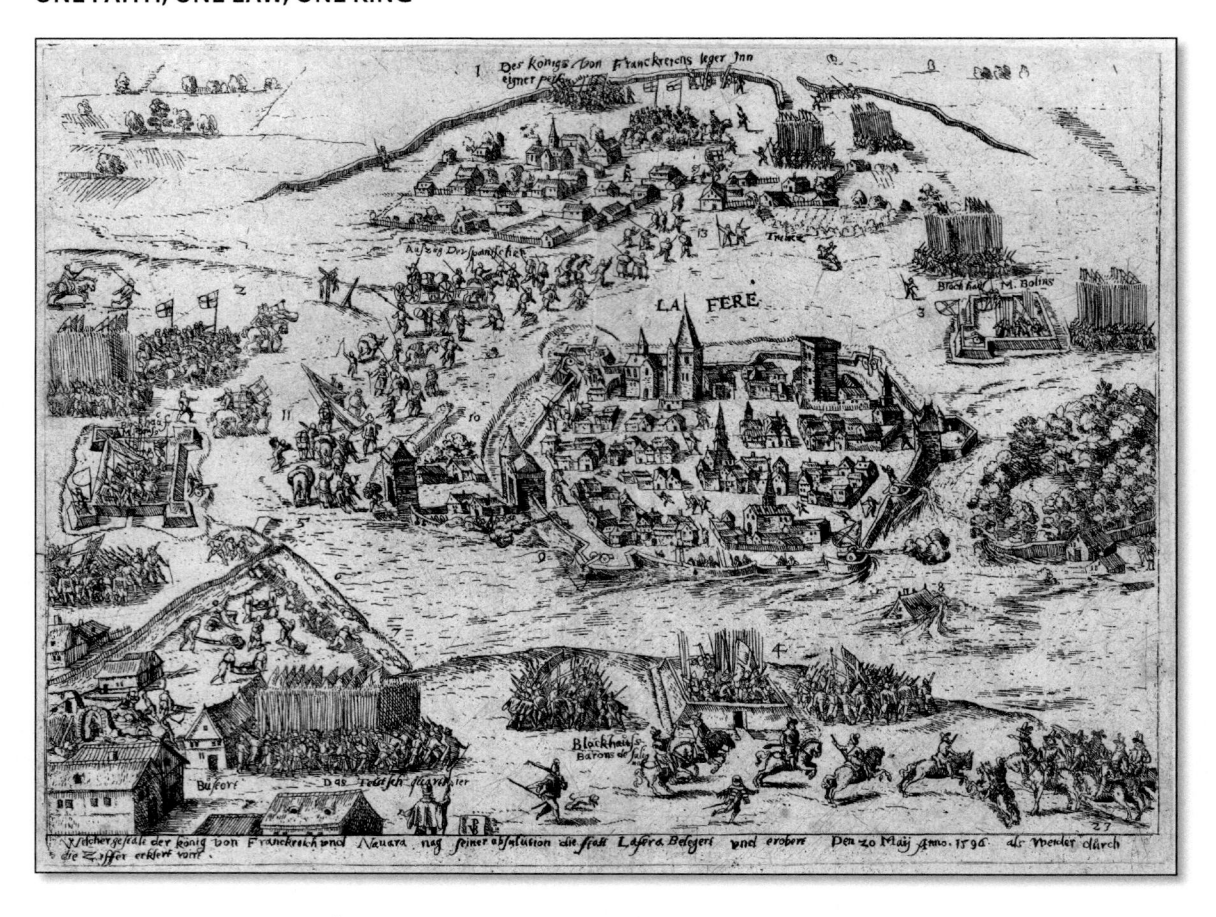

Hogenberg print of the Siege of La Fère. (Rijksmuseum, Amsterdam)

(13 May 1596 to 25 September 1597) in an attempt to recapture the city, the loss of which was a great blow to France's prestige. He was joined by Henry in June with significant reinforcements. He eventually ringed the city with a series of forts. On 15 September 1597, a large Spanish force under Cardinal Erzherzog Albrecht tried to break the siege, but his attempts were beaten off by Biron and Mayenne (now fighting on Henry's behalf).[37]

During these events, King Henry had unsuccessfully tried to cut the flow of Spanish reinforcements from Italy, by dispatching Lesdiguières with a force of 500 horse and 6,000 foot against Savoye. Whilst he failed to achieve this aim, he did defeat the Savoyard army twice at the Combats of Chamousset (19 July 1597) and Les Mollottes (14 August 1597).

---

37 It was during the events surrounding Amiens that Henry sent his famous letter starting with: 'Brave Crillon, pendés-vous de n'avoir été icy près de moy lundy dernier à la plus belle occasion quis se soit jamais veue' (Brave Crillon, hang yourself for not having been here with me last Monday on the best occasion ever). Due to Voltaire's creative use of history, this quote, with variations, is often wrongly associated with the Battle of Arques, though it must be admitted that Henry did use the phrase 'hang yourself...' on other occasions. The recipient in question was Louis des Balbes de Berton Seigneur de Crillon, a Catholic soldier from the Papal enclave of Avignon who fought at Calais, Dreux, Sainct Denys, Jarnac, Moncontour, Lepanto, La Rochelle and Ivry. He was Mestre de Camp of the Gardes Françaises from 1584 and known as 'le brave des braves' long before Maréchal Ney.

The last act of the wars came in early 1598. Henry set off to settle accounts with Mercoeur in Bretaigne. Towns along his march quickly expelled Ligue garrisons and Mercoeur saw that his defeat was inevitable. He yielded while he still had something to bargain with and received a handsome reward. On 13 April 1598, Henry issued the Edict of Nantes, which established the rights of the Huguenot minority until its revocation by his grandson, Louis XIV, in 1685. On 2 May 1598 France and Spain signed a peace treaty at Vervins.

2

The Commanders

The Great Offices of State

Ultimate military authority within the kingdom of France rested with its monarch. During the period of the wars both Henry III and Henry IV commanded armies in person and Charles IX was present with his forces on occasion. More frequently, however, actual command was devolved to leading nobles who held one of the main military posts. These can be seen as belonging to two categories: permanent or semi-permanent honours and temporary military posts.

Chief amongst the permanent honours was the Connestable de France. This venerable title dates back to the early feudal era, and its literal meaning, 'count of the stable' clearly associates it with the kingdom's noble cavalry. Only two individuals, father and son, held this position during the wars, though with a vacancy of 26 years between their tenures. Except during the brief ascendancy of Antoine de Bourbon, the connestable exercised executive command of the royal army if he was present. These men were:

- Anne de Montmorency, Seigneur, later Duc, de Montmorency: 1538–1567
- Henry de Montmorency, Seigneur de Damville later Duc de Montmorency: 1593–1614

Of similarly ancient lineage, the title of mareschal was granted in recognition of service. The following mareschaux held the rank during the wars, even if they did not actively command.

Appointed during the reign of Henry II:
- Jacques d'Albon, Seigneur de Sainct André: 1547–1562
- Charles I de Cossé, Comte de Brissac: 1550–1563

In the reign of François II:
- François de Montmorency, later Duc de Montmorency: 1559–1579

In the reign of Charles IX:

- François de Scépeaux, Seigneur de Vieilleville: 1562–1571
- Imbert de La Plâtrière, Seigneur de Bourdillon: 1564–1567
- Henry de Montmorency, Seigneur de Damville: 1566–1614
- Artus de Cossé-Brissac, Seigneur de Gonnor: 1567–1582
- Gaspard de Saulx, Seigneur de Tavannes: 1570–1575
- Honorat de Savoye, Marquis de Villars: 1571–1580
- Albert de Gondi, Duc de Retz: 1573–1602

In the reign of Henry III:

- Roger de Sainct Lary, Seigneur de Bellegarde: 1574–1579
- Blaise de Lasseran-Massencôme, Seigneur de Monluc: 1574–1577
- Armand de Gontaut, Baron de Biron: 1577–1592
- Jacques de Goyon, Seigneur de Matignon: 1579–1597
- Jean d'Aumont, Baron de Estrabonne: 1579–1595
- Guillaume de Joyeuse, Vicomte de Joyeuse: 1582–1592
- François Gouffier, Seigneur de Crèvecœur: 1586–1594

In the reign of Henry IV:

- Henry de La Tour d'Auvergne, Vicomte de Turenne, Duc de Bouillon: 1592–1623
- Charles II de Cossé, Duc de Brissac: 1594–1621
- Charles de Gontaut, Duc de Biron: 1594–1602
- Claude de La Chatre, Baron de la Maisonfort: 1594–1614
- Jean de Montluc de Balagny: 1594–1603
- Jean de Baumanoir, Marquis de Lavardin: 1595–1614
- Henry de Joyeuse, Duc de Joyeuse: 1595–1608
- Urbain de Montmorency-Laval, Marquis de Sablé: 1595–1629
- Alphonso d'Ornano: 1597–1610
- Guillaume de Hautemer, Comte de Grancey: 1597–1613

The admiral de France was also one of the great officers of the Crown, but, despite the title, its holders concerned themselves but little with naval warfare. The actual maritime role, when required, was mainly carried out by the regional admiraux of the Levant, Bretaigne and Guienne and the general des galeres (general of the galleys). Instead, the post of admiral was endowed with significant fiscal, judicial, military and political powers akin to those of the connestable or mareschaux. Those who held the rank during the Wars of Religion were as follows:

- Gaspard de Coligny: 1552–1572
- Honorat de Savoye, Marquis de Villars: 1572–1580
- Charles de Lorraine, Duc de Mayenne: 1580–1582
- Anne de Batarnay de Joyeuse, Duc de Joyeuse: 1582–1587
- Jean Louis de Nogaret de La Valette, Duc de Espernon: 1587–1589

- Antoine de Brichanteau, Marquis de Nangis: 1589–1590
- Bernard de Nogaret: 1589–1592
- Charles de Gontaut, Duc de Biron: 1592–1594
- André de Brancas: 1594–1595
- Charles de Montmorency, Seigneur de Merú: 1596–1612

Coligny was occasionally deprived of his rank during periods of conflict (Villars was temporarily appointed in 1569, for example), but effectively held it until his assassination.

Unlike the previous posts, which were typically lifelong appointments, the position of lieutenant general was of specific duration and often limited geography. In terms of authority, the holder was seen as the king's deputy and, therefore, outranked all others within their mandate. If the position was 'du Royaume' (of the kingdom), it was normally held by a prince du sang (literally a 'prince of the blood', more prosaically, a direct male descendant of Louis IX). During the wars, the following were appointed:[1]

- Antoine de Bourbon, Roy de Navarre: 1561–1562
- François de Lorraine, Duc de Guise: 1562–1563
- Henry de Valois, Duc d'Anjou: 1567–1573
- Charles III, Duc de Lorraine: 1574–?
- Charles de Lorraine, Duc de Mayenne: 1589–1595

Although the scions of the house of Lorraine later came to be regarded as princes du sang, this was not the case during this era. Guise's elevation to the position was as a result of the army's acclamation, and later confirmed in recognition of his dominant position at court as well as his military capacity. He had held the position twice before, in 1558, during the Connestable's imprisonment, and in 1560, during his ascendancy over François II. The Duc de Lorriane, a foreign prince with little military experience but favoured by the Queen Mother, was appointed to keep the office out of the Duc d'Alençon's grasp. Mayenne's authority did not devolve from the King, but was ratified by the Parlement de Paris, at that time under the control of the Ligue.

Each of the 11 border provinces of the kingdom was entrusted to a gouverneur with local military responsibility. He was assisted by a lieutenant-gouverneur. These individuals had wide-ranging military, political and judicial powers within their province.

Bourgógne:

- Claude de Lorraine, Duc d'Aumale: 1550–1573
- Charles de Lorraine, Duc de Mayenne: 1573–1595

---

1 Stuart Carroll, *Noble Power During the French Wars of Religion* (Cambridge: Cambridge University Press, 1998), p.181, indicates that François Duc d'Alençon, and by that time also Duc d'Anjou, was also appointed to this rank in 1580.

Bretaigne:

- Jean de Brosse, Duc d'Étampes: 1543–1565
- Sébastien de Luxembourg, Duc de Penthièvre, Vicomte de Martigues: 1565–1569
- Louis de Bourbon, Duc de Montpensier: 1569–1582
- Philippe-Emmanuel de Lorraine, Duc de Mercoeur: 1582–1598
- (in opposition) Henry de Bourbon, Prince de Dombes: 1589–1598

Champaigne:

- François de Clèves, Duc de Nevers: 1561–1563
- François de Lorraine, Duc de Guise: 1563
- Henry de Lorraine, Duc de Guise: 1563–1588
- Charles de Gonzague, Duc de Rethelois: 1589–1631

Daulphine:

- François de Lorraine, Duc de Guise: 1520–1563
- Charles de Bourbon, Prince de la Roche-sur-Yon: 1563–1565
- Louis de Bourbon, Duc de Montpensier: 1565–1569
- François de Bourbon, Prince de Dombes: 1569–1588
- Henry de Bourbon, Prince de Dombes: 1588–1591
- (de facto) Henry de Savoye, Duc de Nemours: 1591
- Jean d'Aumont, Comte de Châteauroux: 1592–1595
- François de Bourbon, Prince de Conti: 1596–1601

Guienne:

- Antoine de Bourbon, Roy de Navarre: 1555–1562
- Henry de Bourbon, Roy de Navarre: 1562–1596

Lieutenans Generaux (during Henry's minority and subsequent imprisonment at court):

- Blaise de Lasseran-Massencôme, Seigneur de Monluc: 1562–1571
- Honorat de Savoye, Marquis de Villars: 1571–1578
- Armand de Gontaut, Baron de Biron: 1578–1582

Isle de France:

- François de Montmorency, Duc de Montmorency: 1556–1579
- René de Villequier, Seigneur de Clairvaux: 1579–1587
- François d'O, Seigneur d'O: 1587–1594

Languedoc:

- Anne de Montmorency, Seigneur, later Duc, de Montmorency: 1526–1563
  - Henry de Montmorency, Seigneur de Damville: 1563–1614

Lionnois:

- Jacques d'Albon, Seigneur de Sainct André: 1550–1562
- Jacques de Savoye, Duc de Nemours: 1562–1571
- François de Mandelot, Seigneur de Pacy: 1571–1588
- Charles-Emmanuel de Savoye, Duc de Nemours: 1588–1595

Normandie:

- Henry-Robert de La Marck, Duc de Bouillon: 1556–1574

This, the richest province in the kingdom, was divided into three for a time after the Calvinist Bouillon's death. Even whilst in office, his authority was undermined by the three lieutenans generaux who administered the province between them. This situation continued until Joyeuse's appointment:

- Jean de Mouy, Seigneur de La Mailleraye (Upper Normandie: the bailliages (bailiwicks) of Caux and Gisors)
- Jacques de Goyon, Seigneur de Matignon (Lower Normandie: Alençon, Caen and Cotentin)
  - Tanneguy Le Veneur, Seigneur de Carrouges (Rouen and Evreux)
- Anne de Batarnay, Duc de Joyeuse: 1583–1587
- Jean-Louis de Nogaret de La Valette, Duc d'Espernon: 1587–1588
- François de Bourbon, Duc de Montpensier: 1588–1592
- Henry de Bourbon, Prince de Dombes: 1592–1608

Picardie:

- Louis de Bourbon, Prince de Condé: 1561–1569
- Léonor d'Orléans, Duc de Longueville: 1569–1573
- Henry de Bourbon, Prince de Condé: 1573–1588
- Louis de Gonzague, Duc de Nevers: 1588–1589
- Henry I d'Orleans, Duc de Longueville: 1589–1595
- Henry II d'Orleans, Duc de Longueville: 1595–1618

Prouvence:

- Claude de Savoye, Comte de Tende: 1525–1566
- Honore de Savoye, Comte de Tende: 1566–1572
- Gaspard de Saulx, Seigneur de Tavannes: 1572–1573
- Albert de Gondi, Comte de Retz: 1573–1578
- François de La Baume, Comte de Suze: 1578–1579

- Henry d'Angoulême, Comte d'Angoulême: 1579–1586
- Jean-Louis de Nogaret de La Valette, Duc d'Espernon: 1586–1590
- Bernard de Nogaret, Duc de La Valette: 1590–1592
- Jean-Louis de Nogaret de La Valette, Duc d'Espernon: 1592–1594
- (in opposition) Charles Emmanuel de Savoye: 1591–1592
- (in opposition) Gaspard de Pontevès, Comte de Carcès: 1592–1594
- Charles de Lorraine, Duc de Guise: 1594–1631

Relatively recent additions to the military hierarchy were the colonels generaux. King François I introduced two colonels generaux of French Infantry (colonels generaux de infanterie Françoise) in 1546 as part of his efforts to create an effective native force of foot soldiers. They replaced the archaic and increasingly honorific mestre des arbaletriers (master of crossbowmen). One colonel general commanded all the infantry bands stationed within France proper, from his headquarters in Picardie. The other commanded those 'beyond the mountains' in Piemont. The two roles were amalgamated under Strozzi after the death of Brissac in 1569.

- François de Coligny, Seigneur d'Andelot: 1555–1562 (Picardie)
- Timoléon de Cossé, Comte de Brissac: 1561–1569 (Piemont)
- Charles de La Rochefoucauld, Comte de Randan: 1562 (Picardie)
- Sébastien de Luxembourg, Duc de Penthièvre, Vicomte de Martigues: 1562–1563 (Picardie)
- François de Coligny, Seigneur d'Andelot: 1563–1567 (reinstated, Picardie)
- Philippe Strozzi, Seigneur d'Espernay: 1569–1581 (Picardie, then sole incumbent)
- Jean Louis de Nogaret de La Valette, duc d'Espernon: 1581–1642 (sole incumbent)

It has been suggested that François de Guise introduced infantry regiments as a means of reducing the powers of patronage enjoyed by the Huguenot Andelot. Regardless of this, the colonels general were able to stamp their authority over the regimental colonels. Henry III raised the rank to one of the great offices of state in order to favour his favourite, Espernon.

The title of colonel general of the various foreign infantry contingents also existed. The most important being colonel general de infantrie suisses (or colonel general des suisses), but essentially the holder of this role was little more than a liaison officer between the Crown and the foreign colonels who commanded in person.

Henry II introduced the rank of colonel general de cavalerie legere in 1548:

- Louis Prévost de Sansac, Seigneur de Sansac: 1562–1567[2]
- Jacques de Savoye, Duc de Nemours: 1567–1571

---

2   Sansac died in 1578, on the point of being named mareschal, but remained active up to this date. His successors are a little unclear. Henry de Guise and Jean de La Valette are sometimes referred to by this title during the Third War.

- Henry de Montmorency, Seigneur de Damville: 1571–1572
- Guillaume de Montmorency, Seigneur de Thoré: 1572–1574
- Jacques de Savoye, Duc de Nemours: 1574–1585
- Charles de Lorraine, Duc d'Aumale: 1585–1586
- Jean-François de la Guiche, Seigneur de Sainct Gerén: 1586–1588
- Charles de Valois, Comte d'Auvergne: 1588–1598
- Paolo Giordano Orsini, Duca di Bracciano: 1589–1595
- Charles de Valois, Comte d'Auvergne: 1595–1604

The final senior military rank was the grand mestre de l'artillerie (grand master of artillery), although this was not technically counted as one of the great offices of the state until after this period:

- Jean d'Estrées, Comte d'Orbec: 1550–1567
- Jean Babou, Seigneur de La Bourdaisière: 1567–1569
- Armand de Gontaut, Baron de Biron: 1569–1578
- Philibert Seigneur de La Guiche: 1578–1596
- François d'Espinay, Seigneur de Sainct-Luc: 1596–1597
- Antoine d'Estrées, Marquis de Coeuvres: 1597–1599

It is interesting to note that Jean d'Estrées was a Huguenot, though he remained loyal to the Crown. Antoine, his son, was La Bourdaisière's son-in-law and father of Gabrielle d'Estrées, Henry IV's famous mistress.

During the Third War, and possibly during other conflicts, the Huguenots appointed their own grand master of artillery, in the person of Jean de Hangest, Seigneur de Genlis.

Military Hierarchy

The following diagram illustrates a theoretical, or perhaps idealised, version of the military hierarchy within a field army. In larger royal armies, the army commander would typically be the monarch, the connestable or a lieutenant general. Huguenot armies generally followed a similar model.[3]

The chain of command was frequently confused by individuals holding multiple roles within the military hierarchy. To use the Duc d'Anjou's army of 1567/68 as an example: Anjou himself was the commander-in-chief, but also commanded the bataille and a tactical regiment of 990 gens d'armes with the bataille, and his own company of gens d'armes within that regiment. In a similar manner, the Duc de Montpensier commanded the avant-garde, a tactical gens d'armes regiment of 1,440 men and his own company. Within the avant-garde, the Duc de Nemours was colonel general de cavalerie legere, who numbered 1,315, as well as leading 990 gens d'armes, including his own compagnie.

---

3   Derived from Wood, *The King's Army*, p.79.

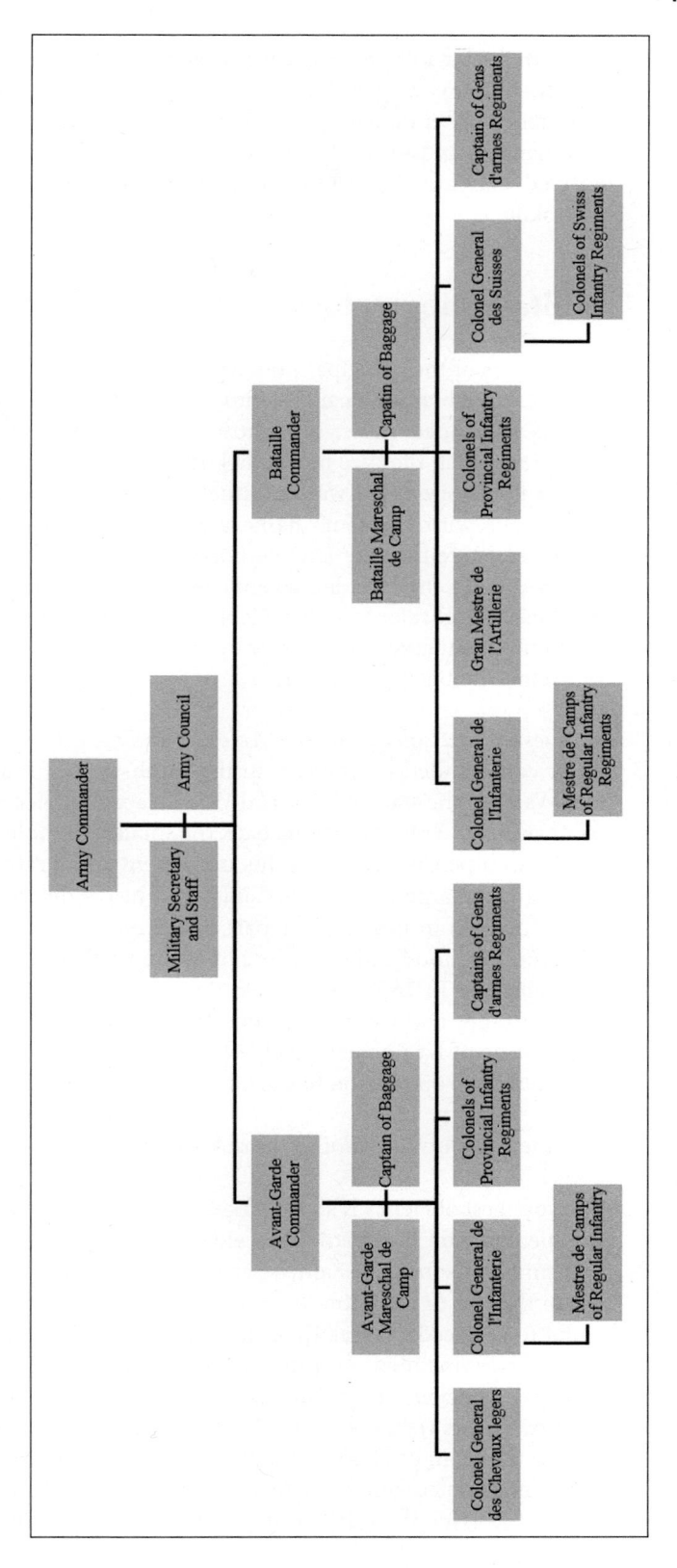

The Chain of Command

Both the bataille and avant-garde would have its own mareschal de camp. Ideally, this was an experienced senior officer with considerable technical experience rather than a high-ranking nobleman. They provided advice to the commanders and issued specific orders to ensure his general directives were enacted. Gaspard de Tavannes and Armand de Biron both fulfilled this role with skill.

Military Biographies

The careers of the principal military commanders of the wars are set out in the following biographical sketches. The full titles of these individuals have not been included, rather only those necessary to identify them clearly. The names by which they are normally known in this work are rendered in **bold** face. The history of the wars is rather confused by the presence of multiple individuals with the same name and/or title. Thus 'Charles de Lorraine' could refer to either the Duc de Lorraine or any of his distant cousins: the Duc d'Aumale, the Duc de Mayenne or the Duc d'Elbeuf. Similarly, the 'Duc de Guise' could refer to either Henry de Lorraine or his father, François de Lorraine (a situation not helped by the fact they were both known by the nickname 'Le Balafré' – scarface).

*Jacques de Crussol, Seigneur d'**Acier**, later Duc d'Uzès (1540–1586)*
Acier commanded local forces in the south-west of France during the first two Wars. At the start of the Third War, he accumulated some 25,000 men in south-western France, pushing back the smaller Catholic forces in the region under Montpensier. However, his movements were rather disorderly and at Mansignac a large detachment suffered a heavy defeat. His troops did not reach the field in time to take part in the Battle of Jarnac, but he retreated with these in good order. He fought at the Battle of Moncontour, where he was captured. In 1573, he escaped the massacre thanks to the intervention of his brother and reconciled himself to the King. He served under Anjou at the Siege of La Rochelle. In 1574, he was appointed lieutenant general in Languedoc, in opposition to the Gouverneur, Damville.

*Hercule François de Valois, Duc d'**Alençon**, later Duc d'Anjou (1554–1584)*
The youngest of Henry II's sons, originally named Hercule but switched to his middle name on the death of his eldest brother, François II. The continuing recriminations from the Sainct-Barthélemy's Day Massacre and the Fifth War led to the rise of a faction known as the Malcontents. Their plans included a plot to replaced Charles IX with his youngest brother, as he was known to be positively inclined towards the Huguenots despite his own religion. The plot was detected, and members of the group were imprisoned. Although his movements were constrained, Alençon eventually managed to break free during the reign of Henry III. Allied with Henry de Navarre, the combined Huguenot–Malcontent force faced down the royal army, and Henry III was induced to issue the Edict of Beaulieu as a result of the so-called 'Peace of

Monsieur' named after Alençon's traditional courtesy title. He was 'rewarded' with lands including Anjou and was thereafter referred to under this name. The provincial estates of the southern Netherlands requested his assistance as 'Defender of Liberties' and with an army he entered Mons in 1578. After failing to court Elizabeth I of England, he was offered the sovereignty of the United Provinces by Willem the Silent in 1581. He arrived with a French army, many of them Huguenots, in 1582. The Spanish feared major French involvement in the rebellion. Alençon was dissatisfied with the limited powers he had been granted and sought to bring some of the more independently minded cities to heel. Under the pretext of a ceremonial entry, he planned to seize Antwerp. The burghers were not fooled, however, and the civic militia massacred his Frenchmen in the streets. He escaped, but never again exercised military command.

François de Coligny, Seigneur d'Andelot (1521–1569)

The younger brother of Admiral Coligny and nephew to Montmorency. He fought in Picardie

Hercule François, Duc d'Alençon. (Scottish National Gallery)

in 1543 and then in Italy at the Battle of Cerisole in 1544. He commanded French troops in Scotland supporting Mary Queen of Scots and her mother, Marie de Guise. In 1551 he served Italy once more, defending Parma but being captured upon its fall. He was not released until 1556. Upon his return to France he replaced his elder brother as one of the two colonels general of infantry, commanding the bands in Picardie. He took part in the defence of Sainct Quentin and later distinguished himself in the capture of Calais. His religion earned him the enmity of the Guise faction and lost him favour at court and he was briefly imprisoned. At the outbreak of the wars he rallied to the Huguenot cause, taking many of his old bands of infantry with him. He was sent to Germany to raise a force of landsknechts and reiters, and with these, despite suffering from a fever, he was able to join his brother and the Prince de Condé and fought at the Battle of Dreux. He commanded the subsequent defence of Orleans. After the peace, he returned to his position of colonel general. Andelot was considered to be one of the instigators of the 'Surprise of Meaux' in 1567 which attempted to seize the King and his court. After its failure, he commanded a detached force of 800 horse and 2,000 foot south of the Seine while Condé and the Admiral blockaded Paris from the North. Thus, he did not fight at Sainct Denys. After the brief peace, he raised troops in Bretaigne in 1569 and crossed the Loire, into the Xainctonge, capturing several towns, before joining the main army at the Battle of Jarnac. After this defeat, he collected part of the remnants of the Protestant army

Above: Henry III. (Musée Carnavalet)

Below: Charles, Duc d'Aumale. (Royal Collection)

before retiring to Sainctes. Here, he was again seized with a fever and died. His death was attributed to poison dispatched by the Queen Mother, but his ongoing illness is equally likely.

Henry (III) de Valois, Duc d'Anjou, later Roy de France (1551–1589)

He was the third son of Henry II and favourite of his mother, Queen Caterina de' Medici. He was christened Alexandre Édouard. After the death of Connestable Montmorency in 1567, the Queen Mother convinced his elder brother, Charles IX, to name Anjou lieutenant general du royaume. He commanded the largest royal force raised during the wars but failed to catch the Huguenots or prevent their juncture with Johann Casimir's Germans. Understandably perhaps, given his age, he did not impose his authority on his military advisors and overrule their hesitancy to give battle. During the Third War, guided by the experienced Tavennes, Anjou's army was able to defeat the Huguenots at Jarnac and Moncontour. The Fourth War saw him tasked with the reduction of La Rochelle. He proved unequal to this and his army wasted away in the trenches. He was wounded slightly during the siege. Upon hearing that he had been elected King of Poland, he was able to extricate himself from the disaster on a reasonable pretext. Charles IX died whilst he was away in his new kingdom, and so he returned to assume the throne of France as well. He commanded again in person during the Fifth War, shadowing Johann Casimir's Germans who had returned during the winter of 1575/76. He exercised joint command with Henry of Navarre over the army which confronted Ligue-controlled Paris in 1589. His assassination put an end to this attempt.

Charles de Lorraine, Duc d'Aumale (1555–1631)

Charles inherited the duchy after the death of his father, Claude (who fought at Sainct Denys in 1567 and against Zweibrücken's Germans in 1569), at the Siege of La Rochelle in 1573. He took part in the Fourth War alongside his cousin, Henry de Guise. He became one of the leaders of Catholic discontent. In 1579 Condé accused him of trying to revive the Picard Ligue in opposition to the King. It was from Picardie that he led a rebellion against royal authority in 1587 as part of the opening stages of the War of the

Three Henrys. He was defeated at the combat of Senlis in 1589 by the allied forces of Henry III and Henry of Navarre. Rejecting the claim of the latter to the throne of France, he was captured by Henry IV's forces at the Battle of Ivry in 1590. He was exiled to the Spanish Netherlands, where he died.

Roger de Sainct Lary, Seigneur de **Bellegarde** (1525–1579)

He fought at the Battle of Gravelines and the capture of Calais. During the First War, he was present at the Siege of Rouen. In 1565 he fought against the Turks in Malta. He accompanied Anjou to the Siege of La Rochelle, where he was wounded. He also accompanied him to his coronation in Poland. Upon Henry III's accession to the throne of France, Bellegarde was created mareschal, much to the consternation of his peers. He was appointed ambassador to Savoye and persuaded Henry III to restore to the Duc de Savoye the fortifications still occupied by France. Ultimately, he fell from favour over these actions and left for the Daulphine, where he was engaged in recovering towns that defied royal authority. He failed to capture Livron. Appointed ambassador of France to Poland in 1575, he refused to go and retired to Savoye, under the pretext of ill health. He returned to France in 1577 and gained joint command of an army in Languedoc alongside Damville. They quickly fell out, and Bellegarde made overtures to the local Protestant commanders. He came into conflict with the Crown over governorship of Saluces, forcibly seizing it in 1579. The Queen Mother intervened with his allies, the Duc de Savoye and Lesdiguières, and obtained his declaration of allegiance to her son, the King. He died shortly thereafter, supposedly poisoned on her orders.

Armand de Gontaut, Baron de **Biron** (1524–1592)

Biron served in Italy under the Mareschal de Brissac. There he received a wound which made him lame for life, gaining him the nickname 'le boiteux' (the limper). Continuing his military career, he held a command with the chevaux legers in 1557 and later was granted a compagnie of gens d'armes. During the early wars he fought at the battles of Dreux, Sainct Denys, Jarnac and Moncontour. In 1569 he was appointed grand maître de l'artillerie. In 1573 he was commanded to take control of La Rochelle, but the townsfolk refused him entry. Prior to Anjou's arrival, he began the blockade of the port. After the peace he made a brief triumphal entry. In 1577 he became a mareschal of France. In 1578, he was lieutenant general of Guienne to counter the influence of Henry de Navarre. Politically, he was loyal to the Crown but opposed to the hardline policies of the Guise faction. He commanded French units under Alençon in the Netherlands in 1582. He then commanded an army against Henry de Condé in 1586. After the assassination of Henry III in 1589, he supported the cause of Henry de Navarre. Fighting for him, he distinguished himself in the battles of Arques and Ivry, but was killed at the siege of Espernay in 1592. He wrote a treatise on the art of war, amongst other works. His son, Charles, also served Henry IV and was also raised to the rank of mareschal.

Antoine de **Bourbon**, *Roy de* **Navarre** *(1518–1562)*

Through his marriage to Jeanne d'Albret, he became Roy de Navarre and flirted with his wife's religion, but appears to have had few firm convictions in this area. Antoine was the most senior prince de sang and, more for political reasons than any proven military capability, he was made lieutenant general du royaume in 1561. He commanded the royal Catholic army during the initial stages of the First War, but was mortally wounded by an arquebus shot (possibly while answering a call of nature) during the Siege of Rouen. He was the father of Henry de Navarre, the first Bourbon monarch of France.

Charles de Cossé-Brissac.
(Louvre)

Charles *de Cossé, Comte, later Duc, de* **Brissac** *(1550–1621)*

He was the son of the famous Mareschal Brissac and nephew of Mareschal Cossé. He inherited the title of Comte de Brissac after the death of his elder brother, Timoléon, in 1569. In 1582 he held a command in the French expedition to the Azores in support of Don António of Portugal. These were defeated by the Spanish at the Battle of Terceira. Henry III blamed Brissac for the failure and did not give him command of the 1583 expedition. As a result, he joined the Guise-dominated Catholic Ligue in 1584. He operated in Poictou. In 1593 he defended Poictiers against the royal army. He subsequently replaced Mayenne as military governor of the capital. No diehard, in 1594 he opened the gates of Paris to the King, and to ensure his continued loyalty Henry IV named him mareschal. He became Duc in 1611.

Timoléon *de Cossé, Comte de* **Brissac** *(1543–1569)*

Another son of Mareschal Brissac, Timoléon was a childhood companion to Charles IX. He was appointed colonel general of the infantry bands on the Italian frontier in 1561. He fought at the Siege of Rouen in 1562. In 1565, he was among the French volunteers at the Siege of Malta. He returned to France to command many of his infantry at the Battle of Sainct Denys in 1567. The next year he fought in the south under Montpensier, defeating Huguenot forces at the Combat of Mansignac. He served with distinction in the avant-garde of Anjou's army at the Battle of Jarnac. He was killed whilst prosecuting the Siege of Mussidan in April 1569, and was much mourned by his men, who slaughtered the garrison in revenge.

Gaspard de **Coligny**, *Seigneur de Chastillon (1519–1572)*

Better known by his title of Admiral, Coligny was one of the two principal commanders during the first three Wars. He was the brother of Andelot and the nephew of Montmorency. He took part in the campaign of 1543 and was wounded at the sieges of Montmédy and Bains. In 1544 he served in Italy and was knighted on the field at the Battle of Ceresole. He was appointed as colonel general of the infantry in 1547. He was appointed Admiral in 1552. In 1557 he undertook the vigorous defence of Sainct Quentin, but was captured upon its fall. By this time, he had become a Protestant and quickly became one of the Huguenot movement's leaders. He commanded the advance guard of the army at Dreux in 1562 and successfully withdrew the defeated army off the field. He commanded the right of the Huguenot army at Sainct Denys during the Second War. After the death of Condé at Jarnac, he assumed command of the army and led it to victory at the Combat of La Roche-l'Abeille in 1569, but mismanaged the subsequent encounter at Moncontour. In the ensuing period, he was able to ingratiate himself with Charles IX and improve the position of the Protestants in the kingdom. He tried to engineer France's involvement in supporting the Dutch revolt. At least indirectly, this led to his assassination in 1572, which triggered the Sainct-Barthélemy's Day Massacre. The Admiral's son, François, took part in the later wars. He commanded part of the Huguenot force at Jarrie in 1587 and then later the same year at Vimory and Aeneau. He also played an important role at Arques, where his timely intervention is credited with saving Henry IV from capture or death.

Henry de Bourbon, Prince de Condé (1552–1588)

Son of the Huguenot leader, Louis de Bourbon, Henry's first military adventure was at Moncontour in 1569. He was presented, alongside his cousin, Henry de Navarre, to the army as the new generation of leaders. Unfortunately, Coligny's insistence that they withdraw from the field prior to the encounter weakened its morale. He was confined in Paris after the massacre in 1573 and temporarily accepted the Catholic faith. After accompanying Anjou in his siege of La Rochelle, he managed to convince the authorities to allow him to exercise his rule as gouverneur of Picardie in 1574,

Above: Admiral Coligny. (Rijksmuseum, Amsterdam)

Below: Henry, Prince de Condé. (Musée Condé)

but instead fled to Germany and returned to Calvanism. He was chosen as governor general and protector by the Huguenot communities of the Midi later that year. After the Peace of Monsieur in 1575 he was able to resume his role in Picardie. However, this caused a reaction by the Catholic nobility of the province, who established the Ligue de Péronne in opposition. During the Sixth War, he commanded the main Huguenot field army alongside Navarre. After a truce had been patched up, he again re-established himself in Picardie. But resistance to his rule had not lessened and his heavy-handed attempts to quell this sparked off the Seventh War: which was essentially a dynastic conflict between the houses of Bourbon and Lorraine. He allied with Navarre and Damville's moderate Catholics in 1585. He repulsed Mercoeur's invasion of Poictou in 1586, but failed to capture Brouage and had to flee to Guernsey. He later opposed Biron. He died after a short illness: his pregnant wife was suspected of his murder and not acquitted until 1596.

Louis, Prince de Condé. (Palace de Versailles)

Louis de Bourbon, Prince de **Condé** *(1530–1569)*

A scion of the house of Bourbon, Condé was the principal Huguenot leader during the first three Wars. His elder brother was Antoine de Bourbon, Roy de Navarre, and he was father to Henry, who succeeded him as Prince de Condé. He served at the Siege of Metz and the Battle of Sainct Quentin. As a Protestant and prince du sang, he opposed the influence of François de Guise and was implicated in the plot to abduct (or free, depending on one's perspective) the royal family in the affair known as the Conspiracy of Amboise in 1560. After being released from a brief imprisonment, he led the Huguenot seizure of Orleans at the start of the First War. He led the main battle of the army at Dreux, where he was captured. After Guise's assassination, he helped negotiate the Peace of Amboise. During the Second War he again led the main Huguenot force alongside Coligny. At the Battle of Sainct Denys he led a devastating cavalry charge and was again captured; on this occasion being rescued. He managed to avoid the pursuing Catholic force and linked up with a large German contingent. During the Third War he led the Huguenot forces at the Battle of Jarnac. With only his cavalry, he rode to the rescue of Coligny's outnumbered force. Despite supposedly breaking his leg immediately beforehand (a horse kicked him), he led a gallant but foolhardy charge into the Catholic army. He was again captured, but this time killed.

Artus de **Cossé**-Brissac, Comte de Secondigny (1512–1582)

He was known as Mareschal Cossé in order to distinguish him from his brother, Mareschal Brissac. He was present at the defence of Metz and was subsequently appointed its governor. He commanded his own company of gens d'armes in 1562. He struggled to make any impression on the kingdom's mountain of debts as Charles IX's finance secretary, but distinguished himself at the Battle of Sainct Denys and was made mareschal in 1567. He then served as second-in-command under Anjou in the subsequent fruitless chase of Condé's army. His personal feud with Montpensier contributed to this failure. He adopted a prominent role in 1569 at the Battle of Moncontour. He was in sole command when held at bay at Arnay-le-Duc in 1570. In 1574 he was arrested, along with Montmorency, on suspicion of supporting Alençon's faction of Malcontents. He remained imprisoned for 18 months.

Henry, Seigneur de **Damville**, Duc de Montmorency (1534–1614)

Son of Anne de Montmorency and younger brother to François, he succeeded to the title of Duc after the latter's death in 1579. After the First War, he was appointed Governor of Languedoc in 1563. He became well established in this province and ruled over it like a personal fief. He was widely suspected of having Huguenot sympathies and came into conflict with the Parlement of Toulouse. He was made mareschal in 1566. His influence over his province had grown to such an extent that he acquired the nickname of 'Roy du Languedoc'. He commanded Royalist cavalry at the Battle of Sainct Denys. He took no part in the massacre in 1572. In 1574 he revolted as a result of the suspicion cast on him and his family by the King and the Guise faction. He allied with local Protestant forces. He was later reckoned to be the leader of the 'Politiques', a derisive term for those of both faiths willing to seek an accommodation with each other and to countenance Henry de Navarre as king. In 1593, Henry IV appointed him to his father's old role of Connestable de France.

Henry de Damville.
(Kunsthistorisches Museum, Vienna)

Jean Louis de Nogaret de La Valette, Duc de **Espernon** (1554–1642)

Espernon was the scion of a minor Gascon noble family. He fought in the Third and Fourth Wars, latterly at the Siege of La Rochelle, where his father was killed and also where he met the Duc d'Anjou. Upon Anjou's return to France as King Henry III, Espernon gravitated back to his side, becoming one of his intimate 'Mignons' by 1578. He was showered with titles and gradually gained ascendancy over his only real rival, Joyeuse. He commanded troops

Jean Louis de Espernon.
(Palace de Versailles)

at the recapture of La Fére in 1580, where he was slightly wounded in the face. He was made gouverneur of Prouvence in 1586 and both admiral and governor of Normandie on Joyeuse's death in 1587. This concentration of power and influence alienated both him and the King from the Guise faction. After the Day of Barricades in 1588, he was forced to relinquish many of these offices. After the death of Guise and, later, Henry III, he opposed Henry IV's succession and tried to establish an independent power base in the south, but he was not trusted by the Ligue. He was eventually forced to submit in 1596. He was suspected of being involved in the assassination of Henry in 1610. He was subsequently active in the court of Louis XIII. His brother, Bernard, served Henry III in the Daulphine commanding the Royalist forces at the Combat of Jarrie in 1587. He succeeded his brother as governor of Prouvence and admiral. He was killed at the Siege of Roquebrune in 1592.

*François de Hangest, Seigneur de **Genlis** (c. 1515–1569)*

Genlis hailed from a Picard noble family but with extensive holdings in Normandie. His family was closely related to both the Montmorency-Coligny clan and several noble houses in the Netherlands. He served under Henry II and was made Chevalier de Sainct Michel in 1560. After adopting the reformed religion, he joined the initial rebellion alongside his brother, Jean, but defected prior to Dreux with 30 of his followers. Despite this, he commanded the left wing of the Huguenot cavalry at Sainct Denys. However, his troops failed to make much impression on Montpensier's French infantry, and he was captured. In 1568 he led a French force to support Willem the Silent's rebellion and was part of the force that defeated the Spanish at the Battle of Le Quesnoy. He died of rabies in 1569, supposedly after sacking the Abbey of Sainct-Hubert, a noted spiritual healer of that disease.

*Jean de Hangest, Seigneur d'**Ivoy** and later Seigneur de **Genlis** (c. 1520–1572)*

Jean was the youngest brother of François de Hangest. He gained a poor reputation during the First War, when his men, under the pretext of abolishing idolatry, sacked the city of Bourges. He failed to capture Issoudun. He subsequently surrendered Bourges to Royalist forces whilst it was thought to be capable of further resistance. He fought at Dreux. Unpopular with other Huguenots, he seems to have converted back to Catholicism, but by the time of the Second War he had recanted. He became Seigneur de Genlis in 1569, after the death of his elder brother François. During the Third War he relieved

Castres and played an important role at the Combat of Arnay-le-Duc. After the Peace of Sainct Germain, he again led a Huguenot force of 6,000–7,000 men in support of the Dutch rebels into the Spanish Netherlands. In this he was encouraged by Coligny, and probably secretly by King Charles as well. He was heavily defeated at the Battle of Sainct Ghislain in 1572. He was captured and held in Antwerp, but was found strangled in his bed on 11 July.

François de Lorraine, Duc de **Guise** *(1519–1563)*

François de Guise was France's leading military figure in the period before the wars. He was the brother to Mary of Guise, who was regent of Scotland on behalf of her daughter the young Mary Queen of Scots. He took part in the Siege of Boulogne in 1545, where he was wounded in the face by a lance, consequently earning the nickname 'scarface' (le balafré). He wed Anna d'Este, daughter of Ercole d'Este, Duca di Ferrara, and granddaughter of Lucrecia Borgia in 1548. In 1551 he was made grand chambellan de France. The following year he successfully defended Metz against Kaiser Karl V and in 1554 defeated his troops at the Battle of Renty. He was made lieutenant general of royaume in 1557 after the defeat of Montmorency at Sainct Quentin. The following year he captured Calais, the last English possession in France. His niece, Mary, was married to Henry II's heir François, making Guise the pre-eminent noble in France. It was Guise's domination of court, as much as any other factor, that led to the outbreak of the wars. He was also responsible for the First War's immediate trigger, the

François de Guise. (Louvre)

massacre at Vassy. During this conflict, he initially allowed Antoine de Navarre and Connestable Montmorency to take the lead militarily, but his actions at Druex probably saved the day for the Royalist cause. Such was his standing at this point, that he effectively appointed himself lieutenant general of royaume once again. He was besieging Orleans when struck down by an assassin.

Henry de Lorraine, Prince de Jonville, Duc de **Guise** *(1550–1588)*

Son and heir of François de Guise, he inherited his father's position as head of the ultra-Catholic opposition to the Huguenot movement. He was also confirmed in his father's old position as governor of Champaigne. He fought in Hungary against the Ottomans in 1565, but returned to France in time to take part in the Battle of Sainct Denys. He came to the fore during the Third War, fighting at Jarnac before winning fame in his defence of Poictiers. He was wounded at the Battle of Moncontour. He failed in his attempt to

Above: Henry de Guise. (Musée Carnavalet)

Below: Anne de Joyeuse. (Pałac Na Wyspie, Warsaw)

marry Marguerite de Valois, the King's sister, and was displeased with the rehabilitation of the Huguenot nobility at court, especially Coligny, whom he blamed for his father's assassination. The escalating conflict between these two noble factions led to Coligny's death in Paris by Henry and his followers: an act that precipitated the Sainct-Barthélemy massacre. During the Fifth War he defeated a portion of Johann-Casimir's reiters at the Combat of Dormons, during which he was wounded in the face. As a result, he bore the same nickname as his father. He opposed the rise to power of Henry III's Mignons and covertly supported the establishment of the early Catholic ligues in various cities. When Henry III recognised Henry de Navarre as his heir in 1584, Guise's opposition intensified. He sponsored the creation of the Saincte Ligue and signed the Treaty of Joinville with Felipe II of Spain. In virtual rebellion, he forced the King to revoke the Edict of Nemours, an act that initiated another round of conflict. During the Eighth War, at the head of the Ligue troops, he successfully defeated the Protestant German allies at the combats of Vimory and Auneau. Despite the King's prohibition, he returned to Paris in 1588. The population rose to support him and after the Day of Barricades (12 May), Henry III was forced to flee his own capital. In desperation he acceded to Guise's demands. But Guise had miscalculated the King's resolve, and answering a summons to attend court, he was murdered by the royal bodyguard.

Anne de Batarnay, Duc de *Joyeuse* (1560/61– 1587)

From 1577, Anne served with his father, the Vicomte de Joyeuse, against the Huguenots in Languedoc and Auvergne. In 1579, he was appointed captain of a compagnie d'ordonnance and later the same year governor of Mont Sainct-Michel. In 1580, he took part in the siege of Fère-en-Tardenois. He became close friends with Henry III and a leading member of the notorious Mignons. In 1581 the King arranged Joyeuse's marriage to his sister-in-law, the daughter of the Duc de Mercoeur. This was celebrated with unprecedented magnificence.

The king elevated his favourite to the dignity of Duc de Joyeuse, with precedence over all other dukes and peers of France, other than the princes de sang. In 1582 he was made Admiral of France. He was appointed governor of Normandie in 1583. He led an armed garrison into Rouen later in the year, but the population pleaded with the King for its removal. As Espernon began to replace him in the King's favour, so Joyeuse hoped that military exploits would help him regain lost ground. He forced Navarre from Poictou in 1587 and into La Rochelle. His massacre of 800 Huguenots during the campaign (at Sainct-Eloi) incurred royal displeasure. He was received coldly at court and, anxious to be restored to Henry's favour, led royal troops against Henry of Navarre once again. He suffered a defeat at the Battle of Coutras and was taken prisoner, but quickly killed in revenge for the massacre of Sainct-Eloi.

François de Bonne, Seigneur, later Duc, de **Lesdiguières** (1543–1626)

During the First War, when the Huguenot uprising broke out in the Daulphine, Lesdiguières became one of the first 'Furmeyer captains' from that region. After the death of his cousin, Antoine Rambaud, he became the leader of local Protestant resistance in 1576. This involved bitter feuds with local Catholics, including the capture of Gap and the massacre of its inhabitants. When Henry III recognised Henry de Navarre's right of succession, Lesdiguières' authority over the Huguenots of Daulphine was formally recognised in 1584. Subsequently, Henry IV named him 'commandant généralement pour le roy du Daulphine' in 1589. He fought against the forces of the Ligue and their ally, the Duc de Savoy. He captured Grenoble in 1590. He defeated a Spanish–Savoyard army at Pontcharra in 1591 and again at Salbertrand in 1593. In 1597 he took the war into Savoye, winning combats at Chamousset and Les Mollottes. In recognition for his services, Henry IV named him Mareschal in 1609.

Henry d'Orléans, Duc de **Longueville** (1568–1595)

Longueville's father had been a Huguenot but had returned to the Catholic faith. Charles IX had recognised him as a prince du sang, despite the illegitimate origins of his house. Henry's grandmother, Jacqueline de Rohan, had been one of the early champions of French Protestantism. Longueville served King Henry III during the Eighth War. In 1588, alongside the veteran La Noue, he defeated Aumale's Ligue army at the Combat of Senlis (17 May), which lifted the siege of this town. After the death of Henry III, Longueville rallied to the support of Henry de Navarre. He opened the gates of the town of Gournay-en-Bray to the new monarch. His noble status, rather than any obvious military talents, subsequently led him to being entrusted with command of a significant portion of the royal forces. He was tasked with subduing Picardie. He was also created Grand Chambellan de France. He took part in Henry IV's failed siege of Paris in 1591, being present at the so-called 'journée des farines' (day of flour – a failed attempt to smuggle forces into the city).

Sébastien de Martigues.
(Bemberg Fondation,
Toulouse)

Sébastien de Luxembourg, Duc de Penthièvre, Vicomte de **Martigues** (c. 1530–1569)

Martigues served under Guise at the Sieges of Metz and Calais and then led an expedition to Scotland in support of Marie of Guise in 1559. During the First War, he participated in the Siege of Rouen and replaced the Comte de Randan as colonel general. In 1565, he was appointed governor of Bretaigne and quickly antagonised the local Huguenot population with his hardline stance. In 1568, he was ordered to advance to the Loire to break up the concentrations of Protestant forces under Andelot. He subsequently joined Montpensier's forces, which became the avant-garde of Anjou's army. He fought at Jarnac and Moncontour, but was killed at the Siege of Sainct Jean d'Angely. He was widely respected for his bravery in battle and was amongst those known by the sobriquet of 'le chevalier sans peur'.

Jacques de Goyon, Seigneur de **Matignon** (1525–1598)

Matignon served initially under Henry II, fighting at the Battle of Sainct-Quentin, where he was captured. He was appointed lieutenant general of lower Normandie in 1559 and governor of Alençon in 1561. During the First War, he opposed the English forces in Normandie. During the Third War, he distinguished himself at the Battles of Jarnac and Moncontour. After the Sainct-Barthélemy massacre he was one of the few governors who actively applied the King's instructions to protect the Protestant communities of Alençon and Sainct-Lô. In 1574 he successfully besieged Domfort and captured Montgomery. He was reappointed lieutenant general of Normandie in 1575 and made mareschal in 1579. During the Seventh War, he recaptured the city of La Fère in 1580. During Henry III's conflict with the Ligue, Matignon was tasked with opposing their forces in Guienne, successfully resisting their attempts to take Bordeaux. He also opposed the Huguenot forces in the same part of the kingdom, defeating them in several minor actions in 1586 and 1587. Despite this, he rallied to Henry of Navarre's side after Henry III's death, and even stood in as acting connestable during his coronation.

Charles de Lorraine, Duc de **Mayenne** (1554–1611)

Charles was the younger brother of Henry de Guise and son of François de Guise. Eager to gain military glory, he left France at the age of 18 to join the wars against the Ottoman Turks. He arrived too late to take part in the Battle of Lepanto, however. On his return to France, the death of his uncle, also Charles, in 1573 allowed him to assume the role of governor of Bourgógne and grand chambellan de France. During the Sixth War he captured Bourage near the Huguenot stronghold of La Rochelle. He gained the office of admiral in

1580, succeeding his father-in-law, the Marquis de Villars. In the same year he successfully besieged La Mure in the Daulphine. The rise of the Mignons cost him the post of admiral in 1582. He fully supported his brother's creation of the Ligue and was a co-signatory to the Treaty of Joinville. In 1588 he, alongside Matignon, was fighting in the south-west of the country when his brother was assassinated. He thus escaped a similar fate and took up leadership of the Ligue. The rebellious government of Paris named him lieutenant general du royaume in 1589. He was implicated in the plot that took the life of Henry III. Unsurprisingly, he was unable to reconcile himself to the succession of Henry de Navarre, but was defeated by him at the Battles of Arques and Ivry. As a result, the Ligue was increasingly dependent on Spanish support. He quelled the excesses of the Parisian council in 1591, hanging a number of their leaders. Although his actions were popular, he subsequently lost the support of the capital when Henry IV converted to Catholicism. He continued the struggle from Bourgógne, but his combined Ligue and Spanish force was defeated by the King at Fontaine-Française in 1595, and he accepted the inevitable and submitted. Well rewarded for this, he fought his former Spanish allies the following year at Amiens.

Phillipe-Emmanuel de Lorraine, Duc de Mercoeur (1558–1602)

On his father's side, Phillipe-Emmanuel belonged to the house of Guise, on his mother's, to that of Savoye. His elder sister, Louise de Vaudemont, was married to Henry III in 1575. He was married to Marie de Luxembourg, who held a claim to Bretaigne. In 1582 he was appointed as governor of that province. He fared poorly in a series of encounters with Huguenots during the Eighth War, earning himself the nickname 'Duc de Recule'. He remained ostensibly loyal to Henry III whilst simultaneously remaining close to his Guise kin. In 1588, however, he fell from favour and only escape the fate of other Guise nobles because he was warned by his sister of the King's intentions. He settled into his lands in Bretaigne,

Above: Charles de Mayenne. (Palace de Versailles)

Below: Phillipe-Emmanuel de Mercoeur. (Musée Condé)

despite being stripped of his office, and refused to give way. He seems to have seriously considered reasserting the independence of that country after the death of the last Valois and the accession of Henry IV. He gained the support of Felipe of Spain, and with Spanish troops he was able to defeat the Duc de Montpensier, the legitimate governor, at Croan in 1592. But this victory was not decisive and English troops arrived to restore the balance of power. With the other Ligue forces giving way, Mercoeur submitted to Henry in 1598, though only upon receipt of significant endowments. In 1599 he marched himself off to Hungary to fight the Turks on behalf of the Emperor, where he enjoyed some success before his death from fever in 1602.

Blaise de Lasseran-Massencôme, Seigneur de **Monluc** (1500–1577)

Monluc began his military career in Italy, fighting for François I and taking part in the Battles of La Bicocca and Pavia. After commanding various infantry compagnies, he joined the guard of the future Henry II. In 1544 he fought at the Battle of Cerisole, playing a leading role in the encounter. He was knighted on the field. In 1554 he took command of Sienna, besieged by the Spaniards. Although the city eventually fell, his dogged defence of the place ensured his military reputation. During the First War of Religion he was commissioned to raise troops in Guienne. By his own admission, his actions in suppressing the local Huguenots were brutal. He was appointed lieutenant general of Guienne in 1562, but continually baulked at the policy of reconciliation adopted by the Crown. He could not countenance any disobedience to the King. During the Second War he again was active in the south-west, countering Protestant forces with his own modest supply of troops. Despite this he enjoyed some local success. He criticised Damville for his lack of vigour in suppressing the rebellion. During the Third War he was shot in the face by an arquebus while besieging Rabastens-de-Bigorre in 1570. This forced him to wear a mask for the rest of his life. His political opponents, including Damville, had him tried for embezzlement and he was stripped of his authority. But the Duc d'Anjou ensured he was acquitted. He subsequently served on Anjou's staff during the Siege of La Rochelle. When the latter assumed the Crown, he made Monluc mareschal in 1574. He conducted some minor operations in 1575 but was increasingly focused on the preparation of his famous *Commentaires*.

Gabriel de Montgomery.
(Château de Beauregard)

Gabriel de Lorges, Comte de **Montgomery** (1530–1574)

Montgomery descended from a Scottish family and commanded the garde écossaise during the reign of Henry II. It was in this capacity that he took part in the joust, during which he mortally wounded his king. Although Henry lived long enough to forgive him, the Queen did not, and he was hounded from court. He retired to Normandie and adopted Calvinism. During the First War he commanded the defence of Rouen, but managed to escape the fall of the city. He retired first to Havre de Grace and then to England. During the Third War, he brought Huguenots from Normandie to serve under Condé. Later, the Queen of Navarre, Jeanne d'Albret, charged Montgomery with the reconquest of her domain. This he accomplished with great efficiency. He subsequently fought at Jarnac, then against Monluc in Guienne and also at Moncontour. In 1572 he fought in the Netherlands, commanding a sizeable Huguenot contingent in the defence of Mons. He narrowly escaped the massacre in 1573 and took refuge with his family on Jersey. Elizabeth I refused the Queen Mother's requests for his extradition. Returning to France, he took part in the Siege of La Rochelle and then moved on to Normandie. However, he was captured at Domfort in 1574. Shortly thereafter, Caterina de' Medici had her revenge: he was executed in Paris.

Anne, Duc de Montmorency (1493–1567)

A close friend and confidant of François I, and later Henry II, he served at Ravenna and Marignano and commanded at Bicocca. Despite his defeat there, he was made mareschal in 1522. He was captured alongside his king at Pavia in 1525. He successfully defended Prouvence against Karl V in 1536 and was named Connestable de France in 1538. His efforts towards peace with the Empire led to his fall from grace, but his fortunes revived with the accession of Henry II. He was defeated at Sainct Quentin in 1557. After Henry II's death and the rise of François de Guise, he fell out of favour once more. Immediately prior to the First War, he was able to patch up his differences and, along with Sainct André, become a member of the 'Triumvirate'. He commanded the Catholic bataille at Dreux, but, like his Protestant counterpart, he was captured while leading his cavalry. During the Second War, he led the Catholic army at Sainct Denys. He refused a call to surrender during the ensuing cavalry melee by knocking teeth from his assailant with the hilt of his sword. He received a pistol shot in response and died two days later in Paris, at the age of 74. Amongst his sons active during the wars were François de Montmorency, Henry de Damville, Charles de Merú and Guillaume de Thoré.[4] Through the marriage of his sister, Montmorency was uncle to the Protestant leaders Admiral Coligny and Andelot.

Anne de Montmorency.
(Musée Condé)

---

4 Somewhat confusingly, upon François' death in 1579, Henry became Duc de Montmorency and Charles took over the latter's old title of Seigneur de Damville. Accounts of 'Damville' being present at the Battle of Arques and the Combat of Craon therefore refer to Charles, not his elder brother.

François de Montmorency. (Museum of Fine Arts, Boston)

François, *Duc de* **Montmorency** *(1530–1579)*

The eldest son of Anne de Montmorency. He took part in the defence of Thérouanne, the Battle of Sainct Quentin and the capture of Calais. He was made mareschal in recompense for his family's loss of position to the Guise faction in 1559. He was also governor of Paris. During the First War, he took part in the Battle of Dreux and was afterwards present at the recovery of Havre de Grace from the English. He was also present at Sainct Denys during the Second War, during which his father was mortally wounded. Succeeding to the title Duc de Montmorency he continued his family's rivalry with the Guises. He was unable to control the turbulent capital and left the city a few days before the Sainct-Barthélemy's Day Massacre. He returned to court in 1574, but conflict with the Guises led him to join with the Malcontents under Alençon. He was imprisoned and not released until April 1575. He died in 1579, to be succeeded by his brother, Henry de Damville.

François de Bourbon, Duc de **Montpensier**, *le* **Prince Daulphin***, Prince de* **Dombes** *(1542–1592)*

He fought, alongside his father, with the royal Catholic armies during the initial Wars. Dombes was entrusted with several provincial governments, first in the centre of France (following his father in Anjou, Touraine, Maine and then in Orleans), and then the Daulphine in 1567. In 1569 he was charged with eliminating the Huguenot forces in Xainctonge, but was unable to do so. In 1574 he replaced Damville as lieutenant general in the Daulphine, Prouvence and Languedoc, causing the latter to fall into the arms of the Malcontents and Huguenots. During the Fifth War he commanded one of the three royal armies, in the Daulphine. He was governor of Normandie in 1588. Despite being staunchly Catholic, he remained a faithful supporter of Henry III and refused to enter into the Guise-dominated Ligue. Upon his king's death, he rallied to the support of Henry IV. He led one of the cavalry wings at Arques and the avant-garde of the royal army at Ivry. He attended the Siege of Rouen in 1591. His son, Henry (1573–1608), also known as the Prince of Dombes during his father's lifetime, fought at Ivry and vied for control of Bretaigne with Mercoeur.

Louis de Bourbon, Duc de **Montpensier** *(1513–1582)*

Prior to the Wars of Religion, Montpensier served under Montmorency against Charles V. In 1536 he fought in Prouvence and Artois. In 1557, he fought again in Sainct Quentin where he was taken prisoner. In 1560, he was made gouverneur of Touraine, Anjou and Maine, repressing the disorders aroused by Protestant revolts. He gained a reputation as one of the cruellest adversaries of the Huguenots, despite his first wife's religious inclinations. He shut his daughters up in convents but one, Charlotte, ran away and married the Protestant Dutch Prince, Willem the Silent. During the First War he led a column of the main Catholic army charged with re-establishing control of the Loire Valley. In 1563 he reconquered Angoulême and La Fère from the rebels. He commanded a body of French foot at Sainct Denys in 1567 and then served as one of Anjou's advisors in the subsequent pursuit of Condé. During the Third War, with a small army in the vicinity of Poictiers, he defeated but did not destroy a Huguenot force marching to La Rochelle. Alongside Brissac, he destroyed a Protestant army seeking to join the Condé's forces. Subsequently, he was joined by Anjou and took part in the battles of Jarnac and Moncontour, commanding the avant-garde on both occasions. He was later appointed governor of Bretaigne. In 1570, he married Catherine de Lorraine, sister of Henry de Guise and Charles de Mayenne. He contributed to the escalation of Sainct-Barthélemy's Day Massacre beyond Paris. In the Fifth War he commanded one of Charles IX's three main armies, in Poictou, enhancing his reputation for ruthlessness. He captured Fontenaÿ and Lusigná with a force largely unpaid and deserting in droves. In 1575 he captured a number of towns in the vicinity of La Rochelle but failed to isolate the Huguenot strongpoint. At this point his enthusiasm for the struggle seems to have waned. The next year, seemingly touched by the state of the common people, he spoke in favour of allowing limited toleration to his enemies: at least until they could be reconverted by more peaceful means. He negotiated the peace that ended the Sixth War in 1577.

Henry IV de Navarre.
(Rijksmuseum, Amsterdam)

*Henry (IV) de Bourbon, Roy de **Navarre**, Roy de France (1553–1610)*

Henry was the son of Antoine de Bourbon and Jeanne d'Albret. After his father's death at the siege of Rouen, he inherited his office of gouverneur of Guienne and his mother's Huguenot religion. His military education began during the Third War. His mother took him to La Rochelle to join the Prince de Condé and Admiral Coligny, with the express view that he should learn the art of war from these captains. He was present at the Battles of Jarnac and Moncontour, though the Admiral sent him and his cousin, Henry de Condé, away from the action before the latter contest. This action disheartened the Protestant forces. He took part in the Combat of Arnay-le-Duc in 1570. His mother died in 1572 and he succeeded her as Roy de Navarre. In the same year he married Charles IX's sister, Marguerite de Valois. The Huguenot nobles gathered in Paris, for the ceremony fell victim to the massacre, thus robbing the Protestants of most of their leaders. Henry was effectively imprisoned at court and forced to convert. During this time, he became associated with the Duc d'Alençon. In 1573 he attended the Siege of La Rochelle as one of the many gentlemen observers in the Catholic army. He became embroiled in the plots of the Malcontents and was imprisoned alongside Alençon in 1574. Henry III pardoned him when he ascended the throne. Navarre took advantage of the disruption caused by the Fifth War to escape and re-join his Protestant supporters in the south-west. The Sixth War was prosecuted by his cousin, Henry de Condé, rather than himself. His lack of religious zeal disappointed many Huguenots and his court contained nobles of both faiths. During this period, he was briefly re-united with his wife, but conducted a number of extra marital affairs. In the Seventh War he attacked and took the city of Cahors in 1580 after bitter street fighting, an event that gained him considerable prestige. After the death of Alençon in 1584, the King sought to reconcile with Navarre and recognise him as heir. This action provoked the hostility of the Guise clan and the hardline Catholics. They forced the King not only to rescind the offer, but to renew the war against the Huguenots. Henry confronted the royalist army led by Joyeuse at Coutras in 1587, winning the first clear major victory by the Protestants over the Catholics (although by this stage these designations were becoming increasingly blurred). Henry III's assassination of Guise allowed the two kings to unite their forces in common cause and they led them against the rebellious capital in 1588. Henry III was assassinated in turn and formally recognised Navarre as his successor from his deathbed. But as a Protestant, Henry IV could not command the respect of all of the kingdom's Catholic lords. The much-diminished army was forced to break off the siege. Moving north, rather than south towards his own power base, he was forced to defend himself against Mayenne at Arques and then Ivry. He still lacked the strength to take Paris, which was supported by Spanish troops under Parma as well as those of the Ligue. However, increased Spanish involvement hardened the determination of Queen Elizabeth of England to support Henry. Together, they sought to capture Rouen. Again, Parma marched from the Netherlands and the two sides conducted a campaign of manoeuvre. Both Henry and Parma were wounded during minor encounters, but the latter more grievously. Accepting that he could never be truly secure in his position as a Huguenot king, Henry bowed to the inevitable and reconverted to Catholicism in 1593. He was formally crowned in early 1594 and Paris opened its gates later that year. Although some Ligue lords still held out, Henry was now firmly in control of France.

Charles Emmanuel de Savoye, Duc de Nemours, Prince de Genevois (1567–1595)

Charles Emmanuel succeeded his father, Jacques, as Duc in 1585. He inherited his parents' association with the house of Guise. He was imprisoned after the assassination of his half-brother, Henry de Guise, in 1588, but escaped. He fought at the Battle of Arques in 1589, and was named governor of the Ligue-controlled Paris the same year. He withstood the siege by Henry III and Henry de Navarre, and continued to oppose the latter after he assumed the crown. He fought at Ivry in 1590 and then withstood a second siege of the capital. Unable to reconcile himself to Henry IV, he broke with his ally and other half-brother, Mayenne, and tried to establish himself in Lionnois, but was forced into exile.

Sack of Lion, 1562

L–R: Arquebusier; Serjent

(Illustration by and © T. J. O'Brien de Clare)

See Colour Plate Commentaries for further information.

Sainct-Barthélemy's Day Massacre, Paris, 1572
L–R: Arquebusier; Officer
(Illustration by and © T. J. O'Brien de Clare)
See Colour Plate Commentaries for further information.

Plate C

The Netherlands 1577–1583

L–R: Lancer; Homme d'armes

(Illustration by and © T. J. O'Brien de Clare)

See Colour Plate Commentaries for further information.

Saincte Ligue Procession, Paris, 1590

L–R: Drummer; Arquebusier

(Illustration by and © T. J. O'Brien de Clare)

See Colour Plate Commentaries for further information.

Plate E

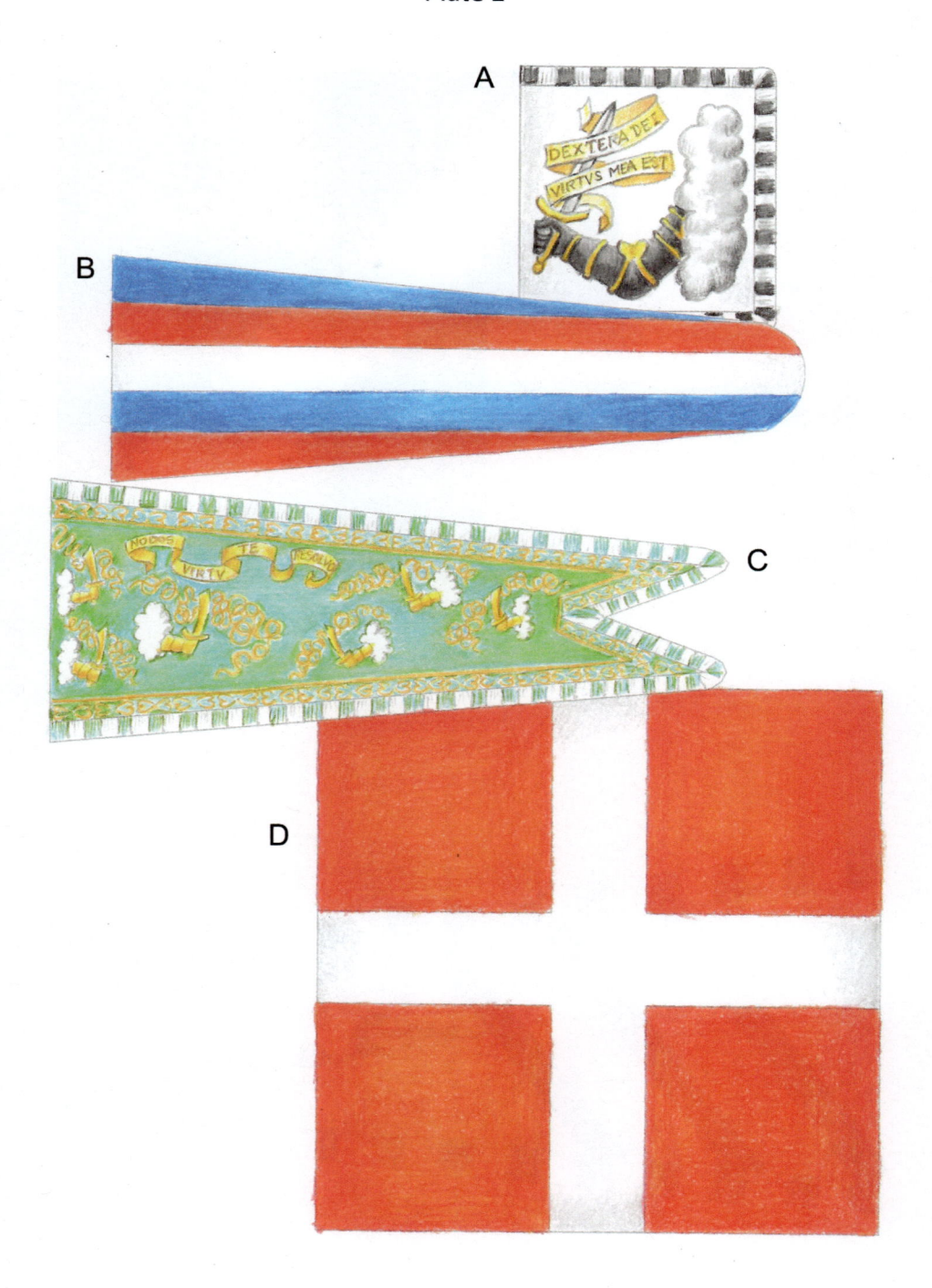

Royalist Flags
A: Cornette of Anne de Montmorency; B: Personal standard of Charles IX;
C: Standard of Sainct Andre; D: French infantry ensign

(Illustration by and © T. J. O'Brien de Clare)

See Colour Plate Commentaries for further information.

Plate F

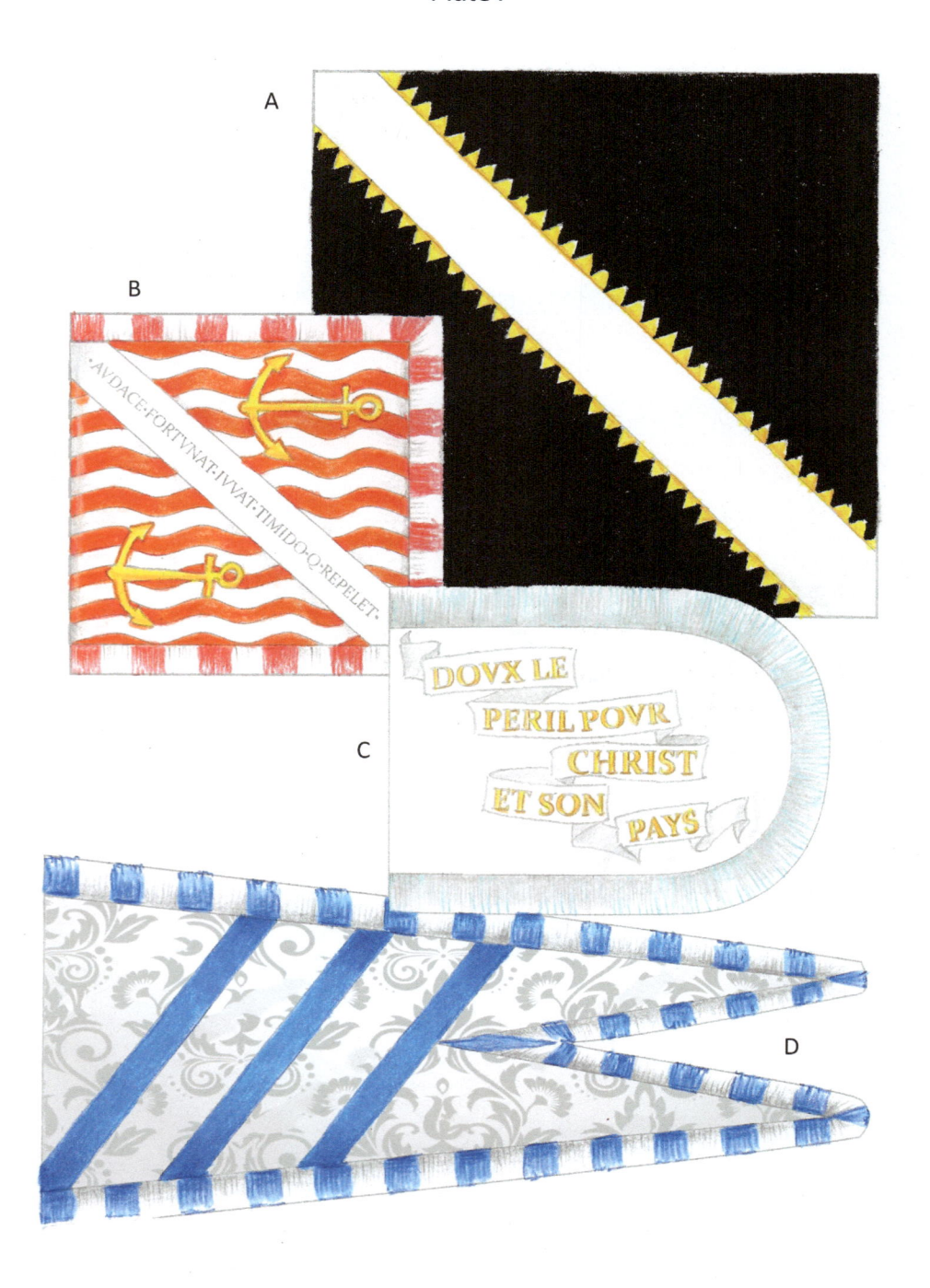

Huguenot Flags

A: Cornette of Admiral Coligny; B: Huguenot infantry enseigne; C: Livery colour of the House of Bourbon; D: Reconstruction of the appearance of Andelot's standard

(Illustration by and © T. J. O'Brien de Clare)

See Colour Plate Commentaries for further information.

Plate G

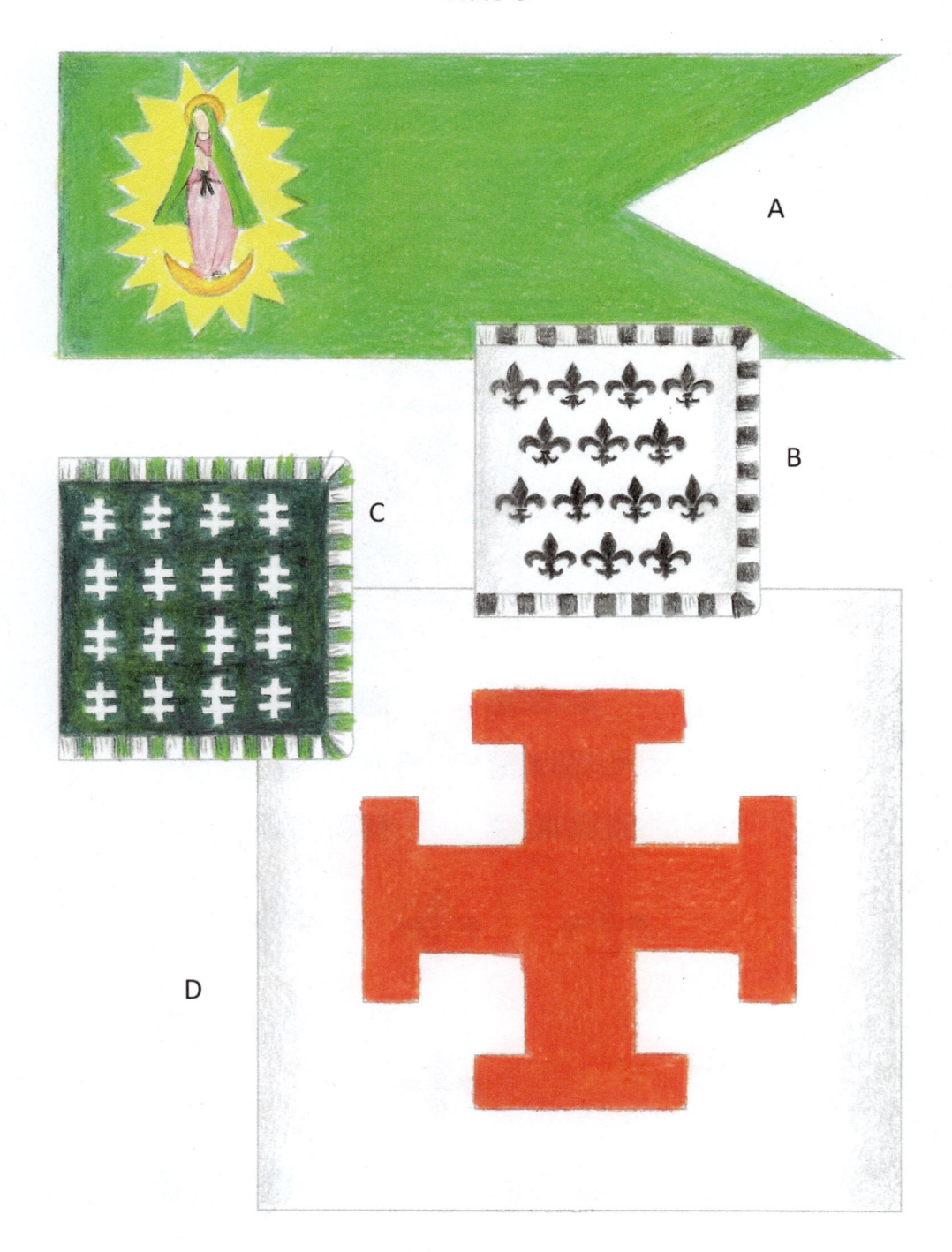

Ligue Flags

A: Standard carried in a Paris procession in 1590; B: Cornette of Charles de Lorraine Duc de Mayenne's compagnie of gens d'armes; C: Conjectural; D: "The cross potent"

(Illustration by and © T. J. O'Brien de Clare)

See Colour Plate Commentaries for further information.

Plate H

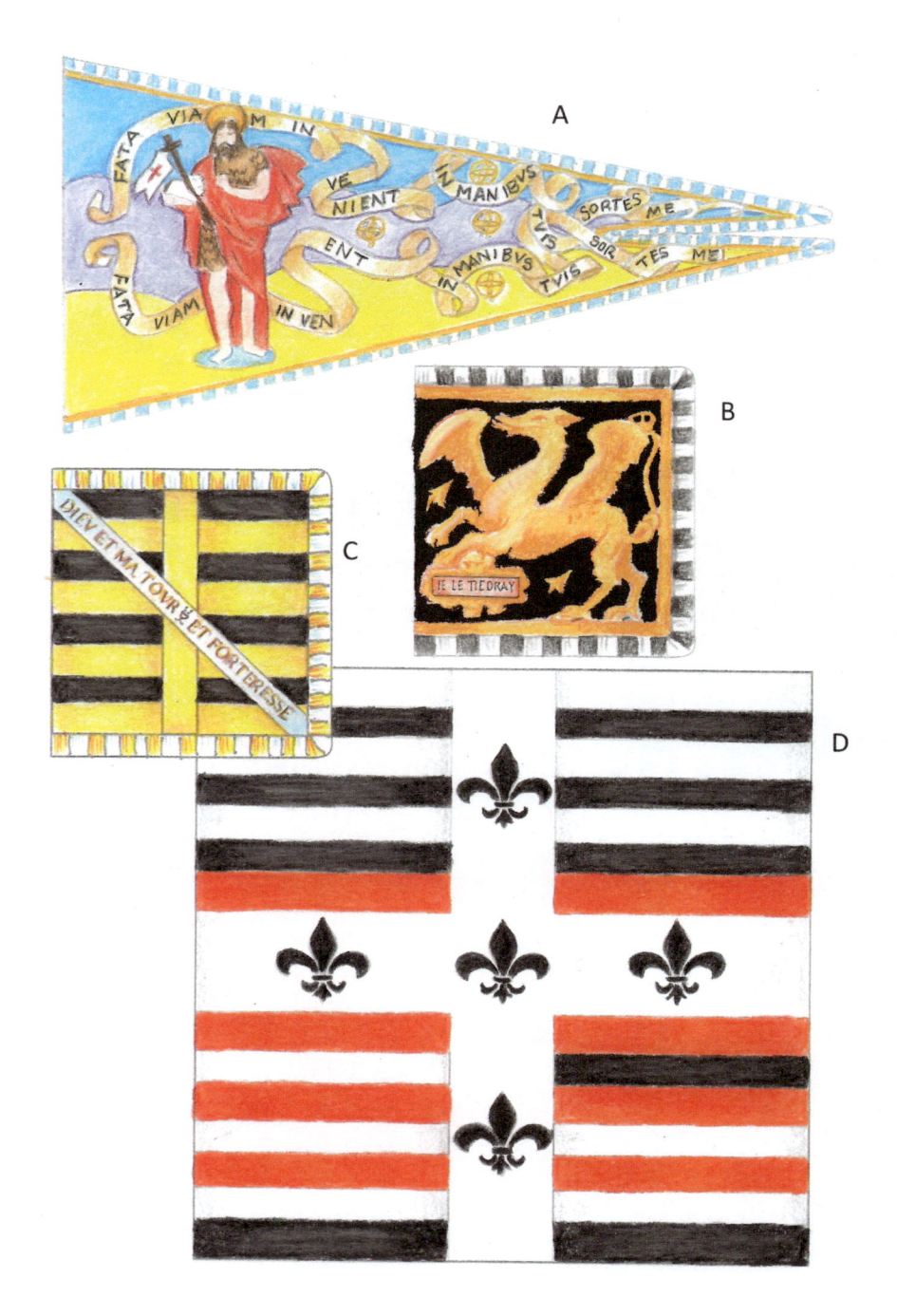

Flags from the Reign of Henry II

A and B: Unknown compagnies/commanders;
C: Cornette belonging to François de la Tour, Vicomte de Turenne; D: Infantry enseigne

(Illustration by and © T. J. O'Brien de Clare)

See Colour Plate Commentaries for further information.

Jacques de Savoye, Duc de **Nemours** (1531–1585)

Nemours distinguished himself at the sieges of Lens and Metz, the Battle of Renty and in the subsequent Piedmont campaign. He held the rank of colonel general of the chevaux legers under Henry II. He was a close supporter of the Guise faction at court. Governor of Lionnois during the First War, he then replaced Antoine de Bourbon in the Daulphine: opposing local Huguenot forces in these areas. He married the widow of François de Guise in 1566. In 1567, he persuaded the court to return from Meaux to Paris, preventing it from falling into Protestant control, and took part in the battle of Sainct Denys. He advised Anjou during the subsequent phase of the campaign and was a vocal opponent of the Peace of Longjumeau. In the Third War, he had some success in repulsing the 'German mercenary invasion' of Burgundy by Pfalzgraf Wolfgang von Zweibrücken. He was succeeded by his son, Charles Emmanuel.

Jacques de Nemours. (Musée Condé)

François de **La Noue** (1531–1591)

Descending from Bretaigne, La Noue was a page to the future Henry II before fighting in the closing stages of the Italian Wars. Despite his association with Andelot and his conversion to Protestantism, he remained a client of the House of Guise, accompanying Mary Stuart to Scotland in 1560. He sided with his faith when war came. In 1562 he fought at Dreux and in 1567 at Sainct Denys. Later in that year he distinguished himself by seizing Orleans at the head of only 50 horsemen. During the Third War he was appointed commander of La Rochelle, Poictou and Santongue by the Prince de Conde and then went on to command the Huguenot rearguard at Jarnac. He was captured at this battle and also at the subsequent encounter at Moncontour. He was exchanged for Strozzi. In 1570, at the Siege of Fontenaÿ, he lost his left arm. This was replaced by an iron prosthesis, earning him the nickname of 'Bras-de-fer'. After the Peace of Sainct Germain, he entered the King's service. In 1572 he fought in support of the Dutch rebels at the Siege of Mons. He thus escaped the massacre in Paris. Charles thought to use him to tempt the rebels in La Rochelle to accept royal authority. But they offered La Noue the role of defender instead, which he accepted, organising the defence of the city. In favour of a negotiated peace, he found himself increasingly at odds with the more hardline Huguenots and left the city before the end of the siege, taking no further part in the affair. He subsequently aligned himself to the Malcontents, representing a moderate Protestant position. During the Fifth War he served as Governor of La Rochelle once more. Disillusioned by the affairs in France, he served with the Dutch rebels against Spain. He was captured in 1580 and spent five years under guard. During these years he wrote his *Discours politiques et militaires* for which he is most famous. He was eventually exchanged for Graaf Egmond in 1585. In 1589 he fought and won the Combat of Senlis on behalf of Henry III. He rallied to Henry IV and fought with him at Ivry. He was sent to assist the Prince de Dombes in Bretaigne, but was mortally wounded at the taking of Lamballe in 1591.

*Alphonso Gieronimo d'**Ornano** (1548–1610)*

Born in Corsica, son of Sampiero da Bastelica, who served Henry II, he took his mother's surname. He spent his youth in France, only returning to his homeland in 1566, where his father fought against the Genoese. After the latter's death the next year, Alphonso continued the struggle until 1569 when he returned to France. He was made colonel and governor of Aix-en-Prouvence in 1578. In 1584 he was appointed colonel general of the Corsican mercenaries serving the kingdom. He remained loyal to Henry III during the Eighth War and played a major role in the victory at Jarrie in 1587. He became lieutenant general of Daulphine in 1589. Rallying to Henry IV, he joined forces with his old opponent, Lesdiguières, to oppose the Ligue forces under Nemours and his Savoyard allies. The King appointed him mareschal in 1595. He campaigned in Catalonia in 1596 but failed to take Perpignan.

François de La Rochefoucauld. (Palace de Versailles)

*François III, Comte de La **Rochefoucauld** (1521–1572)*

Rochefoucauld took part in the campaign of Metz (1552) as a captain of chevaux legers. He fought, and was made prisoner, at the Battle of Sainct Quentin (1557) where he served as lieutenant in the Duc de Lorraine's company of gendarmes. As a Protestant, he was not popular within the court of King François II, but the Queen Mother persuaded him to stay. In 1562, he took a leading role in the Huguenot rebellion and participated in all the major struggles of the first three Wars. He commanded the 100 gentlemen that escorted Condé to the peace talks at Toury. He took Beaugency and Pons, fought at Dreux and then helped defend Orleans. In 1567 he fought at Sainct Denys and then accompanied the Prince de Condé in Touraine. In the Third War he raised a large force to succour the Prince de Condé at La Rochelle and subsequently accompanied him to Languedoc to link up with the troops led by Acier. He fought at the Battle of Jarnac in 1569. He went on to fight at La Roche-l'Abeille and Port-de-Piles, but was ill and did not participate in Moncontour. As was often the case, contemporaries attributed this illness to the Queen Mother's poisons. In the peace that followed, he returned to court, becoming a favourite of King Charles IX due to his charm and wit. This did not save him from the massacre, however. François' younger brother, Charles, Seigneur (or Comte) de Randan, was a Catholic and replaced Andelot as colonel general of infantry. He was mortally wounded in 1562 at the capture of Bourges and died later at Rouen. Unusually, François and Charles married sisters, Silvia and Flavia Pico della Mirandola, respectively. For his part, Charles is often confused with his cousin of the same name. The latter was Seigneur de Barbezieux, Lieutenant General of Champagne, and who fought on the Catholic side at most of the battles of the first three Wars.

Jacques d'Albon, Seigneur de **Sainct André** (1505–1562)

Sainct André was a childhood companion of Henry II and was appointed first gentleman of the king's household in 1547. Later the same year he was named mareschal. In 1550 he became governor of Lionnois. From 1552 to 1555, he fought against the Hapsburgs in Lorraine. In 1557 he was captured by the Spaniards at the Battle of Sainct Quentin. In March 1560, he participated in the repression of the conspiracy of Amboise. In 1561, with Anne de Montmorency and François de Guise, he created the 'triumvirate'. On 4 July 1562, he took Bloys from the Protestants and followed this up on 29 July at Poictiers and 31 August at Bourges, repressing all resistance with extreme brutality. By taking these cities he prevented the southern Huguenots from joining those in the north. He took part in the Battle of Dreux, commanding the advance guard of the army. During this encounter, he was captured by Huguenot chevaux legers and shot by their captain.

Jacques de Sainct André.
(Palace de Versailles)

Filippo di Piero **Strozzi**, *Seigneur de Espernay* (1541–1582)

Filippo was born in Florence to an exiled condottiero and Mareschal of France, Pietro Strozzi. Accompanying his family to Paris, he became page of the future King François II. He took part in the capture of Calais. In 1560 he was sent to Scotland to fight for the regent Mary of Guise and was subsequently made Seigneur de Espernay in recognition of his services. He commanded an infantry compagnie during the First War. Always something of an adventurer, in 1564 he then served the Emperor Maximilian II during the Ottoman invasion in Hungary, and the following year he again faced the Ottomans at the Siege of Malta, where his uncle served as a Knight of the Order. From there he served in his homeland distinguishing himself in the defence of Ancona against the Turks. He later fought also in Transylvania. Returning to France in 1567, he commanded an infantry regiment in the Second War. This regiment was later converted into the Royal Guards. In 1569 he was appointed colonel general, initially in France proper, then as sole incumbent. Later in the year, at the Combat of Roche l'Abeille his detachment was roughly handled when it became isolated from the main Catholic force and he was captured. In 1573, he took part in the siege of La Rochelle where he is said to have tried to introduce the musket into the French army. Later that year he fought alongside the Dutch against the Spaniards. In 1581 he served Dom António, Prior of Crato (claimant to the Portuguese throne against Spanish King Felipe II) as a private mercenary. With a contingent of French, Dutch, English and Portuguese volunteers, he set sail to the Azores. His fleet was, however, destroyed in the Battle of Terceira (26 July 1582). Taken prisoner, he was executed as a pirate.

Gaspard de Saulx, Seigneur de **Tavannes** (1509–1573)

An experienced soldier who had served under François I and Henry II at Pavia, Ceresole, Metz, Renty and Calais. German by birth, his uncle was the commander of the infamous landsknecht 'Band Noir'. He was gouverneur of Bourgógne at the start of the wars, where he had already gained a reputation for his severe persecution of the Huguenots. He was the guiding intellect behind the Catholic army that won the victory at Jarnac in 1569 and, nominally again under the Duc d'Anjou's command, at Moncontour later the same year. In recognition of his achievements, he was made mareschal in 1570. In 1572 he became gouverneur of Prouvence and admiral of the seas of Levant. A close confidant of the Queen Mother, he was implicated in the Sainct-Barthélemy's Day Massacre. His memoires were published in 1620 by his third son, Jean, who served Mayenne in Bourgógne and Normandie and as the Ligueur Mareschal de Camp at Ivry. His second son, Guillaume, reconciled to Henry IV in 1589 and distinguished himself at the combat of Fontaine-François.

Henry de La Tour d'Auvergne, Vicomte de **Turenne**, jure uxoris Duc de Bouillon (1555–1623)

Turenne was the grandson of the Anne de Montmorency, through his eldest daughter, Eléonore. He was a Protestant like many of his kin, but remained on good terms with his mother's family. He accompanied his uncle François de Montmorency on a diplomatic visit to London in 1571. He abjured after the massacre and served in the royal army at La Rochelle during the Fourth War, but thereafter recanted. He was compromised in the conspiracy of La Mole and lost influence at court. He joined the party of the Malcontents headed by his friend, Alençon, in 1575. In 1576 he joined the Protestant party of Henry of Navarre and negotiated the Peace of Nérac in 1579. He was much favoured by Navarre and appointed lieutenant general of Languedoc in 1580. As part of Alençon's mixed confessional force, he took part in the expedition to the Netherlands, but was captured. He only regained his freedom in 1584 after paying a ransom of 50,000 écus. He took part in the Battle of Arques in 1589, the 2nd Siege of Paris in 1590, and conquered Stenay from the Ligue in 1591. Later that year, he married Charlotte de La Marck, heiress to the duchy of Bouillon. In 1592 Henry IV made him a mareschal. After the death of his first wife in 1594, he married Elisabeth, a daughter of Willem the Silent and granddaughter of Louis Duc de Montpensier. He was defeated at Doullens in 1595 by Fuentes and was subsequently sent to England to renew the alliance of France with Queen Elizabeth in 1596.

3

The Armies

A large field army, including its non-combatants, exceeded in population all the cities of France save Paris. Such a mass of humanity required careful management if it was to be an effective instrument of war.

Manoeuvres

Even when actively campaigning, armies spent a great deal more time in camp and marching than they did fighting one another. When some form of combat did occur, it was normally in the context of a siege or small-scale encounter between opposing scouts and foragers. Formal battles were rare events. A study of Anjou's royal army during the Third War concluded that, during the 457 days the army was together:[1]

- 264 days were spent in encampments with no enemy contact (which includes the time the army spent in its winter quarters)
- 107 days were spent marching with no enemy contact
- 51 days were spent besieging Sainct Jean d'Angély
- 35 days were in contact with the enemy, but serious combat only occurred during 11 of these (including the fights at Mensignac, Jazeneuil, Jarnac, La Roche l'Abeille and Moncontour)

The army might occupy a camp for several reasons. The principal one being the difficulties associated with physically moving and obtaining supplies during the winter months. The army might also occupy a position to deny it to the enemy or force them to manoeuvre in response. After any

---

1   Wood, *The King's Army*, pp.237–245, provides a detailed analysis of the movements of the main royal army during the Third War, from its mustering at Samur in September 1568 until the completion of the Siege of Sainct Jean d'Angély in December 1569. The study does not include the activities of the detached column undertaking the Siege of Niort. The statistics can be taken as indicative of most large forces during the period (possible exceptions being the all-mounted expeditions launched by Coligny and Henry IV) but is less applicable to the smaller local forces engaged in the endemic cycles of raid and counter-raid that generated a significant amount of the wars' violence.

period of movement, the army must also come to a halt to allow stragglers and supplies to catch up, rest soldiers and animals and repair equipment. There was also an inevitable amount of dither and delay as commanders tried to locate the enemy, guess their intentions and then formulate a response.

When the army did eventually stir itself, it took on the guise of a vast serpent of men and animals winding through the countryside over tracks and unmetalled roads. If they were moving along the same route, the avant-garde would precede the corps de bataille. The avant-garde would normally be arranged with the chevaux legers or other light cavalry stationed in front, followed by the remainder of the cavalry in several tactical regiments. Then would come the infantry and, finally, its baggage train. The bataille would normally follow with at least a portion of its cavalry, then the artillery train, then the infantry and finally its baggage. There might be cavalry flanking the march of the artillery and guns and a small mounted rearguard as well. In an army containing a Swiss contingent, these troops customarily marched with the artillery.[2]

The size of the army was swelled by numbers of non-combatants, animals and wagons. The former consisted of civilian officials, contractors, servants, craftsmen, drovers, teamsters, sutlers, prostitutes and opportunists. In addition to the horses of the cavalry, there were spare mounts, pack animals, draft animals and beef 'on the hoof'. The number of wagons could be huge. The Huguenot army in the Third War, after they had been joined by their German allies and consisting of 7,000 mounted troops and 8,000 foot, was encumbered by as many as 6,000 wagons.[3] This whole force, if strung out along a single route and marching under normal conditions, would have a length of at least 25 miles (40 kilometres).

To keep the whole army moving simultaneously it was, therefore, normal to utilise as many parallel roads as possible. Of course, this was not always possible, especially when the army was required to pass through a major defile or over a single bridge. If multiple routes were available, then the avant-garde and bataille could follow parallel courses. If not, they could move with a day or more's interval between them.

The speed at which an army moved was dependant on a wide range of factors, not least of which was the commander's intentions and those of the enemy. Using Anjou's army in the Third War again as an example, of the 122 days spent marching (107 with no enemy contact and 15 with contact):[4]

- 21 marches were of five miles (eight kilometres) or less
- 33 marches were of six to 10 miles (nine to 16 kilometres)
- 33 marches were 11 to 15 miles (17 to 24 kilometres)
- 27 marches were 16 to 20 miles (25 to 32 kilometres)
- Eight marches were 21 to 25 miles (33 to 40 kilometres)

---

2   Wood, *The King's Army*, pp.68–70.
3   Gigon, *La troisième guerre*, p.376.
4   Wood, *The King's Army*, p.239.

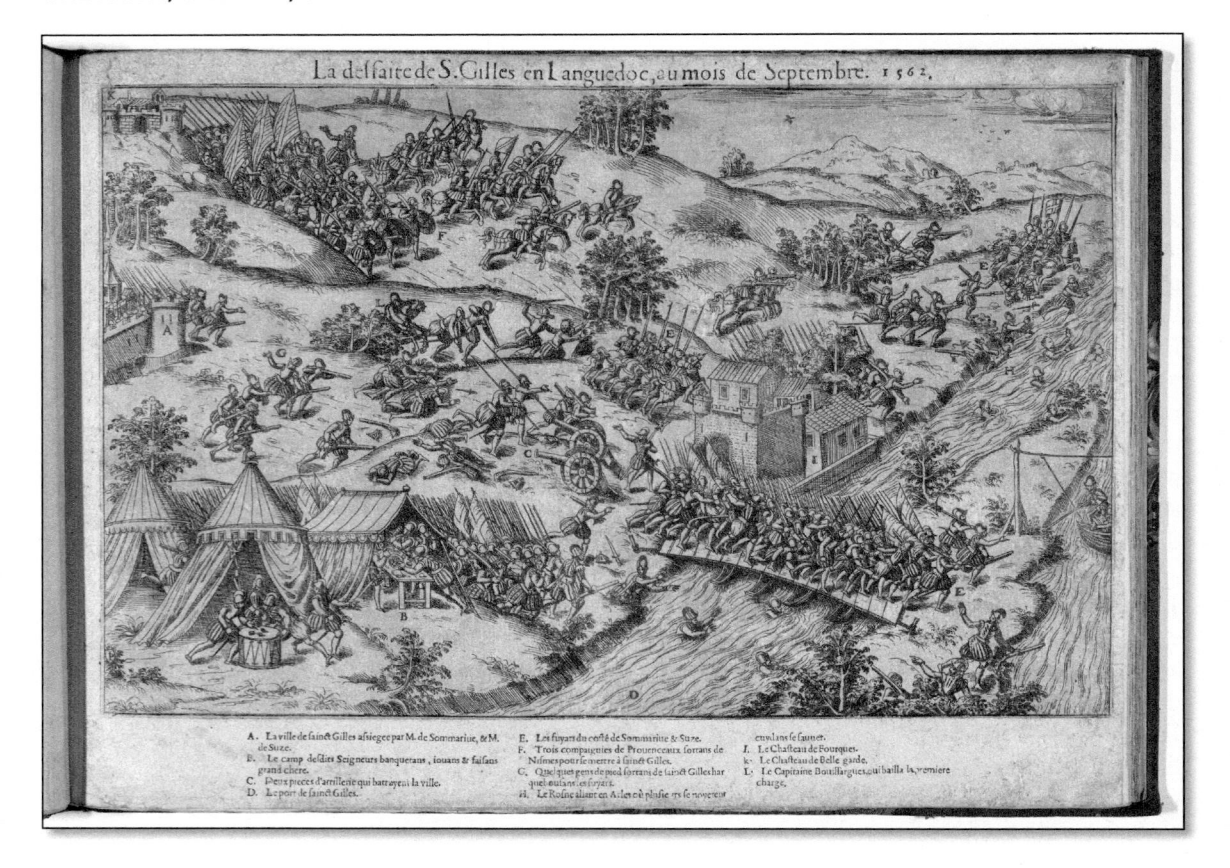

La deffaite de S. Gilles en Languedoc, au mois de Septembre. 1562.

A. La ville de sainct Gilles afsiegee par M. de Sommariue, & M. de Suze.
B. Le camp defdits Seigneurs banquetans , iouans & fufans grand chere.
C. Deux pieces d'artillerie qui batrayent la ville.
D. Le pont de sainct Gilles.
E. Les fuyars du cofté de Sommiriue & Suze.
F. Trois compagnies de Prouenceaux fortans de Nifmes pour fe mettre a fainct Gilles.
G. Quelques gens de pied fortans de fainct Gilles har quebutans en fuyant.
H. Le Rofne allant en Arles ou plufie rs fe noyerent.
cut dans fe faunet.
I. Le Chafteau de Fourquet.
k. Le Chafteau de Belle garde.
L. Le Capitaine Bouilfargues qui bailla la premiere charge.

Tortorel and Perrissin print showing Huguenot forces relieving the Siege of Sainct Gilles, 1562. (Author's collection)

Twenty-five miles (40 kilometres) per day should be considered the maximum for a large army during this era, and this pace could not be maintained for long. Short bursts of speed were generally reserved for those occasions when the enemy was near and a tactical advantage was sought. A more sustainable maximum was nearer 14 to 16 miles (22 to 26 kilometres) per day.[5]

Both the avant-garde and bataille had their own mareschal de camp, who would be responsible for determining the route taken, the length of the march, the position of units in the marching column and (as his title suggests) the quartering of troops upon reaching their destination. To fulfil this role, the mareschal de camp often travelled with the advance parties of the army. This could be a position of some danger, as François Comté de Belin found to his cost when he was captured prior to the Battle of Arques while serving in this capacity for the Ligue.

When the army camped, it did so in the same formation as it marched, except that the baggage moved up to provide sustenance to the units it belonged to. If in the vicinity of the enemy, a temporary entrenchment could be thrown up around the resting troops. As soon as the camp was set, the cavalry would typically fan out in search of fodder for their mounts.

---

5   22 kilometres in Gigon, *La troisième guerre*, p.376 and 16 miles in Wood, *The King's Army*, p.239.

La Noue was resigned to the poor practices adopted by armies when they settled into a position for any period of time:[6]

> Now must I speak of the lodging of the army which they were forced to scatter abroad, and that for two principal reasons. The one for the commodity of victuals, the other that it might be under cover, whereby to be defended from the injury of the winter: for without this help it could not survive. I know this to be a very bad kind of lodging: also that in war between emperors and kings men would beware of committing such oversights, least they might be straight ways surprised: But in civil wars both parties were forced and accustomed so to do, at the least in France. The footmen were lodged in two bodies, viz. in a main bataille and an avant-garde, and the horsemen in the villages next to hand. Upon any earnest alarum the horsemen drew to their quarters: likewise, if one several lodgings were assailed, the others went straight to the rescue.

Supplying the Army

While actively campaigning, as opposed to peacetime garrison duty, troops received rations of three basic items: bread, meat and wine. However, they were expected to purchase these items out of their pay. The army was only responsible for making sure they were available. When the soldiers pay was not forthcoming, as was very frequently the case, rations were provided at a discount or even free against the arrears. In addition to these rations, the army also required, as basic necessities, fodder for its horses and firewood for its men.

The requirements of the army were, in theory, met by the Commissaire General de Vivres. This civilian official was responsible for procurement, preparation and delivery of rations to the army. This was to be achieved through the establishment of étapes (stages or depots) filled by a network of munitionnaires (merchants contracted to source and transport the goods in question). These depots could be close to the army's line of march, so materials could be delivered to the troops in short stages.

La Noue describes the attitude of Admiral Coligny to logistics and the expedients adopted by the Huguenot army:[7]

> The Admiral had a special care above all things to have expert commissaries, and to cause them to have enough transport to meet the Protestant's needs, and was wont to say, whenever there was any question of forming the body of an army: "Let us begin the shaping of this monster by the belly".
>
> Now because our horsemen did commonly lodge scattering abroad in the good villages, the said commissaries besides their ordinary wagons kept, in every cornette, a baker and two pack horses, which no sooner they arrived in their quarters than they fell to making bread, and so sent it to the footmen. All these small helps

---

6   La Noue, *Discours politiques et militaires*, p.628.
7   La Noue, *Discours politiques et militaires*, p.627.

proceeding from forty cornettes (for thereabouts we then were) being gathered together, amounted unto a great deal: yea, and thence sometimes they sent both meat and wine, whereto the Gentry were so affectionate that from their lodgings they would not spare their carriages for conduct of whatsoever was required. The small towns that were taken were reserved for the munitionnaires, and they threatened the rest that kept no garrisons to fire all a league round about if they sent in no provision: whereby our footmen who lodged close were ordinarily well provided. I did not here talk of the booty which the footmen as well as horsemen won from the adversaries, neither is there any doubt but this devouring animal (that is, the army) passing through so many provinces… so sore did necessity and desire to catch incite those that wanted no excuses to colour their spoil. Of these fruits were many provided of those things which besides food the soldier is to buy, such as garments and weapons which are most necessary things.

La Noue highlights the problems in supplying the army with bread. Unlike other commodities, this required a considerable amount of processing before it could be consumed. Not only did the flour need to be baked, but wheat needed to be milled to produce the flour. The wheat and flour also had to be transported. The availability of these resources, or lack thereof, often contributed to the movement of armies in the field.[8] It also made mills legitimate targets for enemy activity. These could also be rendered useless by the onset of winter, when the water that powered them froze, or during long dry spells in the summer.

During the initial stages of the First War, La Noue was pleasantly surprised by the good behaviour of the Huguenot army, in which 'no man forsook his enseigne to go foraging, but were content with such victuals as were distributed among them, or the small pay that they received.'[9] The Admiral, however, was more sceptical and foresaw that 'these people will pour forth all their goodness at once, so as within these two months they will have nothing but malice left: I have governed footmen a great while and know them well. They will fulfil the proverb: a young saint; an old devil.' He was proved correct:

Thus did our footmen lose their virginity, and this unlawful conjunction caused the procreation of Mademoiselle Picoree (Miss Plunder), who is since grown into such dignity that she is now called Madam: and, if this civil war continues, I do not doubt she will become a Princess. This perverse custom immediately crept in among the nobility: whereof part having tasted the first delicacies here administered, would never after eat any other meat. Thus, this particular mischief grew general, and infected the whole body more and more.

Even salutary justice handed down to plunderers by conscientious commanders had only a temporary effect on the army. Others were more sympathetic to their perceived needs. Brantôme, after listing their faults in

---

8   Gigon, *La troisième guerre*, pp.381–382
9   La Noue, *Discours politiques et militaires*, pp.575–576.

this regard, commented that 'it is necessary that they live and profit'.[10] There was a tacit acceptance that the soldier's life was not bound by the same social and legal constraints as a civilian. They expected, for example, to plunder a town taken by assault. It did not matter to them that the town might contain many subjects loyal to their own notional cause. Their determination to exact their due could be carried out in the teeth of their own commander's prohibition, as occurred after the taking of Rouen in 1562.

When elements of the army were detached from the main body, or local forces were raised to protect or pacify their own region, they had less access to organised supply systems and, inevitably, there was also less control over their activities. Men hardened by violence and fuelled by sectarian grudges were quick to turn upon peasants and burghers alike. They took what they wished and committed casual acts of torture, rape and murder along the way.

Even when the army was in hand and funds were adequate to their needs, the sheer mass of humanity they represented could strip an area of its food reserves in a frighteningly short time. This in an era when agricultural surpluses were limited and the means of food preservation few. As a result, its commander had two choices. Firstly, he could set up a static base on the periphery of the campaigning area, choosing a location with good transport routes. Here, in reasonable security, regular supply lines could be set up and maintained, drawing in food from a much wider area. A winter camp was invariably established on this basis. An army besieging an enemy stronghold also represents a static camp. Its security derives from the fact that the enemy is bottled up in the city or fortress. However, the approach of a relief force typically meant abandoning the siege because of the threat to the besieging force's vulnerable supply lines. The commander's second choice was to keep the army moving, so new resources could be continually exploited. The richer the region, the more leisurely these moves could be. But with his opponent doing the same thing, a whole region could become exhausted during a campaigning season. As much as any other factor, the availability of supply determined the movement of armies in the field.

Losses and Reinforcements

Reasonably detailed figures are available for the fluctuations of strength experienced by Anjou's army during the Third War.[11] During the period between September 1568 and October 1569 (prior to the Battle of Moncontour), the French elements of the army suffered an attrition of 63 percent. This equates to a rate of 4.8 percent per month. Though in fact the rate is higher since the army was only joined by 37 of the cavalry compagnies in November 1568 and 28 of the infantry compagnies in January 1569. Nor was the rate of loss even. The three-month period between March to May 1569 saw the average strength of an infantry compagnie drop from 78 men

---

10 Quoted in Wood, *The King's Army*, p.303.
11 Wood, *The King's Army*, pp.229–235.

to only 36, a 54 percent reduction.

Comparable figures are available for the Spanish army fighting in the Netherlands.[12] Between 1570 and 1572, a period which saw the Spanish troops remain largely unpaid, the units lost on average 0.7 percent of their strength per month. To 1573, this increased to two percent per month and peaked at three percent during 1574 to 1576. These increases correspond to the intensity of the fighting the troops experienced. It can be seen, therefore, that the rate of attrition experienced by French troops was significantly greater than that of the Spanish.

There were three principal causes for these losses: battle casualties, disease and desertion.

During the period discussed above, the royal army fought four significant actions, with casualties as follows: [13]

Table 1. Royalist Casualties October 1568 to June 1569

Action	Date	Royalist Casualties
Mensignac	26 October 1568	200–500?
Jazeneuil	17 November 1568	250–700
Jarnac	13 March 1569	200–300
La Roche l'Abeille	25 June 1569	500+

Most of these losses were suffered by the native French elements within the army. These actions do not represent all the fighting that occurred; there were several small-scale sieges and numerous skirmishers, but nevertheless they do give an indication of the scale of losses resulting from enemy action. All in all, it is unlikely that more than 4,000 men were killed during this phase of the campaign. This is less than 15 percent of all the losses for the army.

There are no detailed figures for losses due to disease during the same period. Soldiers were typically men in the prime of life who would have already weathered the rigours of childhood mortality. But hard marching and poor diets undermined the health of many, as did the generally unsanitary conditions of a marching camp. Infections from relatively minor wounds are likely to have carried off other souls days or weeks after the actions in which they were sustained, thus are unlikely to be recorded in the casualty figures above. Bubonic plague was endemic in Europe from the fourteenth-century Black Death onwards. Although France did not experience a nationwide outbreak of the disease again until 1628, localised outbreaks were common. Paris experienced at least some infection one year out of every three, with

---

12 Geoffrey Parker, *The Army of Flanders and the Spanish Road 1567–1659* (Cambridge: Cambridge University Press, 1984), pp.207–210.

13 Gigon, *La troisième guerre*, p.108 states that as a result of the Montpensier's operation that failed to relieve Angoulêmeand then engaged Acier's column at Mensignac and Sainct Astier, the Duc lost 2,000. Given the intensity of the fighting and the loses sustained by the defeated Huguenots, it is likely that this number actually reflects his losses from all causes, including desertion and straggling as a result of hard marching, rather than purely combat losses.

particularly virulent periods in 1560–62, 1580 and 1595–97.[14] Conditions to be found within army camps and experienced by both sides during a siege could lead to infestations of rats that carried the disease. It was justly feared by commanders and plague towns were avoided lest the contagion spread to the fighting troops. However, there are no records of widespread losses due to illness in Anjou's force. An upper limit on losses due to disease could be set at one percent per month, which is still more than the total losses suffered by the Spanish troops in the Netherlands while relatively unengaged.

The most significant period of loss suffered by the army was between March and May 1569. Anjou's army contained 23,000 foot at Jarnac. By the end of April 1569 Anjou, despite winning a battle in which few of these units suffered significant losses, was already complaining that he was growing desperately short of infantry. On 24 May he had only 7,000–8,000 infantry with him and 10,000–12,000 available in total. When he joined Aumale on 2 June after marching over poorly provisioned routes, he had only 10,000. What happened to the lost 13,000?

In the days after Jarnac, Anjou established a few minor garrisons, but his numbers were swelled by the arrival of a regiment of foot under Montluc. On 20 March he distributed the sick and wounded from the army into neighbouring towns. There were some hundreds of these. His troops suffered some loss at the abortive siege of La Fère, but probably less than the 200 men claimed.[15] Over the next few days the bataille moved relatively slowly while the avant-garde remained at Jarnac. These latter troops fought a successful action on 6 April, but only cavalry was involved. By 14 April, the whole army had moved, by short marches, to Montmoureau and then Villebois. Here it conducted some minor siege operations, the most significant of which was against Mussidan. There were losses here, including the Colonel General, Timoléon de Brissac, but these were not particularly heavy. The town fell on 1 May. During this period two very understrength regiments were returned to their recruiting grounds to rebuild their numbers. As a result, the total number of enseignes fell from 138 to 108. This represents a loss of hundreds of men, but undoubtedly less than 2,000, given that they were the weakest in the army. Around this time, Anjou makes mention of the desolation of the countryside caused by the movement of armies. On 5 May the army moved to La Rochefoucauld. By 19 May, he refers to the state of the royal army as 'dilapidated'.[16] This is well before the hardest march of the period to meet Aumale.

Given this information, the inevitable conclusion is that most losses suffered by this army were due to desertion. Only days after a victorious battle, on 17 March, Anjou wrote that: 'I could hardly do anything else but contain those inside (the villages chosen as billets) to prevent them from running and taking to the countryside.'[17] He was, of course occupying the ground north of the Charente River previously occupied by the Huguenot army since the last

---

14 Vanessa Harding, *The Dead and the Living in Paris and London, 1500–1670* (Cambridge: Cambridge University Press, 2002), p.25.

15 Gigon, *La troisième guerre*, p.103.

16 Gigon, *La troisième guerre*, p.112.

17 Gigon, *La troisième guerre*, p.102.

day in February. They had undoubtedly already picked these villages clean of available victuals. The army was also desperately short of funds.

While all military forces in this era were subject to desertion on a scale unimaginable a couple of centuries later, the situation was made easier for those soldiers who took part in the Wars of Religion because of two important factors. Firstly, they were not foreigners in a hostile country. They could slip back into civil society relatively easily if they chose to do so. Secondly, the increasingly extended periods of civil unrest, even outside the periods of formal war, caused a breakdown in the system of judicial enforcement. Soldiers could become bandits and prey on the local communities with relative impunity. Such activities did not preclude them rejoining the army at some future date, once their thirst for plunder was slaked.

Although far from immune from such tendencies, the aristocratic gendarmerie suffered significantly less attrition than their infantry colleagues. A study of documented gens d'armes compagnie strengths during the Third War shows that they started the campaign with an average strength of 85 percent of that authorised (though the few double compagnies in the sample account for most of this, the other compagnies were at 95 percent). By May 1569, despite the poor state of the army as a whole, they still attained 72 percent. During November 1569, the average had actually increased a little, to 75 percent.[18]

Reinforcement

Individual compagnies were not generally reinforced by additional men while campaigning with the army. There was no pool of drafted manpower which could be assigned to units according to need. The armies of the Wars of Religion existed partly in the world of feudal hosts and partly in that of military entrepreneurs. In either paradigm the compagnie was, in a very real sense, the property not of the state, but of its captain. The Crown might authorise the recruitment of men, by issuing a commission, but it was the captain who not only personally recruited the rank and file, but also chose the compagnie's officers. This was a valuable facet of the commission, as it allowed him to extend his personal patronage base by selecting his relatives and clients for these roles. He was responsible for making sure the men were fit for service. If their pay was late, as was normally the case, he was expected to dip into his own coffers to cover their expenses until it eventually turned up. The position of captain, especially in the gendarmerie, was almost hereditary. Sons, brothers and nephews frequently succeeded to the post on the death or retirement of the previous holder. The appointment of an 'outsider' could cause a significant amount of ill will. Therefore, the

---

18 Gigon, *La troisième guerre*, pp.356–362. This is summarised in Wood, *The King's Army*, p.141, who compensates for Gigon's errors regarding the authorised strength of the compagnies. However, Wood assumes that all of the compagnies in the November sample have an authorised strength of 75 men, and consequently calculated the average at 65 percent. It would seem more likely that the compagnies with a notional strength of 30 lances had an authorised strength of only 20 lances or 50 men. Though of course a reduction in the authorised strength of the compagnies is also an indicator of dwindling manpower.

captain would not have been pleased to have unknown men foisted upon his compagnie as reinforcements. The men, who tended to be drawn from the same region, would be equally unhappy for Picards to be incorporated into a Gascon company. The same might also be true at a regimental level.[19]

Individuals or groups of deserters might be returned to their compagnies by the authorities, if the pleas of army commanders are based on a genuine expectation. Those who temporarily absconded from their units to engage in plundering expeditions might well return to the colours of their own volition. The sick and wounded who recovered would also find their way back to their comrades. So, the strength of compagnies could rise as well as fall, but the general trend was inevitably downward.

An individual compagnie or, as noted above, whole regiments might be sent back from the army to their home region to look for more men. This process obviously took time, as the unit had to march to a potentially distant corner of the kingdom, then set about the recruiting process, which involved raising funds and providing equipment, and then march all the way back again. During this period, the veterans of the company would be unavailable for operations and would still have to be paid and fed.

A more common expedient was simply to raise new compagnies. Thus, after the clash at Dreux that so damaged the Royalist gendarmerie, Guise's first thought was not the recovery of the existing units, but to raise 17 new ones.[20] Individual compagnies could be incorporated into existing regiments. While during the Siege of La Rochelle in 1573 an unusually large and disorderly compagnie 500-strong was used as a pool for other units, but this seems to have been an exceptional instance.

As a result of normal practice, compagnie strength within an army varied greatly, with the newly joined elements being considerably stronger than those with hard months' campaigning under their belts. It also meant that the character of the army changed over the course of a long campaigning season. The core units would be joined from those hailing from the more distant provinces and, eventually, their foreign allies and auxiliaries. The latter could eventually outnumber the native French troops. Anjou's army during the Third War reached this point in early June 1569.[21]

Finally, a compagnie stationed in or close to its own recruiting district always had the option of ongoing recruitment. A detailed study of the changes of personnel in Montluc's compagnie of gens d'armes during the Third War, which only briefly served outside Languedoc, shows that more than half their number only joined during 1569.[22]

---

19 Oman., *War in the Sixteenth Century*, p.407.
20 Wood, *The King's Army*, pp.202–203.
21 Wood, *The King's Army*, p.233.
22 Wood, *The King's Army*, pp.142–143.

The Army in Battle

One contemporary writer summed up the typical manner of deploying armies as follows:

> The French way is to divide the mass of an army into two parts which are called avant-garde and bataille. If the army is very large, we add an arriére garde, which is three parts: the latter is to support the first two, it also serves to rally, to stop fugitives and compel them to fight. This way of acting seems taken from the Romans.[23]

Despite these comments, in none of the battles described above was there sufficient strength in reserve to qualify for an arriére-garde. When encountered, such small bodies that were formed (such as under Guise at Druex or Biron at Ivry) are normally referred to as an ost de reserve.

It was the duty of the mareschal de camp to arrange the formations of the army in accordance with the instructions of the army commander. The activities of Biron, who served in this capacity before the Battle of Ivry, are described thusly:

> The King having invented the Form wherein the Army was to be drawn up and embattled, gave the design thereof into the hand of the Baron de Byron Camp-Master-General; and chose Monsieur de Vicy, an old Colonel of the French Infantry, and a man of great valour and experience, Serjeant-Major-General; an Office, for the high importance of it, not wont to be conferred but upon such persons as by their approved knowledge and long practice in remarkable occasions, had gotten the credit and reputation of Command, and consequently both knew and were known of all… The Sieur de Vicy, and the Baron de Byron, together with the Sieur de Surene, and Captain Favas, who that day executed the Office of Adjutants, being all rode before into this place, drew up the Army as it came, and disposed it in such manner.[24]

Despite Biron's valuable contribution, Henry IV took great care checking the placement of each unit, wearing out three horses while reviewing his army.

In contrast with these careful arrangements, Jean de Tavannes, acting in this capacity for the Ligueur forces at the same battle, was implicated in their defeat because he packed the units too close together, preventing the reiters from executing their caracole tactics without impeding other units. This was, in part, blamed on Tavannes' poor eyesight.

Within the overall scheme set out by the commander and his mareschal de camp, individual infantry units were formed up by their serjens major, also called serjens de bataille, who were specialists in this vital task. Their authority within this specialised domain could not be challenged. At the

---

23 Henri de La Popelinière, *La vraye et entière histoire des troubles et choses memorables avenues tant en France qu'en Flandres, & pays circonuoisins, depuis l'an 1562* (Basle: Pierre Davantes, 1573), p.312.

24 Avila, *History of the Civil Wars*, p.443.

Battle of Ceresole in 1544, Serjeant Major Pierre de La Berthe struck dead a noble volunteer who repeatedly failed to take his assigned place.[25]

The avant-garde was normally deployed to the right of the bataille unless circumstances dictated otherwise, as at Jazeneuil. It could vary from being of equal strength to the bataille to only a small fraction of its size. Both elements of the army contained the same combination of cavalry and infantry, but normally the chevaux legers would be found in the avant-garde and the artillery, if deployed in a single battery, in the bataille. The avant-garde and bataille could form up as a single line, that is with a depth of only a single regiment, or else more deeply, where additional regiments formed behind the first.

Normally cavalry and infantry units were interspaced along the length of the line. While there were exceptions, such as the Huguenots at Sainct Denys and both sides at Coutras, the alternation of horse and foot remained the norm from Dreux to Ivry.

The battle would normally start with a preliminary artillery barrage. Where this desultory fire had any tactical effect, it was to goad an opponent into attacking rather than enduring it. Whether because of such goading, or more normally of their own volition, the next stage of battle was a general assault by the mounted units against their opposite numbers. Sometimes the cavalry of one wing might be ordered to move first, but normally all the cavalry attacked at once. The results of these encounters were normally reached before the infantry got to grips with their opposite numbers, though they could find themselves being attacked by enemy cavalry or, as in the case of the Swiss at Moncontour, intervening to tip the scales in favour of their own horsemen.

Infantry could have another contribution to a battle, small units of arquebusiers could be deployed to defend rough ground or defensive works to provide localised fire support.

Horsemen have considerable striking power but lack stamina and are poor at defending ground. Combined with the volunteer nature of many of the troops involved, this meant that most battles were of fairly short duration. The most notable exception is, perhaps, Dreux, at which victory and defeat hung in the balance for some considerable time. Arques is another example, but this was a fight around fortified positions in a narrow defile rather than an open battle.

Although they often played little active role in the battle itself, the foot soldiers often suffered disproportionate casualties during its immediate aftermath. Whole units were often forced to surrender and, given the bitterness engendered by a civil war centred around religious issues, massacres were not uncommon. Foreign troops were often singled out for cruel treatment.

---

25 David Potter, *Renaissance France at War: Armies, Culture and Society, c. 1480–1560* (Woodbridge: The Boydell Press, 2008), p.195.

The Army in Siege

Although of limited use in most field battles, a siege required the presence of heavy guns if there was to be any reasonable chance of success. Only towns with antiquated or dilapidated fortifications could normally be taken by storm without their contribution. This represented a dilemma to army commanders. In May 1569, the Duc d'Anjou pointed out to his brother, the King, that an army encumbered by a siege train and other impedimenta could not move quickly and so could not conduct an active campaign in the field.[26] Therefore, when the army moved, the heavy guns were normally left behind at some strongpoint until they were needed. An army, victorious in the field, would then have to await the arrival of the siege train before it could capitalise on its success. This delay inevitably gave the defeated army a chance to retreat to its strongholds and recover its losses. This occurred most notably after Dreux and Jarnac. The Huguenots were doubly inconvenienced in this matter, for not only could they not campaign with a siege train, they often lacked such resources to begin with. They were without not only the heaviest guns, but also plentiful ammunition and pionniers.[27]

Once a siege was decided upon, there followed a relatively predictable series of steps; though these had not yet evolved into the military science perfected by Vauban and his contemporaries a century later. Even the skill the French had previously enjoyed in this area had decayed, and they were forced to employ Italian engineers to compensate for these deficiencies.[28] Scipione Verano had the distinction of building the La Rochelle bastions in 1569 and losing his life while besieging them in 1573.

The first step was to invest the strongpoint by seizing the villages, bridges and other strategic sites in the vicinity, in order to cut off the defenders from any source of succour and also to prevent them from making any use of resources in these areas. The attacker would draw on the resources of these environs to supply not only foodstuffs, but also other materials used for the construction of the trenches and batteries. Against a city located on a river, this could also include diverting watercourses, to expose weak points in the defences and prevent them using watermills. Against a port, it could involve sinking hulks in the harbour or approaches to prevent resupply by sea.

The next step was to draw the net tighter by establishing fieldworks and batteries near the city. These would be used to protect the besiegers and provide a platform from which long-range fire would destroy the battlements on top of the walls and overwhelm the defender's guns located on them. In the meantime, active defenders would do all in their power to prevent or slow down these efforts by skirmishing and raiding against the besiegers, forcing them to divert men and energy into guarding and containing these attacks and away from prosecuting the siege proper.

---

26 Gigon, *La troisième guerre*, p.233.
27 Christopher Duffy, *Siege Warfare: Siege Warfare, The Fortress in the Early Modern World 1494–1660* (London: Routledge, 1979), p.106.
28 Duffy, *Siege Warfare*, p.110.

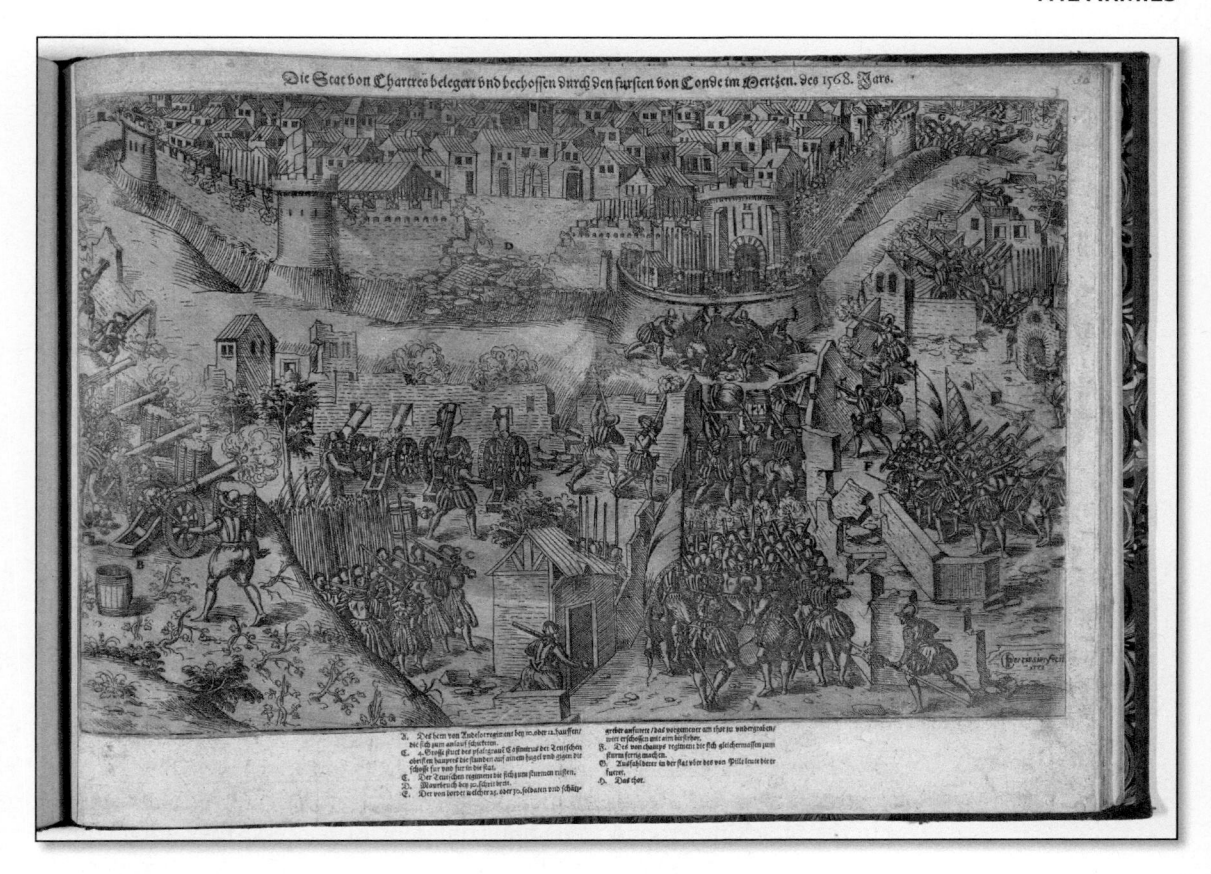

Tortorel and Perrissin print of the Siege of Chartres, 1568. (Author's collection)

Once the defender had been contained, and his guns suppressed, the attacker would then start the process of digging trenches ever closer to the walls. As they advanced, new batteries would be built that allowed the heavy guns to fire on these directly. Eventually these trenches would extend to within a short distance of the city. Once the guns had pounded the walls long enough, they would collapse, and a breach would be formed. The defender would continue to conduct sorties against these trenches, those digging them and those guarding the batteries with the aim of destroying them and delaying the point when such a breach occurred. For when it did, the final bloody act of the siege occurred. The attacker would launch an assault on the breach and the defenders would mass their own forces to keep them out. Both sides would deploy their guns to support these efforts, resulting in a close-range maelstrom of hand-to-hand fighting.

There were, of course, variations on this theme. The attacker might have to reduce outlying defences such as bastions, casements and hornworks before focusing on the main wall, conducting mini sieges within the siege to do so. However, these features were not yet a common feature of French strongholds. If the ground was suitable, the besieger might dig tunnels under the walls to set mines (explosives) or simply undermine the foundations. Either way, with the intention of bringing down the walls so an assault could be launched. A relatively recent innovation was the petard, an explosive device fastened to the fortress gates with a view to blowing them apart when detonated. Henry de Navarre, sometimes credited with its invention, used one to take Cahors in

1580 and Semannes in 1589. If the attacker was confident of his own supply situation and felt the defender was less well prepared, then the city might simply be starved into submission. Regardless of the methods used, a regular siege could be a time-consuming operation, lasting weeks or even months.

In a civil war, there was also the possibility of treachery. A population sympathetic to the besiegers might betray the garrison and contrive to let the attackers enter. A city might be taken by means of a ruse, usually soldiers entering disguised as women or peasants or concealed within carts. Such as occurred at Mascon (Mâcon) in 1562, the Salenas Tower in 1570, Joigny in 1585 and the Milamperle Tower in 1590. Henry IV was trying the same tactic to take Paris during the 'Day of Flour' in 1591.

Regardless of the method chosen, the morale of the city's defenders was of the utmost importance to the result. If an assault was successful the most common outcome was for the city to be thoroughly sacked and the garrison put to the sword. It was normal, therefore, for the garrison to negotiate a surrender if their situation looked hopeless. The terms of this surrender would normally be more lenient if the garrison either surrendered quickly or put up a very gallant show, as at Sainct Jean d'Angely in 1569.

Siege warfare was a continuous, exhausting and demoralising process. It placed significant demands on the nerve of the attacker as well as the defenders within. They had to remain in a constant state of vigilance while casualties mounted from sniping, sorties and disease that inevitably arose in the cramped and unsanitary conditions they found themselves in. Storming a breach was just about the most dangerous operation troops could mount. If the attacking troops were not confident of success, they might point blank refuse or else give up after only a token attempt. Even success could lead to horrendous casualties. Many prominent leaders on both sides were killed or seriously wounded during siege operations, including Antoine de Bourbon, Randan, Timoléon de Brissac, Claude d'Aumale, La Noue, Montluc, Martigues, Humières, Biron and Espernon. The pent-up fear and frustration caused by siege operations explains, if not exculpates, the brutal behaviour of troops if the city was taken.

Native French soldiers were not generally expected to actually dig the saps, parallels, mines and batteries required during formal siege operations. These tasks fell to the army's pionniers. The mercenary landsknechts could be persuaded to help, but only if they received additional pay for doing so. Arquebusiers were kept busy manning the besieger's trenches and the city's walls, keeping up harassing fire to either cover or discourage the progress of the pioneer's work. Pikemen could guard the siege works and were invaluable in assault, because of their heavier armour, but were less useful overall. For this reason, Swiss troops, with their preponderance of these arms were only of limited value. The gens d'armes were also frequently employed as dismounted shock troops when a breach was assaulted.

Henry IV and especially his trusted minister, Sully, worked hard to reverse the deficiencies within both artillery and fortification. They had a large measure of success, including taking the 'impregnable' Savoyard fortress of Mantmélian in 1600. But these measures, and their impact, lie beyond the scope of the Wars of Religion.

4

The Soldiers

The army of France immediately prior to and during the initial periods of peace between the Wars of Religion differed little in composition from that of other Western European powers. It consisted of a permanent nucleus of trained soldiers, around which a larger number of mercenaries and volunteers would be recruited in times of war, and these could be supported by militias of limited quality and enthusiasm. As the wars dragged on, and a low level of conflict became the norm over parts of the country, the distinctions between these various categories blurred.

The Maison du Roy and Other Guards

Household troops that attended the person of the monarch consisted of several distinct bodies of troops. The Gentilshommes de la Maison (or de l'hotel) numbered 200 fully equipped cavalry on barded horses. The Cent Suysses, as their name suggests, numbered 100 footmen armed with halberds. The Archers de la Garde were the largest body, with 400 men, equipped much as their counterparts in the gendarmerie, with a helmet, breastplate and backplate and a shirt of mail but carrying a halberd when on palace duties. Despite their name, they had not actually carried bows for decades before the wars began. Finally, the Gardes-ecosse, 100 strong, were equipped like the Swiss when at court, but probably more like gens d'armes should they be required to serve on campaign. Individual gentilhommes might hold commands or serve as volunteers in field armies, and the archers were actively engaged in the Sainct-Barthélemy's Day Massacre, but the Maison du Roy did not take part in any battles during the wars.

At the end of the first war and the recapture of Le Havre, the Huguenots demanded the disbanding of the infantry regiments established by Guise. The Queen Mother acquiesced but retained 11 compagnies of Strozzi's regiment as a guard unit. Although this is seen as the founding date of the the Gardes-françaises infantry regiment, the unit was actually briefly disbanded in 1574 during peace negotiations, as it had played a prominent role in the massacre. At the same time as the Strozzi regiment was retained, the Swiss regiment of Pyffer was also not disbanded as promised. This large unit became the

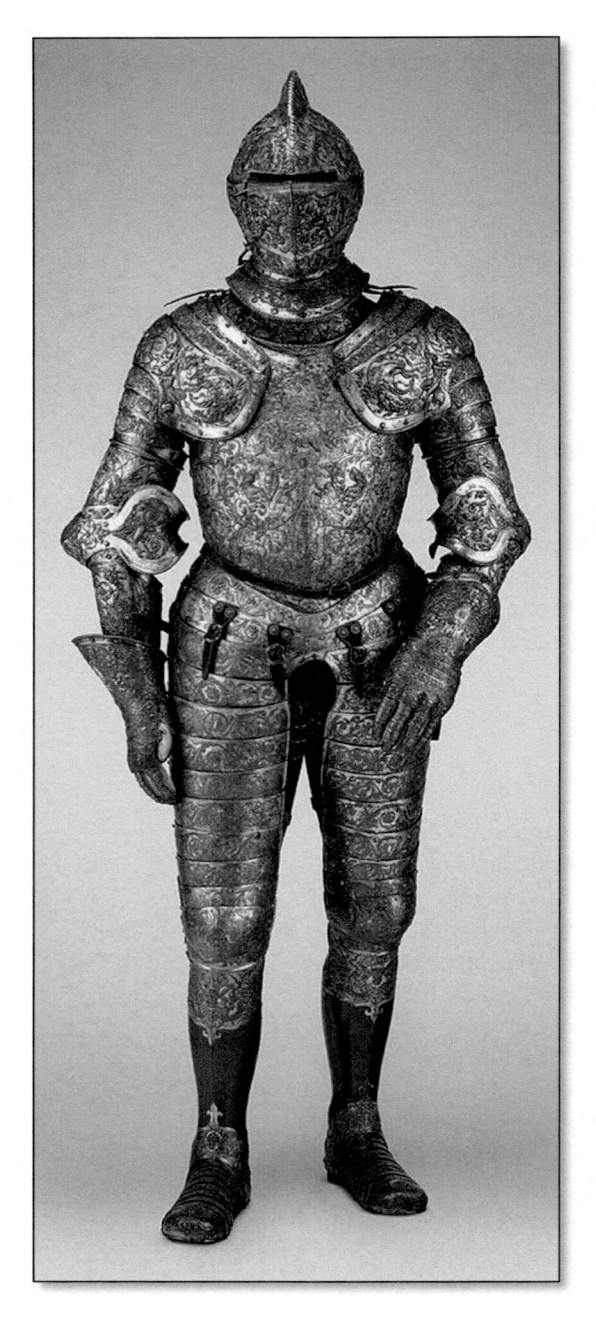 

Armour of Henry II, front and rear views. (Metropolitan Museum of Art, New York)

Gardes-suysses but was distinct from the inner bodyguard of the Maison du Roy. Both guard infantry regiments were very much battlefield formations, serving at Jarnac, Moncontour and Ivry. The Swiss also fought at Arques.

Les Quarante-cinq (The Forty-Five) were recruited by Espernon to provide Henry III with a more reliable bodyguard during the War of the Three Henrys. They were drawn from the lesser nobility, mainly Gascons. Fifteen were always on duty, day or night. They were responsible for the assassination of Henry Duc de Guise and his brother. After Henry III's own assassination, they switched allegiance to his successor, Henry IV.

Henry IV, as Roy de Navarre, maintained a guard of both horse and foot soldiers. The infantry unit was originally formed in 1558 from the Bandes de Guienne and commanded by Colonel du Tilladet. After 1562, and the death of Antoine de Bourbon, the regiment was assigned to guard his son, taking the title of Garde du Roy de Navarre. It later became the Regiment Navarre in the French national army.

Individual commanders could also have personal bodyguards. Colingy, Anjou and Mayenne (the latter two endowed with the title lieutenant general du royaume at the time) had a picked body of gens d'armes referred to as a 'cornette blanche'. The Seigneur Acier's guard consisted of 40 arquebusiers à cheval during the Third War.

The Cavalry

Many commentators have characterised warfare during the renaissance period as representing a watershed in the development of battlefield tactics, during which the aristocratic cavalry which dominated the medieval era were forced to yield prominence to commoners fighting on foot with pikes and firearms.[1] Whilst this argument may have merit when applied to Europe-wide trends, it has only limited applicability to the civil wars that wracked France during this period. Cavalry continued to dominate French military thinking, whether

Field Armour, c. 1575.
(Chicago Institute of Art)

---

1   This being one of the principal themes in the influential lecture by Michael Roberts, *The Military Revolution 1560–1660* (Belfast: Boyd, 1956). Also, Michael Howard, *War in European History* (Oxford: Oxford University Press, 1976), p.34, and Martin van Creveld, *Technology and War* (London: Macmillan, 1991), p.95.

Right: Armoured Saddle, *c.* 1540. (Chicago Institute of Art)

Left: Curb Bit, *c.* 1580. (Cleveland Museum of Art)

the lance-armed gens d'armes at the beginning of the conflicts or the pistol-armed cuirassiers who replaced them. Virtually every battle and combat was decided by their performance. Indeed, in some encounters, the mass of infantry often appears to be little more than bystanders.

The core of every royal cavalry force was built around the regular compagnies. These were supplemented, as need arose, by volunteers or members of the aristocracy drafted in accordance with their ancient duties to serve in the local or general levies (Ban or Arrière Ban). This noble militia was called because of a proclamation issued by the King to all his feudal vassals and sub-vassals. These men were obliged to provide two months' service at their own expense.

Compagnies d'Ordonnance

Since their inception in 1447, the compagnies d'ordonnance formed the backbone of France's standing army. King Charles IX formally recognised them as the 'principal force' of his army that he raised in 1574.[2] When first constituted, they contained both cavalry and soldiers who normally fought on foot, but by the outbreak of the Wars of Religion, they consisted solely of heavy cavalry known as the gendarmerie. There were 65 of these compagnies in existence at this time. Many additional compagnies were raised by both sides during the conflicts, rising to a maximum of 180 royalist compagnies during the Third War, but these were invariably reduced once peace was restored.[3]

Each compagnie had an authorised strength expressed in 'lances'. The lance, or 'lance fournie' (equipped lance) was an archaic medieval term: originally encompassing the homme d'armes and his immediate military retainers and servants. By the period of the Wars of Religion, it had become a purely notional accounting standard representing two and a half men. One of these men was a fully equipped homme d'armes, while the remainder were slightly less well-armoured cavalry known, again by an archaic throwback, as archers. Both the homme d'armes and the archer were noblemen, or at least of gentle birth.[4]

The overwhelming majority of compagnies contained 30 lances (and so 75 men). A few 'double-compagnies' had 60 lances (150 men). The latter were outnumbered four to one by the former. A small number of compagnies contained even more lances, and, as the wars progressed, some 20-lance compagnies were also raised. Confusingly, 30- and 60-lance compagnies were often referred to as 50- and 100-lance compagnies, respectively. This related to their purely nominal, rather than authorised, strength.[5]

Each compagnie contained a cadre of five officers regardless of size. In order of seniority these were: its capitaine, his lieutenant, an enseigne (sometimes called a cornette), a guidon and a mareschal de logis. These officers were all considered gens d'armes in their own right. Therefore a normal compagnie

---

2   Quoted in Wood, *The King's Army*, p.127.

3   Wood, *The King's Army*, p.128.

4   Carroll, *Noble Power During the French Wars of Religion*, p.71.

5   Wood, *The King's Army*, pp.134. 30- and 50-lance compagnies are sometimes referred to in the same documents. It is possible that the former is actually the nominal strength of 20-lance compagnies.

contained an additional 25 gens d'armes as well as 45 archers, while a double-compagnie had 55 and 90, respectively. The capitaine was invariably a noble of significant rank. Many held other military responsibilities, and even the most senior army commanders retained the captaincy of their own compagnies. As a result, effective command was often left to the lieutenant.

Although referred to as compagnies for administrative purposes, the units of heavy cavalry of the ordonnance, in common with other cavalry, were frequently called cornettes or occasionally troupes when referring to tactical formations. As they were relatively small bodies of horsemen, five to 12 cornettes were typically grouped together into an ad hoc regiment on the march or battlefield.[6] These would be commanded by the most senior capitaine, though unlike his infantry counterpart, he received no additional pay or staff for carrying out this role. Such regiments could occasionally be made up of a variety of types of cavalry. Admiral Coligny's regiment is recorded, just prior to the Battle of Moncontour, as consisting of two compagnies of gens d'armes, four cornettes of chevaux legers, two cornettes of mercenary reiters and the cornette of arquebusiers à cheval that constituted the Seigneur d'Acier's bodyguard.

Although they were paid soldiers, the men of the gens d'armes compagnies were imbued with the spirit of medieval chivalry and regarded honourable service as the raison d'etre for their class. Unquestionably brave, they were often poorly disciplined: often following their own instincts rather than orders.

The Huguenots adopted the same organisational structures as the royal army. Of the compagnies that existed at the outbreak of the wars, at least four deserted to the rebellion en masse (those of Condé, Admiral Coligny, La Rochefoucauld and Jean Seigneur de Sénarpont). In addition, individual members of other compagnies sided with their confessional or local loyalties rather than the Crown.[7] Since the number of nobles eager to serve always exceeded the number of places available, especially since the reductions authorised by Henry II following the Peace of Cateau-Cambrésis in 1559, local Protestant magnates had little difficulty in attracting recruits to their newly formed compagnies. Their size was probably quite variable. Eighteen compagnies made up the 1,500 Huguenot horsemen at Sainct Denys: 'in my own compagnie there were 75 (men), some are much larger, but the one supporting mine had only 40 or 45'.[8] These nobles were frequently veterans of recent wars. As with the royal gens d'armes and archers, they were also expected to provide their own mounts and equipment. Thus, the rebels were able to field a highly effective cavalry force from the outset.

The Crown normally reduced the number of compagnies back to a peacetime force of 60 odd after each flare up of military activity. The principle exception to this was the unprecedented rise to over 90 compagnies between the First and Second Wars. This was primarily a political move designed to mollify both Catholic and Huguenot nobles who had raised units during the First War. As they failed to achieve a stable peace, the net result was

---

6   Wood, *The King's Army*, p.138.
7   Wood, *The King's Army*, p.122.
8   D'Aubigné, *Histoire Universelle* (1626) vol. 1, p.302.

that the Crown effectively maintained a portion of the rebel forces at its own expense. Although this measure was not repeated after subsequent wars, a number of resulting peace agreements did specify that the Crown would pay off the mercenary units contracted by the Huguenots. Such agreements ultimately allowed the Huguenots to continue to hire mercenaries despite the impecunious situation, since the latter could be confident that they would eventually receive their pay from one side or the other.

Although Huguenots only ever formed a relatively small minority of France's total population, perhaps only 10 percent of adults, they counted many members of the petty rural nobility amongst their numbers.[9] The Dowager Queen, Caterina de' Medici, once commented that the better half of this class supported their cause, and modern commentators have generally concurred with her estimate.[10] It was from precisely this group that the gendarmerie drew most of its numbers. One source lists a total of 3,872 horsemen (including 600 regular gens d'armes and 300 arquebusiers à cheval) available to the Condé in the summer of 1562, but this probably excludes their forces in the south of the country.[11] Whilst the Huguenots were often defeated by the royal army during the early wars, this was never ascribed to the inferiority of their cavalry; quite the reverse in fact. They seem to have gained a rapid ascendancy over their Catholic counterparts that is hard to explain. Perhaps it is simply because they not only won the first encounters, skirmishing outside the suburbs of Paris and at the Battle of Dreux where they enjoyed a numerical superiority, but also inflicted a disproportionate number of casualties upon their opponents: as many as a third of those engaged.[12] Equally plausible are the notions that King Charles wished to preserve the political support of the Catholic nobles in his gendarmerie and so tried to shelter them from losses, thereby engendering a subtle taint of timidity, and that the Huguenot nobles, as rebels, had less to lose and more to gain.[13]

Equipment

A decade prior to the start of the wars, an observer, de Rabutin, described the gendarmerie gathered before the city of Metz in 1552:

> The hommes d'armes were mounted on big roussins or couriers of the kingdom, turks and horses of Spain, with bards painted in the colours of the sayes worn by the captains, armed from the top of their head to their toes. With hautes pièces and plastrons, a lance, a sword, an estoc, a coutelas or a mace. Without yet counting their suite of other horses, upon which were their coustiliers and valets. And, on all, the chiefs and members of these compagnies, and other noblemen,

9   Knecht, *The French Civil Wars*, p.59.
10 Wood, *The King's Army*, p.144 and Knecht, *The French Civil Wars*, p.52.
11 David Potter, 'The French Protestant Nobility in 1562: "The Associacion de Monseigneur le Prince de Condé"' in *French History*, Volume 15, Issue 3 (Oxford: Oxford University Press, 2001), pp.307–328. Potter gives the total as 4,272 but assumes each of the four regular gens d'armes compagnies contained 250 men (that is, 100 lances). The figure above assumes 150 men (that is, 60 lances) as an actual rather than nominal strength.
12 Wood, *The King's Army*, p.121.
13 Wood, *The King's Army*, p.124.

were armed very richly with gilded and engraved harnesses of all sorts. Their horses, strong and skilful, protected and caparisoned with bards and plates of steel, light and rich, or strong and flexible mail, covered with velvet, gold and silver sheets, gilded and embroidered in unspeakable sumptuousness. The archers were lightly armed, carrying a demi-lance, a pistol on the saddle, a sword or coutelas, mounted on cavalines and horses of small size, very nimble and swift.[14]

A similar description of the gendarmerie is given in the Ordonnance of 1574, which required them to be equipped as follows:

Let us have the homme d'armes equipped with an armet, or closed helmet (without allowing any morions, even if they have a baviere), good body cuirasse, brassars or avant-bras, tassettes, cuissots, with genoüillieres and greves to the front, a good and strong lance, an estoc and an espee d'armes, a saddle armoured before and behind, having two good service horses, one of which will be barded, bearing a chanfrain, and frontal barding with flancars of boiled leather. And he will have at least a courtaut, or a baggage horse, not being allowed to bring any cart with him.[15]

In contrast:

The archer shall wear an armet or a bourguignote, but not a morion without a baviere; he will have a good body cuirasse, avant-bras or brassars, tassettes and cuissots, with a good and strong lance, an espee d'armes, and a good horse, besides that of baggage. Also not allowed to have a cart.[16]

Surprisingly, the 1574 ordonnance omits any mention of pistols. But the earlier 1549 ordonnance issued by Henry II lists a pistol amongst the required equipment of an archer, and suggests that the homme d'armes could carry one from his saddle 'if it pleases him'.[17] There are certainly many anecdotes and contemporary illustrations of such gentlemen carrying pistols in battle, even during the First War.

Both these descriptions give the impression of a fully armoured medieval knight, or, as one ordonnance puts it, a 'monster of iron'. Doubtless, for some individuals, this image was accurate, but it is unlikely that the majority were as well equipped as this. Contemporary images invariably show unarmoured horses and almost always boots rather than greaves. At the Battle of Moncontour in 1569, the Duc d'Anjou's gens d'armes were proceeded by a squadron of 50 gentlemen on barded horses.[18] That this is noteworthy suggests it was not the norm.

---

14 Rabutin, *Commentaires*, p.67
15 *Les ordonnances militaires tirees du code de Henry III. Roy de France et de Pologne* (Paris: Fougé, 1625), p.159.
16 *Les ordonnances militaries*, p.161
17 '… et si bon lui semble aura un pistolet a l'arcon de la selle.'
18 Oman, *War in the Sixteenth Century*, p.451. Interestingly, they are picked out in the T&P engraving of the battle, but not shown with barding.

Armet, 1555–1560, front, side and rear views.
(Metropolitan Museum of Art, New York)

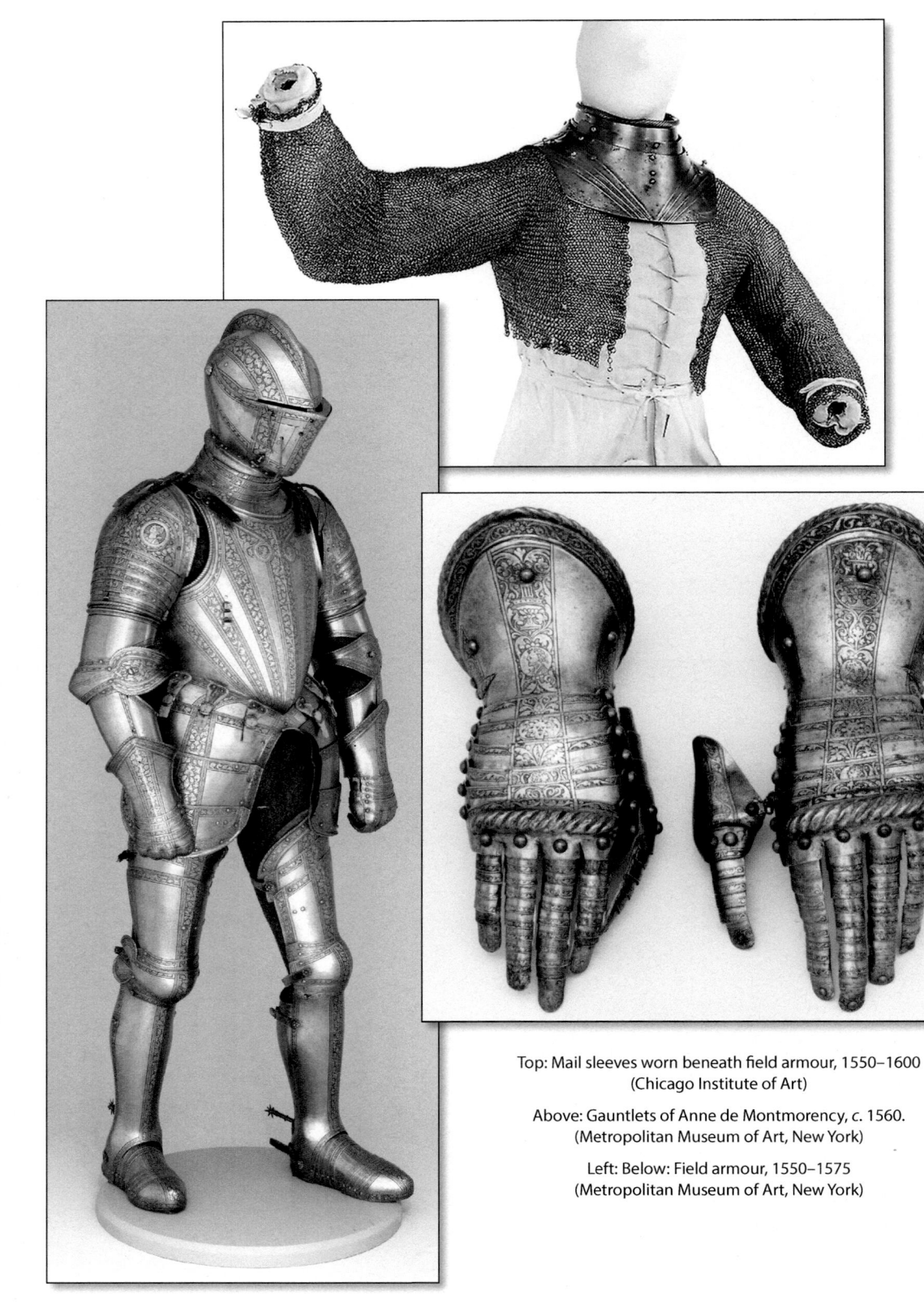

Top: Mail sleeves worn beneath field armour, 1550–1600
(Chicago Institute of Art)

Above: Gauntlets of Anne de Montmorency, *c.* 1560.
(Metropolitan Museum of Art, New York)

Left: Below: Field armour, 1550–1575
(Metropolitan Museum of Art, New York)

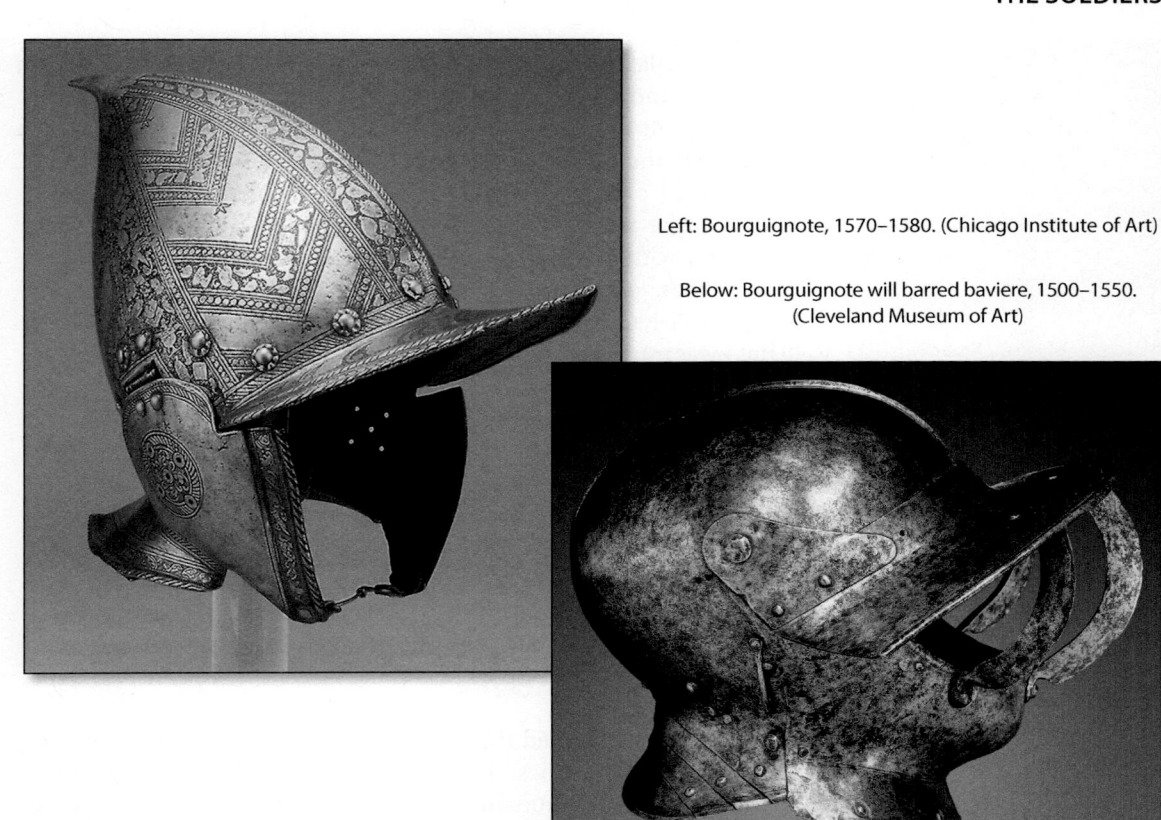

Left: Bourguignote, 1570–1580. (Chicago Institute of Art)

Below: Bourguignote will barred baviere, 1500–1550.
(Cleveland Museum of Art)

Below: Pistols, 1577. (Chicago Institute of Art)

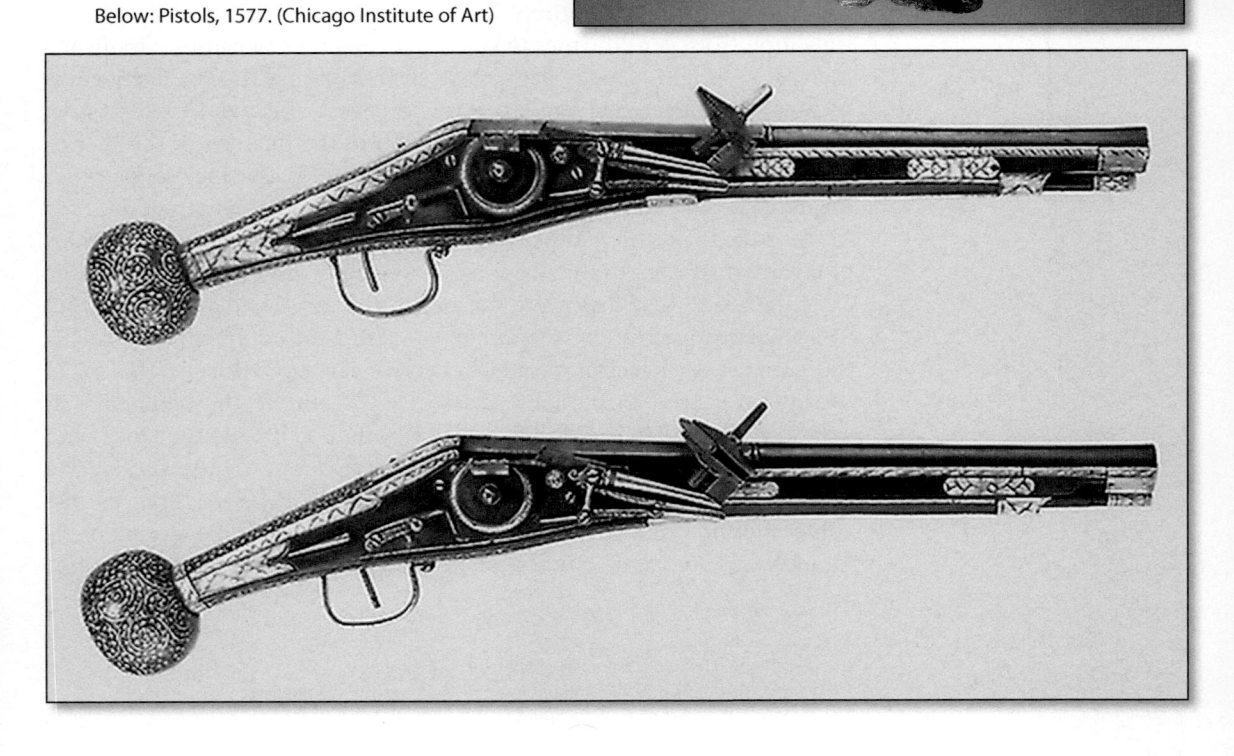

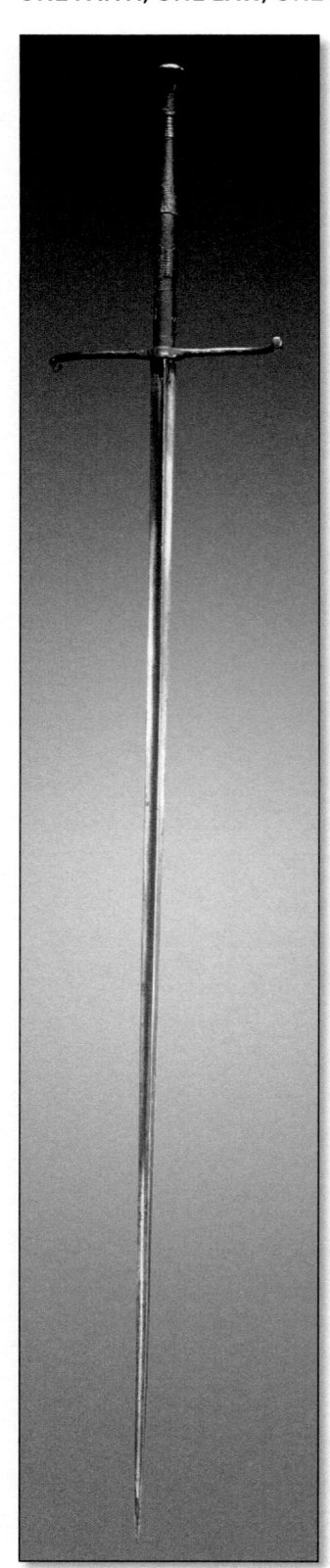

The term 'à la Huguenotte' means 'extemporised' or, less flatteringly, 'on the cheap', and this could be applied to at least a proportion of their cavalry forces. At the Battle of Sainct Denys in 1567, a Protestant prisoner reported that: 'the ranks behind the flag [presumably, he means beyond the front rank] of this troupe are filled up with men who have only a casaque blanche and pistols; of gentlemen wearing cuirasses and closed helmets, and with a horse worth fifty écu, there are, except in the very largest troupes, not more than ten or a dozen.'[19] Another nobleman complained: 'I had in truth a good Arabian horse that served me very well; but I was much at a disadvantage in my weapons, having only a mere cuirasse … without a helmet, no brassars, no boots.'[20]

La Noue bemoaned this situation:

> Afterwards, all the beauty of the horseman turned into a deformity, for his head covering is like an iron pot. On the left arm he bears a large gauntlet, which covers it to the elbow, and to the right a small mougnon, which only hides the shoulder; and ordinarily he wears no tassettes; and instead of casaque, a mandille; and without a lance. Our gens d'armes and chevaux leger, in the time of King Henry the second, were much more beautiful to see, bearing the salade, brassars, tassettes, casaques, lances and banderolles…[21]

The Huguenots adopted the pistol in place of the lance rather more quickly than their enemies. This process was accelerated after Henry de Navarre assumed command of their forces. His own followers had abandoned the lance entirely by the Battle of Coutras in 1587. The transition from gens d'armes to cuirassiers had several causes. Firstly, the increasing weight of body armour, itself in response to the effectiveness of firearms, meant that the lance was also less effective in penetrating these defences. Secondly, the deterioration in the finances of the French Crown and the continual impecunious nature of the Huguenot cause, meant that the gendarmerie compagnies increasingly went without pay. At the same time, the number of compagnies actually grew. The captains of these bands were drawn from an increasingly diverse socio-economic caste, meaning that they were no longer able to subsidise any shortfall. Consequently, their men were unable to afford the equipment, especially the courser, so necessary for an effective lancer.[22] Thirdly, the social disruption caused by the long series of wars reduced the availability of candidates who had the skill at arms to be able to handle the lance with sufficient proficiency.[23] The aristocratic joust gave way to more proletarian marauding. The 'gentilshommes' (gentlemen) degenerating, as the contemporary pun had it, into 'gens-pille-hommes' (people looting men). In addition, the compagnies were normally retained for shorter periods

19 D'Aubigné, *Histoire Universelle* (1626) vol. 1, p.302.
20 Seigneur de Sainct-Auban quoted in Love, 'All the King's Horsemen', p.513.
21 La Noue, *Discours politiques et militaires*, p.409.
22 Phillips, 'Of Nimble Service', pp.75–78, on the evolution of warhorses and horsemanship.
23 Phillips, 'Of Nimble Service', p.61.

and, even then, often on reduced pay scales. So, they could not compensate for this lack of skill with training of their own. Finally, the quality of horses required to carry a fully armoured warrior with sufficient momentum to use the lance effectively also fell away.

Despite his nostalgia for the cavaliers of Henry II, La Noue was of the opinion that the change in equipment was a positive move. He stated the matter plainly in the 1580s: 'The pistol is capable of buckling defensive weapons (armour), but the lance is not. It is nothing short of a miracle when someone is killed by a lance.'[24]

The gendarmerie were required to wear a tunic over their armour. The royal ordonnances of 1533, 1549 and 1574 all require both gens d'armes and archers to wear 'the hocqueton of their capitaine's livery.' The ordonnance of 1584 renews this obligation but uses slightly different terminology for the garments: 'casaques and sayes'. The casaque consisted of a thigh-length tunic which was pleated from the waist down and had false, hanging sleeves.[25] They were usually lined and trimmed in a contrasting shade. The hocqueton and the saye were probably identical: consisting of a heavily pleated skirt attached to a doublet, more typical of the Italian Wars era. The skirt worn alone, referred to as a demi-saye, was also frequently encountered.

The Huguenots initially differed from their opponents, in that they uniformly wore casaques of white, though these could still be trimmed in other colours. White was chosen to both symbolise the purity of their cause, but also to avoid any charge of treason against the Crown by wearing the colours of a noble house.[26] These garments gave rise to the nickname of 'Millers' by which these troops are famously known. The origin of the term has been attributed to Caterina de' Medici.[27] At the talks of Toury in 1562, the gens d'armes escorting the Catholic leaders were dressed in casaques of crimson and carried lances

Above: Espee d'Armes, 1540–1560. (Rijksmuseum, Amsterdam)

Facing page: Estoc, early sixteenth century. (Cleveland Museum of Art)

---

24 La Noue, *Discours politiques et militaires*, p.312.
25 Denise Turrel, *Le Blanc de France – La contruction des signes identitaires pendant les guerres de Religion (1562-1629)* (Droz: Geneva, 2005), p.25, states that 'During the first civil wars, the riders wore over their armour a tunic, called a casaque if it has no sleeves, and mandillo (or mandil) when its open sleeves form wings. These floating sleeves are very well on engravings of battles of Tortel and Perrissin and on the tapestries of the museum of Ecouen.' However, it is clear from the ordonnances that the casaque had sleeves. As early as 1533, it is noted in Pierre Guenois, *La Conference des Ordonnances Royaux* (Boun: Paris, 1707), p.1012 that 'Archers, who shall wear a casaque with a sleeve of the Captain's livery.' Turrel may actually be distinguishing between a saye and a casaque. It must be acknowledged, however, that contemporaries may not have used these terms with precision and their meaning may have altered over the decades.
26 Turrel, *Le Blanc de France*, pp.28–29.
27 Aubigne, *Histoire*, p.196.

with red banderoles. In contrast, their Huguenot counterparts had white casaques and banderoles. Observing them, the Queen Mother commented sarcastically: 'Your people are millers, my cousin?' Less well remembered is the Prince de Condé's pithy retort: 'The better to beat your donkeys, Madame.' Despite the popularity of the term with more recent authors, the name does not appear to have been widely used by contemporaries. In any event, after the Sainct-Barthélemy's Day Massacre in 1572, the Huguenots became less concerned with displaying their loyalty towards the Crown. In addition, they were gradually joined by moderate Catholics of the Politique and Malcontent movements. So it is likely that the casaque blanche was joined by those of other colours. The Huguenot forces fighting in aid of the Dutch rebels seem to have worn orange and continued to do so on their return to France.[28]

Royalist capitaines might also select white as their own livery colour. This could cause confusion, as at the Battle of Dreux:

> Having got mixed up with the compagnie of Mareschal de Sainct-André, who wore white casaques with a little green embroidery which hardly showed at all, I thought for a long time that they were our soldiers; for the Huguenots all had white casaques; on mine I had some yellow and black braid which also made the enemy think that I belonged to their compagnie.[29]

During the Battle of Sainct Denys three 'escadrons' of Catholic cavalry are referred to in contemporary accounts by colours (presumably of their casaques): Les Rouges, Les Bleus and Les Dorés (the reds, the blues and the golden).[30] Whilst it is possible that this refers to the colours worn by individual compagnies, the context suggests larger bodies of horsemen than this. It is possible that compagnies with casaques of a similar colour were grouped together.

The Royalist gens d'armes typically also wore a white cross of Sainct Denys on the front and back of their casaques. This symbol had been a national field-sign of France since the Hundred Years War. It was retained by the Royalist forces but avoided by Calvinists because of its association with soldiers who wore it during some of the massacres that preceded the outbreak of war. Not until Henry IV took the throne did it become used by them again: in this instance to demonstrate that the Catholic Ligue and their Spanish allies were fighting against France rather than for it. The Ligue suffered a propaganda defeat by adopting a red cross in its stead, as this colour was associated with their Spanish allies. They also wore the double-ended cross of Lorraine in various colours.

---

28 D. Turrel, *Le Blanc de France*, p.31, who quotes Sully describing himself as wearing a mandille of 'velous [velvet] orangé et broiderie d'argent' at the Battle of Arques.

29 J. de Mergey, 'Mémoires du Seigneur Jean de Mergey, gentilhomme champenois' in *Collection Complète des Mémoires relatives a la Histoire de France* (Paris: Foucault, 1823), vol. 34, pp.51–52

30 All three are shown in a plan of the battle by André Thevet in Etienne Vitelli, *Commentaires sur la guerre civile de France: de la surprise de Meaux à la Bataille de Saint Denis, 1567* (Paris: École de chartes, 2005) translator Anne Lombard-Jourdan, p.23. The T&P engraving shows only Les Rouges: Benedict, *Tortorel et Perrissin*, p.28.

The scarf, as both a badge of rank and a symbol of allegiance, originated during the later Italian Wars and the Valois–Habsburg conflicts that followed. The colour of the scarf came to be associated with particular nations or causes. From the beginning of the wars, a white scarf was associated with the Huguenot movement. Commenting on the situation at the end of the Battle of Dreux, the Huguenot La Popelinière wrote regarding the troops scattered on the field that: 'so one could scarcely discern between the Admiral's (men who) wore white scarves, from the red scarves of his enemies'.[31] However, red was not universally associated with Royalist forces since it was the colour worn by their traditional enemies, the Spanish. As noted above, the forces of the Ligue were criticised for adopting it to mark their alliance with Felipe II. Henry de Navarre retained the white scarf upon ascending the throne, and it became the symbol of French officers up until the Revolution. Green was the livery colour associated with the House of Guise. Scarves in this colour were worn by their adherents, especially after Henry de Guise's assassination. Though in the period immediately after, black was worn as a symbol of mourning. At the Battle of Moncontour, the Huguenot army adopted yellow and black scarves in remembrance of their erstwhile ally, Wolfgang von Pfalz Zweibrücken.

Initially, scarves were mainly restricted to officers but towards the end of the wars, Henry's cavalry increasingly abandoned wearing a casaque or mandille over their armour and replaced these garments with a scarf instead.

Tactics

The gendarmerie normally deployed on the battlefield in a formation known as 'ligne en haye' (a line like a hedge). Although often referred to as a 'single line', this essentially medieval formation normally consisted of two ranks of horsemen, some 12 metres apart.[32] The Protestant writer and soldier La Noue was critical of this approach. He felt it was adopted only to give the honour-conscious nobility the opportunity to all fight in the front rank.[33] Typically, the first rank was made up of gens d'armes and the second rank of archers.

The gendarmerie cornettes normally launched a vigorous charge early in the battle. This could be devastating to enemy cavalry and infantry alike. At the Battle of Dreux in 1562, Huguenot gens d'armes managed to cut their way through the Swiss pike block (though still failed to break it, despite the heavy casualties they inflicted). Similarly, the Turkish ambassador observing their charge at Sainct Denys, remarked that: 'if his master, the Sultan, had only a thousand of those 'white-coats' to put at the head of each of his armies, he could become master of the whole universe'.[34] However, the long thin lines of cavalry were difficult to control, and the charge was sometimes launched too far away from the enemy, as was the case at Coutras. In these cases, the

---

31 La Popelinière: 'qu'à peine pouvoit-on plus discerner les escharpes blanches qui portoit l'amiral, de avec l'escharpe rouge de ses ennemis' quoted in Gustave Desjardins, *Recherches Sur Les Drapeaux Français* (Paris: A.Morel, 1874), p.55.

32 R.S. Love, 'All the King's Horsemen: The Equestrian Army of Henri IV, 1585–1598' in *Sixteenth Century Journal*, XXII, No. 3, 1991, p.514 and Gigon, *La troisième guerre*, p.16.

33 La Noue, *Discours politiques et militaires*, p.614.

34 Aubigné, *Histoire Universelle*, volume 1, p.307.

cornettes could arrive piecemeal and blown. The effectiveness of their charge also decreased as the battle wore on, as riders discarded their broken lances and their mounts grew tired.

Although the change to deeper cavalry formations is normally credited to the Huguenots, it seems that the royal Catholic army was the first to use this expedient: at Moncontour in 1569.[35] This is clearly shown on near-contemporary prints of the battle.[36] On this occasion, they were accompanied by many German, Italian and Spanish-supplied Burgundian/Walloon cavalry, which may have influenced their tactics. Equally possible, however, is that the line was rather cramped. In this encounter, the Huguenot cavalry were still deployed in the traditional en haye manner.[37] Though each line was followed by another in the same formation. Possibly with this encounter in mind, La Noue advises against such an arrangement: 'although three or four troupes of horse be arranged en haye one at another's heals, yet shall a squadron (that is, cavalry in a deeper formation) overthrow them all almost as easily as the boule does many ranks of skittles'. The horsemen he commanded at this battle suffered just such a fate and he was captured. Shortly thereafter, however, at the Battle of Arnay-le-Duc in 1570, the Huguenots were drawn up into six 'square troops' instead.[38] A deeper, tighter formation, typically containing five to seven ranks,[39] seems to have become their normal arrangement in subsequent encounters, though La Noue implies that at the time he composed his work (1580–1585) French cavalry were still wedded to using the lance in shallower formations, that is, en haye. He maintains that the best formation for 100 men (he is still discussing lance-armed cavalry in this case, not pistoliers) would be a front of some 14 or 15 horsemen, six or seven ranks deep.[40] The French mercenary horse fighting for the Dutch republic fought in squadrons of 100 horsemen in six ranks of 15 and the few odd horsemen left formed a small reserve to the rear. Despite their success at Moncontour, the Catholics frequently reverted to attacking in a long, thin line. Perhaps the innovation was initiated by Tavannes and lost once he departed the army.

Superficially, the deeper formations adopted by French cavalry resembled the formations of the German mercenary reiters. La Noue certainly refers to these troops when making his recommendations, so they almost certainly influenced the transition. But the French formations remained dedicated to shock action, as opposed to the reiters' mounted fire tactics. Nor did the size or depth of either Huguenot or Catholic cavalry units approach those

35 Aubigné, *Histoire Universelle*, volume 2, pp.108-114. La Noue, *Discours politiques et militaires*, p.288, states that 'the king's horse being brought into squadrons of lancers, at their enemies the Protestants, who were ordered en haye and without lances'.

36 Benedict, *Tortorel et Perrissin*, p.36. Note, however, the Huguenot gens d'armes are carrying lances in this engraving.

37 La Noue, *Discours politiques et militaires*, p.289.

38 Aubigné, *Histoire Universelle*, volume 3, pp.174–175.

39 Williams, *A Briefe Discouse of Warre* (London: Thomas Orwin, 1590), p.38.

40 La Noue, *Discours politiques et militaires*, p.288. He also mentions that a squadron of 300 horsemen deployed en haye would have a frontage of almost 1,000 paces, whereas the same number of men in three deeper squadrons of 100 men each would have a frontage of only 120 paces.

of the Germans. This reliance on close combat did not change even after the Huguenot cavalry abandoned the lance in favour of pistols.

It has been suggested that Henry IV taught his men to charge 'at the gallop' delivering fire with their pistols at close range before following up with the sword.[41] But it is difficult to see how this would have worked in practice. The effectiveness of fire delivered by cavalry moving at this speed would have been very limited; hardly worth the effort. Similarly, given the range of a pistol, estimated at as little as three paces by contemporaries, there would have been little opportunity to build up speed after the discharge.[42]

It is more likely that Henry's cavalry charged with sword drawn and reserved their pistols for use in the subsequent confusion of the melee.[43] In fact, he seems to have emphasised the regularity of their order rather than speed in his commands. This regularity did not imply a close formation, however, but rather the opposite. At Amiens in 1597, he gave instruction that the cavalry should 'leave a good space between one another, which having been done, they found that the shock of the lancers, not meeting a firm opposition, proved for the most part in vain'.[44] One can imagine the unpleasant fate of lancers threading through the gaps between the files of Huguenot horsemen and being subject to numerous, close-range pistol shots. The relatively open files would have allowed Henry's cavalry to cope well with any irregularities of terrain, whilst their relatively deep formation and emphasis on maintaining order would have made them easier to control than long lines.

As noted above, the evolution of the homme d'armes from lancer to pistolier was not due to a top-down directive but was rather a trend driven by several related factors. No one was really in a position to take a firm decision on the matter of lance verses pistol until the end of the period. Charles IX could not dictate policy to the Huguenots. Henry III had even less control, since even many of the Catholic forces were loyal to the Ligue rather than the Crown. Henry de Navarre had to wait until Henry de Condé's death before he was acknowledged sole leader of the Protestant cause. Even then, his authority over some Huguenot communities and Catholic allies was limited until he became king. A commander such as Coligny, Tavannes or Anjou did enjoy considerable authority over sufficiently large forces for short periods

---

41   John A Lynn, 'Tactical Evolution in the French Army, 1560–1660', in *French Historical Studies*, volume 14 (Durham, NC: Duke University Press, 1985), p.183.

42   Brent Noseworthy, *The Anatomy of Victory: Battle Tactics 1689–1763* (New York, NY: Hippocrene,1992), pp.122–124. Although dealing with a later period, the mechanics of the issue remain constant. Gervase Phillips, '"Of Nimble Service": Technology, Equestrianism and the Cavalry Arm of Early Modern Western European Armies', in Paul E.J. Hammer (ed.) *Warfare in Early Modern Europe 1450–1660* (Farnham: Ashgate, 2007), pp.59–80.

43   Love, *Sixteenth Century Journal*, p.517. He asserts that: 'There is no evidence to support John A. Lynn's contention that at Coutras and Ivry Henry's cavalry "used their firearms for an initial shot" before charging with the sword. The "initial shot" was fired by arquebusiers placed in intervals between the various squadrons of royal horse.' Sully mentions, in a skirmish in 1589 near Chartres, that he resorts to his pistols only after breaking two swords.

44   Avilia quoted in Love, *Sixteenth Century Journal*, p.517.

of time, but there is no evidence any ever attempted to make the break with traditional equipment.[45]

Possibly an expedient, Henry de Navarre and his fellow commanders chose to make a virtue of necessity and developed a form of warfare that made the most from the material they had to hand. The new type of cavalryman, the cuirassier, when deployed in multiple ranks, found he could take on and defeat those gens d'armes who clung on to their traditional methods. Their example undoubtedly accelerated the process. It is a matter of conjecture, however, as to how they would have fared against the compagnies that charged so boldly at Dreux and Sainct Denys.

Notwithstanding the above, not all military commentators were convinced of the inherent value of the lance armed cavalryman. La Noue, in the first paradox goes into a lengthy discussion regarding the relative merits of a 'lancier' verses a reiter.[46] He was firmly of the opinion that the reiter was the superior of the two, though conceded that he was in a minority among 'those who profess arms'.

Chevaux Legers

In addition to the gendarmerie, France also raised other categories of native cavalry. At the beginning of the wars, the most common of these were the 'chevaux legers' (light horse). They first arrived in the French army during the Italian Wars, probably mimicking local practice as initially most seem to have been Italians or Albanians. By the 1540s, however, native Frenchmen predominated. As these troops normally served in the van of the army, the opportunities for both glory and plunder were greater. Senior nobles, many of whom already had gendarmerie compagnies, lobbied for commands. King Henry II even had himself depicted as a captain of these troops. By 1552 there were 2,940 chevaux legers in 36 compagnies. In the same year, they were also at the Siege of Metz, and were described by the same observer as noted above.: 'As for the light cavalry ... there could have been nearly two thousand chevaux legers, who were lightly armoured with corselets, brassars and bourguignottes, the demi-lance, or a pistol or a coutelas, as they see fit, or the Gelderland épieu, mounted on cavalines, double courtauds or horses of light size and lively.'[47]

By the start of the Wars of Religion, the chevaux legers were constituted from noble volunteers in compagnies of 100, or sometimes 50, men. Gigon regards all those called up by the ban or arrière ban as belonging to this class of cavalry as well.[48] These men were organised into cornettes by the capitaine-general de l'arrière ban once they reached the army's assembly point. Gigon also assumes that many of the Huguenot cavalry were effectively chevaux legers. Although more lightly equipped than the gendarmerie, the chevaux legers were drawn from the same social class. Tactically, their compagnies

---

45 Although two T&P prints show whole units of Huguenot gens d'armes in 1570 carrying pistols rather than lances. Bendict, *Tortorel et Perrissin*, pp.34 and 40.
46 La Noue, *Discours politiques et militaires*, pp.307–314.
47 Rabutin., *Commentaires*, p.67.
48 Gigon, *La troisième guerre*, p.49.

could be drawn together to serve as a single regiment on the battlefield, under their own colonel general, as at Dreux. As the conflicts dragged on, many chevaux leger compagnies would find themselves upgraded to gendarmerie by commanders eager to bulk out their cavalry. Whether this was reflected by any change in their equipment is debateable, especially considering the parlous state of many gendarmerie units, as noted above.[49]

Although this tendency to convert them into gendarmerie reduced their significance as an independent category of cavalry, they never disappeared entirely. Henry IV operated between 1585 and 1587 with a mobile force of 2,000 arquebusiers à cheval and 500 gens d'armes but also 300 chevaux legers.[50] There were units of such troops on both sides at Arques and Ivry. After the end of the wars they remained part of the military establishment.

It has been suggested that chevaux legers fought in deeper formations than the gendarmerie at the beginning of the wars, typically three to six ranks deep.[51] If so, this might also have provided a model for the later pistol-armed cavalry. They were certainly also deployed en haye on occasion.

Argoulets

The name argoulet is first encountered during the Italian Wars, referring to a type of native light cavalry. It was applied to: 'troops carrying firearms of the smaller sort, which they could use without dismounting'.[52] They were increasingly known by a variety of different names that all referred to the distinctive weapon they carried: petronels, carbins and arquebusiers à cheval. It is by this latter term that they are described at the Siege of Metz. 'Arquebusiers à cheval, there were from twelve to fifteen hundred, equipped with jacques with sleeves of mail or cuirasses, a bourguignotte or a morion, an arquebuse 3 feet (97 centimetres) long on the saddle-bow, mounted on good courtauds, each according to his puissance.'[53]

It is necessary to draw something of a distinction here between two different types of troops; cavalry armed with a short arquebus and infantry armed with a weapon of standard length given a riding horse to increase their operational mobility. Both were known to contemporaries imprecisely as arquebusiers à cheval, as well as by other names, but they were probably distinct categories. It is likely that one served as the inspiration for the other, since references to arquebus-armed cavalry diminish as the wars progressed, whereas mounted infantry are regularly recorded, especially under Henry IV. Given the gendarmerie's own metamorphosis from heavy lancer to lighter pistolier, perhaps the need for old-school argoulet waned.

Despite assertions to the contrary, it is clear that the argoulet was expected to remain mounted and use his firearm from the saddle.[54] The erroneous

49 Wood, *The King's Army*, p.130–131.
50 Love, *Sixteenth Century Journal*, p.524.
51 Gigon, *La troisième guerre*, p.16, but Conyart, *Dreux*, Légende du Plan No. 1, suggests a single rank.
52 Oman, *War in the Sixteenth Century*, p.228.
53 Rabutin, *Commentaires*, p.67.
54 Potter, *Renaissance France at War*, p.86. The same curious assertion has also been made in relation to mounted crossbowmen, from whom firearm *argoulets* descend.

view probably stems from the aforementioned confusion with Henry IV's later mounted infantry.

It would seem that these troops were not maintained on a permanent basis. Describing the preparations for war in 1553, Rubatin notes that:

> The arquebuserie à cheval were not in individual compagnies, because, a little beforehand, the King (Henry II) had given an order to each of the capitaines of a hundred hommes d'armes, to raise fifty arquebusiers à cheval, armed with corslets, morions, brassars or sleeves of mail, with the scopette or an arquebuse proper with a match or with a wheellock, in a scabbard of boiled leather, mounted on good courtauds, and to those (capitaines) of fifty, twenty-five in this same type, led by a homme d'armes, of the most experienced sort, who would be chosen from their company.[55]

Such an arrangement was useful on the march, or in smaller engagements, where the gendarmerie might be vulnerable in close terrain or to sudden ambush. However, they were later drawn together into a single body, under the same commander as the chevaux legers, as battle approached.[56] During the Wars of Religion argoulets were deployed in both these ways.

It is clear, however, that these troops were relatively well armoured and mounted and were not simply mobile infantry. That said, they did occasionally dismount and fight on foot. Martigues did so with 200 when he forced his way along the Loire at Angers in 1568. The narrowness of the route meant he could only deploy 20 mounted gens d'armes on the road itself.

These relatively cheap horsemen were useful in the endemic low-level skirmishing that occurred throughout the wars. Monluc, for example, recruited 200 arquebusiers and 100 argoulets in Guienne in an attempt to put down the initial wave of Huguenot risings in 1562.

The Artillery

During the first half of the sixteenth century, the reputation of France's artillery rivalled that of her cavalry. This reputation was laid down a century earlier, during the latter stages of the Hundred Years War, when French guns played an important role in breaking English control of Normandie and Guienne. It was cemented during Charles VIII's invasion of Italy in 1494. Italian commentators were aghast by the speed at which castles and city walls could be breached. Francesco Guicciardini provided some insightful comments regarding these achievements:

> The French developed many pieces, which were even more manoeuvrable, constructed only of bronze. These were called cannoni, and they used iron balls instead of stone as before. Furthermore, they were hauled on carriages drawn not

---

55 Rabutin, *Commentaires*, pp.212–213.
56 Rabutin, *Commentaires*, p.242.

by oxen, as was the custom in Italy, but by horses, with such agility of manpower and tools that they almost always marched along with the armies and were led right up to the walls and set into position there with incredible speed; and so little time elapsed between one shot and another and the shots were so frequent and so violent was there battering that in a few hours they could accomplish what previously in Italy used to require many days. They used this diabolical rather than human weapon not only in besieging cities, but also in the field, together with similar cannon and smaller pieces.[57]

He noted that the French advantage stemmed not only from their technological achievements in casting cannon and balls, but also from the logistics that supported their use. Monluc echoed these comments at the Siege of La Rochelle, noting that an army that deploys its batteries quickly will dismay the defenders.[58]

The cannon's dominance over medieval fortifications stimulated the development of countermeasures. Low, thick walls of rammed earth proved to be an effective means of absorbing the power of the cannon's shot, but also useful platforms from which the defender could deploy his own guns. These principles led to the creation of ever more complex works that became known as 'trace Italienne'. Thus, the attacker's advantage over the defender proved relatively short lived, but only if the latter was protected by such works.

On the field of battle, France's use of guns, despite Guicciardini's comments, was less revolutionary. Arguably, only the Battle of Ravenna in 1512 was defined (if not decided) by the use of artillery. At this encounter, however, many of the guns were provided and deployed by France's ally, Alfonso d'Este, Duca di Ferrara. On other occasions, notably Cerignola, Novara, Marignano and Biccoca, the French guns played little part despite being present in considerable numbers. They were often masked by the impetuous charges of either their own cavalry or Swiss mercenaries.

The Guns

The guns that Charles VIII took into Italy were of diverse character with little uniformity and carrying names reminiscent of monstrous beasts, such as serpentines and basilisks. By the reign of François I, a degree of theoretical standardisation had developed. This was codified in the ordonnance of Henry II issued in 1550, though not substantially implemented until 1572. Even after this date, large pieces of non-standard calibre were still to be found in garrisons and cities for many years thereafter. The artillery proper consisted of six calibres:

- Canon or Canon Royal, firing a ball of between 33 livres four onces and 34 livres in weight (16.27–16.64 kg)
- Grande Coulevrine, with a ball of 15 livres two onces to 15 livres four onces (7.4–7.48 kg)

57 Francesco Guicciardini, *The History of Italy* (Princeton NJ: Princeton University Press, 1984), translator Sidney Alexander, pp.51–52.
58 Quoted in Wood, *The King's Army*, pp.246–247.

- Coulevrine Bâtarde, with a ball of seven livres two ounces to seven livres three onces (3.49–3.51kg)
  - Coulevrine Moyenne, a ball of two livres (979g)
  - Faucon, a ball of one livre one once (520g)
  - Fauconneau, a ball of 14 onces (428g)

To these may be added a seventh category, the arquebus à croc, which was a large-calibre arquebus fitted with a hook used to defend walls.

Of these weapons, only the cannon and larger coulevrines had any value in pounding fortifications during a siege. Both could be used on the battlefield, and the lighter coulverines had utility in this arena as well. But the faucon and fauconneau were relegated to anti-personnel use from fortifications or, in extremis, by local forces deficient in heavier guns.

The Grande Couleuvrine and Coulevrine Bâtarde were long guns. Such pieces were cast in a vertical position, meaning that the bronze was denser around the breach. This allowed for a larger charge and, consequently, greater range. They were favoured when accuracy was important.

Contemporary estimates of range are numerous, but very inconsistent. The following table gives indicative average values.

Table 2. Artillery Ranges

	Range (metres)	
	Point Blank	Maximum
Canon Royal	675	3,600
Grande Coulevrine	765	4,500
Coulevrine Bâtard	540	3,600
Coulevrine Moyenne	360	2,400
Faucon	288	2,250
Fauconneau	252	1,350

Most guns used in the field were able to manage 10, or at the most 12, shots per hour. After this number they would need a similar period for the barrels to cool down or they would risk a premature ignition of a charge. The barrels could be soaked to aid this process. While most battles open with an artillery barrage, the guns ceased to have much impact beyond this point, being effectively immobile. Their chief contribution seems to have been to force the enemy to either seek cover or attack prematurely. Few troops were stoic enough to remain stationary under artillery fire for any length of time. In this manner, artillery fire (by only three guns) made a significant contribution to Henry IV's victory at Coutras.

In terms of absolute numbers, the weight of artillery available in France was considerable. Guns were to be found throughout the realm but were concentrated in three main areas: Paris and the two important frontiers of Picardie and Piedmont. In 1561, the latter held 583 guns including 49

cannons royal and 23 grande coulevrines. At a later date, *c.* 1580, Picardie held 360 guns, of which 45 were cannons and 44 coulevrines.

The Paris arsenal was originally built by the city authorities themselves, in 1396. It became known as les Granges de l'Artillerie de la Ville. King Francis I took over part of the structure as a royal foundry in 1533. Later, Henry II took over the entire site, establishing apartments for the artillery staff as well as seven gunpowder manufactories.

In 1568 the planned peacetime strength of the Paris arsenal, under the direct control of the Grand Mestre de l'Artillerie amounted to 233 individuals, of whom 130 were trained gunners and 30 were skilled craftsmen of various sorts. Should such a force take the field, it was anticipated that they would require, in addition, 387 teamsters and 2,000 pionniers.

On 28 January 1563, the site was devastated by a huge explosion that also damaged adjoining parts of the city. Four of the seven manufactories were destroyed. This event occurred just as Guise was preparing to besiege the Huguenot stronghold of Orleans. The loss of both powder and the means

Top: Coulevrine Bâtard, cast for Henry II *c.* 1550, muzzle. (Metropolitan Museum of Art, New York)

Above: Coulevrine Bâtard, cast for Henry II *c.* 1550, breech. (Metropolitan Museum of Art, New York)

to produce more greatly impacted his ability to conduct this endeavour. Subsequently, gunpowder had to be purchased and transported from as far afield as Vlænderé (Flanders) to make up the shortfall. The cause of the explosion was never discovered. A new arsenal was built on the same location.

Though the Paris arsenal represented the centre of the French artillery administration, the actual casting of its guns was often carried out elsewhere. Many foundries were in the east of the country, especially around Nancy, Sainct Dizier and Langres. This was Ligueur territory: a fact that caused Henry IV no small difficulties. He was increasingly obliged to call upon England's resources to make up the shortfall. Well over 100 guns were shipped over the channel during the Ninth War. In previous wars the Huguenots had also requested similar assistance.

Logistics

Despite the quantity of guns available, neither the royal army nor any of the rebellious factions were ever able to deploy a sufficient force to achieve enough of a superiority to dictate events. The largest number of heavy guns ever brought together for a single action was the 42 cannons and larger coulverines at the Siege of La Rochelle in 1572. There were 45 guns of all types at the Siege of Rouen in 1562 and 32 at Orléans the following year. Field trains accompanying the army were generally smaller still. 22 guns were with the Royalist army at Dreux in 1562 and Anjou had 20 with him in 1568. Contemporaries regarded these forces as well-equipped as far as artillery is concerned. Huguenot and regional factions were unable to field such numbers. This disparity between the number of pieces available and the number actually employed was due to the vast amount of support paraphernalia that was required to service them, and the scarcity of this material.

Although the gun crews were rather small by later standards, the number of labourers and horses required to move them were considerable.

Table 3. Artillery Gun Crews

	Gunners	Pionniers	Draught Horses
Cannon	5	30	23
Grande Coulevrine	4	24	17
Coulevrine Bâtarde	3	12	13
Coulevrine Moyenne	3	6	9
Faucon	3	6	3
Fauconneau	3	6	2

To this must be added the men and animals and wagons, required to move the ammunition, powder and tools. Anjou's 20-gun train in 1568 consisted of 241 gunners and other artillery personnel, 1,814 pionniers, 316 teamsters and 1,653 horses. The artillery personnel were relatively highly paid and the teamsters were generally independent contractors. Both had a habit of refusing to co-operate if not paid.

Many of the guns that were available in arsenals lacked suitable carriages that would allow them to be used in the field. An inventory of guns located in Piemont in 1573 reported that of the 72 cannons and grande coulevrines, 43 percent lacked carriages, and this rose to 60 percent of the bâtardes and all but four of the 102 smaller pieces.[59]

Both the guns themselves and the carriages that bore them were heavy constructions, as the following table shows.

Table 4. Artillery Gun Weights

	Weight in Livres (kg)	
	Barrel	With Carriage
Canon Royal	5,200 (2,548)	8,000 (3,920)
Grande Coulevrine	4,200 (2,058)	6,500 (3,185)
Coulevrine Bâtard	2,500 (1,225)	4,400 (2,156)
Coulevrine Moyenne	1,500 (735)	2,200 (1,078)
Faucon	800 (392)	1,340 (657)
Fauconneau	500 (245)	800 (392)

The draught horses that pulled these weapons were harnessed between shafts (á la limonière) which is relatively inefficient compared to later practice. For the lighter pieces at least, guns could be moved a short distance on the battlefield by means of drag ropes known as 'combleau'.

Pionniers

The pionniers provided the manual labour and less skilled trades upon which the movement of the artillery depended. They were also charged with emplacing batteries for a siege and digging the trenches and tunnels upon which a successful assault or mining attempt depended. This was unglamorous, ill-paid and frequently dangerous work. Not unreasonably, men drafted into such a role served with ill-will and frequently deserted.

The loss of large numbers of pionniers, either through enemy action or desertion, could render the army's guns immobile and reduce the pace of a siege to a snail's pace. The operations at La Rochelle were imperilled as their numbers fell from 1,500 to only 600.

At least some wore uniforms. One of those contingents raised for the Siege of La Rochelle were described by Biron on their arrival:

> Pierre Sixlivres, merchant of Bernay, presented us in this city of Niort the number and quantity of 50 pionniers and a capitaine, including three carpenters, a standard bearer, and a drummer, ordered raised by the King in the election of Bernay … fit to serve the King in the artillery train … Each one was attired and arrayed in red caps, and cassocks and hose of green woollen cloth with two white

---

59 Wood, *The King's Army*, pp.180–181.

crosses and the first and last letters of the name of their election sewn on the front and back of their garments.[60]

Tactics

The army's guns were normally deployed in one or two batteries. These were placed a little forward of the main line and, if a suitable site was available, on an eminence to improve their range and field of fire. In Royalist forces, the guns were normally deployed near any Swiss infantry present, as these troops had traditional responsibility for guarding the artillery.

The artillery would often open an engagement with their fire. This was frequently designed either to provoke an enemy into a premature attack or else demoralise and disorganise their lines in preparation for an attack by one's own side. Given the slow rate of fire of the guns and their limited mobility once deployed, such fire was short in duration and ceased as soon as the two army's cavalry and infantry units engaged. It could, nevertheless, have a significant impact on troop's morale and movements.

There may be a few exceptions to this generally static use: some accounts credit the Grand Mestre La Bourdaisière with deftly repositioning a portion the Royalist artillery during the Battle of Moncontour. Near contemporary illustrations of the event show guns moving across behind lines even as the battle rages.[61] Similarly, the royal artillery at Jazeneuil managed to split the single battery in the centre of the line into two, in order to support the wings.

Contemporary military manuals that cover the activities of cavalry and infantry in a significant amount of detail are all but silent on the subject of artillery. Those specialist works that address this arm focus instead on logistics and ballistics.

The losing side in any encounter almost always lost any guns it deployed, since they were incapable of outpacing any pursuit.

Despite the relatively minor role guns played on the field of battle, an effective siege train was absolutely necessary to bring about the rapid reduction of enemy strongholds. As previously noted, the results of battles, such as Dreux and Jarnac, were largely wasted because the victorious force was unable to capitalise on their momentary advantage due to the lack of available heavy guns. It should again be emphasised that sieges in this era were far more common occurrences than battles.

The Infantry

Unlike the cavalry and artillery arms, the infantry of France did not enjoy much of a reputation prior to the Wars of Religion. During the Italian Wars,

---

60 Wood, *The King's Army*, p.165. He has suggested that this uniform served in the manner of a convict's garb so they could not easily desert. Equally plausibly, given the banner and drum, it was intended to instil an esprit de corps in the men.

61 The significance and even direction of this movement is unclear. Gigon, *La troisième guerre*, pp.329–340, merely notes that Anjou 'moved his artillery to his flanks' without further comment. His account of the battle emphasises rather the effectiveness of the Huguenot artillery.

commentators suggested this was because the nobility opposed military training for commoners: for fear that they would revolt. Whatever the truth of this, successive monarchs made several, largely unsuccessful, attempts to develop a competent force of native infantry. By the time of the Wars of Religion, infantry could be drawn from several different sources that were the relics of these efforts.

The best troops belonged to the compagnies of the vieilles bandes. These troops were embodied and paid in both peace and war, and thus were trained, equipped and available for immediate use. The principle problem with these troops did not relate to their quality, but quantity. Generally, only between 40 and 50 such compagnies were retained in peacetime, and even these were typically at reduced strength, so that they constituted only about half of the 6,000 to 6,500 men the Crown maintained. They were generally grouped along France's north-eastern frontier or in the rump of its Italian possessions. In 1562 several of the northern bandes followed their colonel general, Andelot, into the Huguenot camp and formed the core of Rouen's defence.

Morion, French, c. 1560. (Chicago Institute of Art)

The remainder of the permanent infantry force was made up of lower-grade compagnies that were specifically raised to act as garrison units. They generally contained older men or youths and were less well equipped. In addition, some garrison infantry, referred to as morte-payes, seem to have only served on a rotational basis. Numbering only 1,300 men in total, they were often dispersed in exceedingly small bodies across the kingdom.

In 1534, François I established a much larger body of territorially based infantry: the legions. There were seven in total, originally based in Bretaigne, Normandie, Picardie, Bourgógne–Champaigne–Nivernais, Daulphine–Prouvence–Auvergne, Guienne and Languedoc but these regions were altered on several subsequent occasions. They were essentially refounded in 1558. Each theoretically contained 6,000 men: by 1562 in 15 compagnies of 400 each. The men received limited tax exemptions in peacetime, but only their officers were paid, except in times of war. They served sporadically and with mixed fortunes under François I and Henry II. During the First War of Religion, 20 (or 16) compagnies of legionnaire troops from Bretaigne and Picardie formed one of the two main bodies of French infantry in the Royalist battle line at Dreux.[62] They were put to flight by Huguenot cavalry early in the battle. Meanwhile, the legion of Languedoc went over to the

---

62 Oman, *War in the Sixteenth Century*, p.416.

rebels. Thereafter, these troops are sporadically mentioned. A regiment composed of six enseignes of legion troops fought at Moncontour in 1569.[63]

The majority of infantry were specifically raised for the duration of a campaign and dismissed upon its termination. These were the men of the new bands and were often referred to in the decades leading up to the Wars of Religion as 'aventuriers' (adventurers), a term which signified both a soldier and a plunderer or bandit. The release of large numbers of such men into the countryside at the end of each war became a significant cause of disorder, which could render large areas unsafe for travel and perpetuate local conflicts.

Finally, some cities had been granted the right of self-defence, typically as a means of avoiding having royal troops billeted in them. This right entailed the obligation of maintaining a local militia. Such troops were extremely unwilling to serve beyond the city walls, but were often called upon to aid in its defence. The Paris militia provided several thousand men to form the left wing of the Royalist forces at the Battle of Sainct Denys; fought virtually on their own doorsteps.

Although initially raised under distinct conditions, it was possible for the status of a compagnie to change. Thus, a unit of aventuriers might find itself employed as a garrison company instead or, if it had performed well, it might be retained after the end of the conflict and join the vieilles bandes. Individual infantrymen were probably even more flexible regarding their terms of enlistment: an experienced adventurer would be welcome in a vieille band looking to bring its numbers up to strength at the start of a campaign. Similarly, he might take up a more sedentary role among the morte-payes once age or infirmities began to catch up with him.

Unlike the nobility, who were obliged to perform military service when it was required of them, commoners were not subject to forced conscription. In theory, all infantrymen were volunteers. For even those who opted for military service, the terms of enlistment were short, as little as three months, compared to later centuries.

As with the cavalry, the compagnie, or enseigne or bande, was the basic organisational unit for French infantry. And it was the compagnie's capitaine who was responsible for its recruitment and maintenance. The internal organisation of infantry compagnies, even prior to the First War, was even more diverse than their origins; 29 different structures being recorded during the 1560s.[64] They ranged in size from 50 to 400 men, though the norm was around the 200 mark. These authorised strengths typically dwindled on campaign more rapidly than their cavalry equivalents. Two examples, both from compagnies stationed in Piemont in 1567, are presented in Table 5.[65] One is a vieille bande and the other a garrison unit.

---

63   Gigon, *La troisième guerre*, p.334.
64   Wood, *The King's Army*, p.103.
65   Wood, *The King's Army*, p.88.

Table 5. Infantry Company Structures

Rank/Type	Vieille Bande	Garrison
Capitaine	1	1
Lieutenant	1	1
Enseigne	1	-
Serjent	2	1
Corporal	4	3
Fourier	1	1
Musician	2	1
Lanspessade pike	16	9
Corseleted pike	37	10
Corseleted halberd	9	-
Pike	17	38
Pike seiches	-	6
Lanspessades arquebus	4	-
Morinées arquebus	55	10
Arquebus	20	19
Total Number	170	100

The lanspessade was either a gentleman of the company, typically a well-to-do young man beginning a military career, or else a veteran soldier. Seiches (literally 'dry' but perhaps better translated as 'exposed' in the sense of a dry riverbed) denotes a pikeman without any defensive equipment. The morinées arquebusier was equipped with a helmet.

The tables of organisation for the various types of native infantry company during the early wars suggest that the desired proportion of pike to arquebus ranged from an ideal of roughly 1:1 down to 1:2. This contrast with their pike-heavy German and Swiss mercenaries who were equipped with 2:1 and 9:1 respectively and, at the opposite end of the scale, their Italians with 1:9. However, it would seem that the proportion of pikes dwindled over the course of the wars, and may never have been achieved for the local Huguenot infantry. Certainly, La Noue bemoaned the lack of pikes amongst the native French infantry and Biron went further: 'I will venture to say that the French infantry have given up carrying pikes. Therefore, they must be joined to them a nation which does carry pikes, for expeditions in great as well as small force, according as the occasion offers itself, as especially for assaults (in a siege).'[66]

---

66 Quoted in Wood, *The King's Army*, p.112.

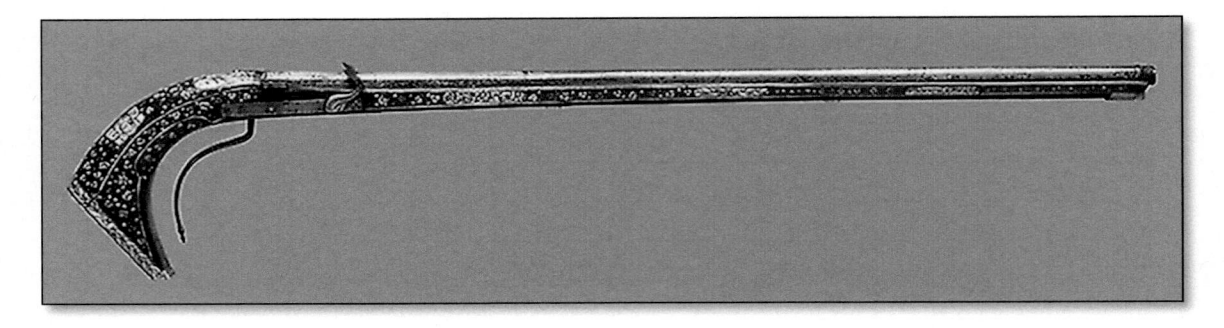

Arquebus, 1570–1580. (Chicago Institute of Art)

Traditionally, French pikemen were drawn from the northern provinces, especially Picardie, and this regionality may have continued to influence the composition of compagnies during the wars.

Although the compagnie remained the principal unit of administration, tactically, these were usually brought together into larger formations, at least while the army marched or prepared to fight a large action, though during the petty encounters that typified much of the conflicts, the independent compagnie remained an important element. The larger formations were increasingly referred to as regiments. Initially these were only regarded as temporary groupings. Normally, each regiment would be formed from men drawn from the same type of compagnie; whether vieille band, legion or aventurier. There were exceptions. During the Siege of Orleans in 1562, Andelot mixed the militia compagnies with those of more seasoned troops.[67] This situation evolved rapidly as the wars progressed. During the First, a body of infantry might be described as '18 enseignes of the vieille bands of Picardie'. By the Third, it was normal for a similar body to be referred to as simply 'Mirabel's Regiment', after its colonel. The regiment was no longer a convenient grouping of independent compagnies, but each took on an identity in its own right. So, six compagnies might be detached from Strozzi's regiment to provide a garrison for a stronghold, but there was an implicit expectation that, at some point in the future, those six compagnies would be returned to their parent formation. That this expectation was not always met does not detract from the general principal. In many respects, the French regiment gained a functional equivalency to the Spanish Tercio in this regard.[68]

The first regiments to be established on a more permanent footing were those Royalist units formed during the Second War. Six of these were available at the start of the Third. The number of enseignes in each regiment varied somewhat but settled in the nine to 12 range. Nearly all the existing vieille bandes were incorporated in these formations. Three were under the authority of Colonel General Strozzi. They were commanded by Cosseins (the Garde also known as Strozzi's regiment), Gohas and Sarrieu. The other three were under Colonel

67 Édouard de La Barre Duparcq, *L'art militaire pendant les guerres de religion* (Paris: Charles-Lavauzelle, 1864), p.16.

68 Geoffrey Parker, *The Army of Flanders and the Spanish Road 1567–1659* (Cambridge: Cambridge University Press, 1984), p.13. Ian Heath, *Armies of the Sixteenth Century* (Guernsey: Foundry Books, 1997), pp.130–131.

General Brissac: Honoux (also known as Brissac's regiment), La Barthe and Muns.[69]

After the death of Brissac in 1569, Strozzi became the sole Colonel General of infantry. At the camp at La Rochfoucauld on 29 May he reorganised the six regular regiments with a variable number of enseignes: Cosseins (Gardes Français) 15 enseignes, Sarrieu 16 (which became known as the Picardie regiment from 1585), Gohas (Champaigne regiment) 25, La Barthe 15, Gohas (the younger, who replaced Muns) 15 and Honnoux 12 (Piemont regiment).[70] The enseignes allocated to these regiments were not necessarily the same ones that they began the campaign with. For example, Sarrieu's Regiment contained 10 enseignes from the gardes and six of the vieille bandes of Picardie.

Morion-Cabasset, *c.* 1580.
(Chicago Institute of Art)

Whilst provincial or volunteer infantry regiments were placed under the command of a colonel, a regular regiment under the authority of a colonel general, such as one of those formed by François de Guise and those that followed, were entrusted to officers with the rank of Mestre de Camp. This was a direct translation of the Spanish term for the commander of a tercio: Maestre de Campo.

French pikemen were armed with a weapon some 4.5 metres (14 pied de roy) long, notably shorter than the 5.5-metre pikes wielded by the Swiss and landsknechts, or the 5- to 5.5-metre pikes of the Spanish, but comparable with the lower end of Dutch practice. Pikemen were, however, almost always heavily outnumbered by their arquebus-armed brethren. This trend was most noticeable amongst the Huguenots and increased as the wars dragged on. English commanders complained that they had to detach their own pikemen to protect French Royalist forces, so lacking were they in these weapons.

The arquebus was a relatively simple firearm. It weighed five kilograms or somewhat less and fired a ball of 15 to 20 grammes. It had a barrel length of less than 90 centimetres to a little over a metre. Unlike modern firearms its butt was generally braced against the chest when fired. They were overwhelmingly matchlock weapons. However, a few arquebus à rouet (with wheellock mechanisms) were also in use. At La Roche-l'Abeille, Coligny ordered those so armed in Rouvray and Pouille's regiments to form a separate body, as they could fire in the rain when the rest of his arquebusiers could not. Their numbers are not recorded.

The mosquet (musket) was supposedly first deployed by Spanish forces at the Siege of Parma in 1521. It was longer than the arquebus and had a wider bore. By the later sixteenth century, the definition included those weapons with a barrel length of 115 to 140 centimetres firing a lead bullet

---

69   Louis Susane, *Histoire de l'ancienne infanterie française* (Paris: Corréard, 1849) Vol. 1, pp.162–163.
70   Gigon, *La troisième guerre*, pp.111–112.

Officer's esponton, *c.* 1600. (Cleveland Museum of Art)

weighing 50 to 70 grams. The size of the firearm, which typically weighed seven to nine kilograms, meant that the musketeer, a new specialist category of infantryman, had to balance the weapon on a forked rest during firing. Spanish forces gradually increased the proportion of foot armed with the musket as the century wore on. By the early 1570s, this meant between a quarter and a third of those armed with firearms. In the same period, however, it was virtually unknown in France. According to Brantôme, the musket was only introduced into French service by his friend Strozzi during the siege of La Rochelle in 1573.[71] The soldiers were initially sceptical of the weapon's value: 'so as to win them over little by little, Strozzi had a page or lackey carry a musket about with him throughout the siege. Whenever Strozzi saw a good target, he fired.' While some of his shots were impressive (he brought down a horse at 450 metres) and he won some converts, the French never incorporated significant number of these weapons into their infantry. Given the shambolic state of the French economy and administration during the wars, part of the reason for this is probably logistical.

Equally likely, however, is that by the time the musket made it appearance in France a better alternative had been found. The caliver (a word derived from the French term for the standardised bore size of firearms: calibre) was halfway between the arquebus and musket in size. Its utility meant that it gradually replaced both other weapons towards the end of the century, though not before it acquired the name of the latter along the way. The caliver was sometimes fired from a rest, but this was also frequently dispensed with.

Huguenot Infantry

Although some of the vieilles bandes from Normandie and Guienne rallied to their cause, the bulk of Huguenot infantry forces were drawn from the local forces organised by the reformed churches for self-defence. In 1562 Condé requested that each community 'use such means as you have to promptly furnish soldiers'.[72] The ecclesiastical structure of consistories and synods was adapted to provide compagnies and regiments. The synod of Guienne resolved to have each church form an enseigne and to group these into regiments by colloquys. There were seven colloquys in 1560. Montluc records his alarm and anger that the Reformed Church in Guienne claimed to have 4,000 men armed, organised and paid in 1562.[73]

Huguenot infantry were typically organised into enseignes of between 100 and 150 men. Initially, no more than a fifth of those men carried pikes.[74] The remainder were armed with arquebuses. As noted above, the lack of

---

71 Pierre de Bourdeille, Seigneur de Brantôme, *Discours sur les couronnels de l'infanterie de France* (Paris: Renouard, 1873), pp.83–84.

72 David J.B. Trim, 'Huguenot Soldiering c. 1560–1685, The Origins of a Tradition', in Glozier, Matthew and Onnekink, David (eds), *War, Religion and Service: Huguenot Soldiering, 1685–1713* (Farnham: Ashgate, 2007), p.11.

73 Blaise de Lasseran-Massencôme, Seigneur de Montluc, 'Commentaires de Messire Blaise de Montluc' in *Collection Universelle des Mémoires Particuliers Relatifs a l'Histoire de France*, Volume 24 (Paris: Roucher, 1786), pp.192–193.

74 Arlette Jouanna, Jaculine Boucher, Dominique Biloghi, Guy Le Thiec, *Histoire et Dictionnaire Des Guerres de Religion* (Paris: Robert Laffont, 1998), pp.672–673.

polearms was a chronic problem, contributing to the destruction of Mouvans' regiments at Mensignac in 1568.[75] Some of the regiments at Moncontour a year later were still without them.

As the wars dragged on, the Huguenots also had access to veteran troops who had served as mercenaries or volunteers outside France. Although the Low Countries was the source of most of this experience, Huguenots were also found fighting for Venice against the Turks and in the Azores aiding the cause of Portuguese independence.

Tactics

French infantry regiments, whether formally embodied or of a more provisional nature, were deployed on the battlefield in a manner typical for the era. The pikemen would be drawn out of their individual compagnies and brought together into a square, or oblong, block. This task usually fell to a professional serjeant major if available. These men were skilled drill-masters rather than lowly non-commissioned officers.

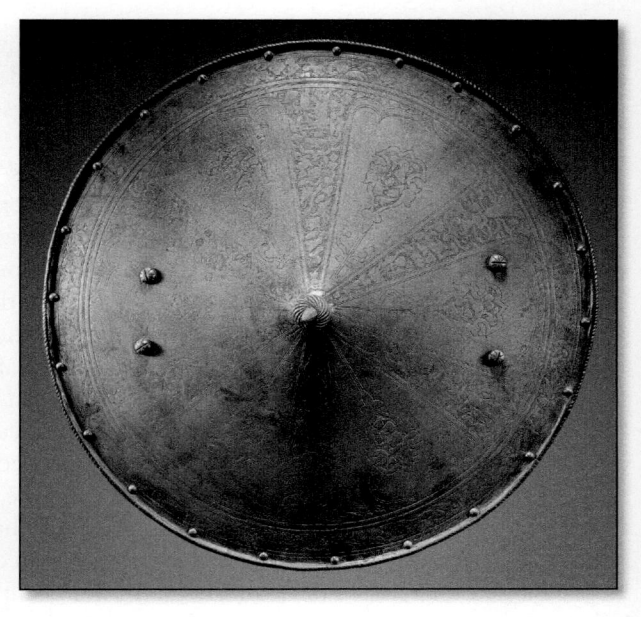

Officer's shield, 1550–1600. (Cleveland Museum of Art)

The dimensions of the pike block could vary according to circumstances, but typically contained as many ranks of pikemen as there were files. So, a block containing 2,000 men would be roughly 45 men wide and 45 deep. This was known as a 'square of men' (quarré d'hommes).

Alternatively, a 'square of ground' (quarré de terrain) could be formed, which had the actual physical dimensions of a square and contained more files than ranks. This was because the space allocated to each man in formation was greater in depth than breadth: Tavannes indicates twice as much. He describes an 1,800-man 'square of ground' 60 files wide but only 30 ranks deep.[76] This was his preferred arrangement, as he regarded the 'square of men' as a waste of manpower.

The actual distances could be varied according to circumstances, that is closed up for melee or more open for manoeuvre. Tavannes suggests three paces (1.92 m) between files and seven (4.48 m) between ranks, which must surely represent the latter. Elsewhere it is recommended that each rank be separated from that behind by three paces (1.92 m), and each man left a gap of one pace (0.64 m) between himself and those on either side.[77] Assuming the man himself occupied a square of roughly a pace on each side, then the

---

75 Gigon, *La troisième guerre*, p.90, states they were all arquebusiers, though Robert J. Knecht, *The French Civil Wars, 1562–1598* (London: Routledge, 2000), p.88 in an unreferenced note states that Acier's force contained 5,000 pikemen (out of a total strength of perhaps 19,000 infantry).

76 Jean de Saulx, Vicomte de Tavannes, 'Mémoires de très-noble et très illustre Gaspard de Saulx, seigneur de Tavanes, mareschal de France, admiral des mers de Levant, gouverneur de Provence, conseiller du Roy, et capitaine de cent hommes d'armes, Tome I' in *Collection Complète des Mémoires relatives a la Histoire de France*, Volume 23 (Paris: Foucault, 1822), p.243.

77 Édouard de La Barre Duparcq, *L'art militaire pendant les guerres de religion*, Section IV, note 86.

2,000-man 'square of men' mentioned above would have a frontage of 56.96 m (45x0.64 + 44x0.64) and a depth of 113.28 m (45x0.64 + 44x1.92). However, even these 'melee' distances seem large when compared to contemporary Spanish or Dutch practice.

The company standards would also be massed within this pike block. The arquebusiers would then be positioned on the flanks of this formation, although they retained some mobility and could advance and retire around the pikemen as the situation demanded. As native French units generally contained fewer pikemen than German or Swiss troops, their regiments were typically shallower and wider. Huguenot regiments, many of which contained few (or any, as at Mensignac) pikemen, may have deployed in formations as shallow as ten men deep. Various recent accounts suggest that the Catholic infantry at Dreux also formed up only 10-deep.[78] This is highly unlikely, as it contradicts contemporary practice as well as contemporary accounts. Avila, for example, states that their 5,000–6,000 Swiss troops were drawn up in a 'double battalia' suggesting a formation twice as broad as deep, or 100 men wide by 50 men deep. He also states that the 2,000 allied Spanish infantrymen were drawn up in a single block 35 ranks deep. This is largely confirmed by the Castilian Captain, Juan de Ayala, who was present and indicates that the pike element of the 2,100 Spanish infantry were drawn up in 36 files.[79]

Each rank of arquebusiers was drawn up at a similar depth to the pikemen, but they left an extra pace between each file. Continuing the example given above, if the number of arquebusiers equalled the number of pikemen, and they were drawn up on either flank, it would extend the frontage by another 83.84 m (45x0.64 + 43x1.28). This would give the whole formation a frontage of 140.8 m (or a bit more depending on the gap left between the pikemen and arquebusiers) and a depth of 113.28 m.

As the wars drew on, there was a tendency for French infantry to be deployed in smaller bodies, typically no more than a 1,000 strong. Though there were those who resisted this trend, Tavannes included, on the basis that such bodies were too fragile to stand against a determined assault. Assuming a 1:1 ratio of pikes to shot, such a small formation drawn up in a 'square of ground', would be no more than 16 ranks deep. As noted above, a force of arquebusiers without any pike might be drawn up shallower still, with perhaps as few as 10 ranks. Contemporary military thinkers regarded this as the minimum necessary for the countermarching files of arquebusiers to maintain continuous fire.[80] The small, shot-heavy French regiments that evolved during this period bear a strong resemblance to contemporary

---

78 The detailed account of the battle in Raymond de Coynart, *L'Année 1562 et là Bataille de Dreux* (Paris: Firmin-Didot, 1894), Lègend du Plan No.1, among them. However, his maps do not show the forces involved at a consistent scale and, given the placement and size of units he suggests, there would not be room for the French, Swiss and Landsknecht infantry to deploy only 10 deep.

79 Julien Coudy (ed.), *The Huguenot Wars, an eyewitness account* (London: Chilton Book Company, 1969), translator Julie Kernan, pp.142–143.

80 Heath, *Armies of the Sixteenth Century*, p.113.

Dutch practice initiated by Maurits van Nassouwe from 1590.[81] Given the large numbers of Frenchmen who fought in the Netherlands a degree of cross-fertilisation is understandable.

Mounted Infantry

The Wars saw the development of mounted infantry, as opposed to cavalry armed with firearms, though confusingly both are sometimes referred to as arquebusiers á cheval. The first instance occurred in 1569, where the Huguenots mounted infantry behind (en crouppe) gens d'armes to capture Nysmes in a surprise attack. In 1570, Coligny took the expedient a stage further and mounted 3,000 of his arquebusiers on nags, which allowed them to keep pace with the cavalry as he undertook his epic march across France. Henry IV regularly made use of similar troops in his fast-moving campaigns. These men were not expected to fight from horseback, however. They were mounted only for operational mobility. When combat ensued, they dismounted and fought like traditional infantry. As such, they were the forerunners of later dragoons.

Enfans Perdus

The term 'enfans perdus', literally 'lost children', was given to soldiers tasked with an especially dangerous mission or placed in an exposed position. It is equivalent of the German verlorene haufe meaning 'lost band' from whence the English 'forlorn hope' is derived. They were invariably bodies of arquebusiers drawn from the infantry regiments present in the army. They were often positioned to protect artillery batteries or garrison important geographical features, such as buildings or woods located in front of the main battle line.

French arquebusiers were quite capable of operating in open order when the occasion demanded, as demonstrated during actions like Jazeneuil and Jarrie. On both these occasions the relative experience of troops was a telling factor.[82] Brissac's regiments at the former combat were able to hold their own against much larger numbers of Huguenot levies. La Noue described it thus:

> Neither side could see anything, being hidden in the hedges and small valleys, and only scattered arquebus fire could be perceived … Our soldiers (the Huguenots) were very courageous, but this was not equalled by their conduct, because they fired in salvos and held themselves too densely organised, and by contrast those of Monseigneur (Anjou) were spread out, firing slowly and moving by small groups, such that 200 arquebusiers stopped a Huguenot regiment.[83]

---

81 Marjolein 't Hart, *The Dutch Wars of Independence, Warfare and Commerce in the Netherlands, 1570–1680* (London: Routledge, 2014), p.40.

82 Experience during the contemporary wars in the Netherlands demonstrated the same point, see Geoffry Parker, *The Army of Flanders and the Spanish Road 1567–1659* (Cambridge: Cambridge University Press, 1984), p.13.

83 La Noue, *Discours politiques et militaires*, p.654.

Commanded Shot

During the seventeenth century, a commonly employed tactic was to post small bodies of troops armed with firearms adjacent to or amongst cavalry units to disrupt the formations of enemy horsemen as they closed. Such infantry where referred to as 'commanded shot'. Though associated with the Swedish King, Gustavus Adolphus, during the Thirty Years' War, he was not the originator of this tactic. Henry IV regularly deployed arquebusiers in this fashion, as at Coutras and Ivry. But it was Coligny who initiated the practice. La Popelinière writing in 1572 concerning the Admiral's dispositions at Moncontour, commented that: 'This manner of doing things was very familiar to him … intermixing infantry and cavalry; he deploys, as enfans perdus, the best arquebusiers in between the cornettes, both French and reiters.'[84]

Armed Peasants

Bands of armed peasants, fighting purely local actions under their own elected leaders, often clergy or petty nobles, are encountered throughout the wars. Their primary concern was protecting their families and property from the attentions of marauding soldiers, especially foreign mercenaries. But they could also act in support of one of the contending factions.[85] Their most notable interventions favoured the Catholic cause. At the outset of the wars, the Duc d'Aumale encouraged the rural population of Normandie to oppose the Huguenots who dominated the cities. Calvinist chroniclers even accused him of fermenting social discord by offering them the opportunity to loot the houses of the Huguenot seigneurs. A body of 2,000 menaced Dieppe in 1562. Coligny faced a similar body during his campaign around Bernay in 1563, but he easily defeated them. After the Combat of Mensignac in 1568, many of the defeated Huguenots were killed by aggressive bands of peasants. Later, the Catholic Ligue was supported by bands drawn from the rural population. In the latter instance they fought alongside Charles de Brissac's troops in Lower Normandie in 1589, where they help relieve Falaise from Montpensier's Royalists. In none of these various instances did such bands take a role in a formal battle, however.

---

84 La Popelinière, *La vraye et entière histoire des troubles*, p.303. Note, once again, that it is the best of the available troops that are employed in this role.
85 Carroll, *Noble Power During the French Wars of Religion*, pp.123–128.

5

Illustrations

Commanders

Connestable Montmorency
Although the Connestable was already old at the start of the wars, the armour he wears is thoroughly up to date. The image is taken from an engraving in the Armamentarium Heroicum dated 1601,[1] but the actual armour he wears has been preserved. This is now in Les Invalides, Paris, and has been dated to 1550. Most of the surface has been blackened and the remaining areas gilded, giving it a striking appearance. The traditional separate tassettes and cuissots have been replaced with articulated bands that would come to characterise cavalry armour well into the next century and give rise to the nicknames 'lobster' or 'crayfish'. The back of his legs are entirely unarmoured, as are his feet and fingers. His armet has a two-part visor, both elements swivelling independently from the same pivot. As connestable, he carries his baton of command. His tomb depicts him in an earlier style of armour and wearing a saye baring his coat of arms, but the use of formal heraldry (as opposed to purely personal symbols, monograms and mottos) seems to have fallen out of military use by the time of the Wars of Religion.

Louis Prince de Condé
The T&P plate depicting the Battle of Jarnac shows the unhorsing and murder of the Prince de Condé.[2] He is shown in distinctively different dress from the gens d'armes that surround him. He wears a (presumably white) scarf over his left shoulder rather than a casaque and an open-faced burgonet with a long peak rather than a closed armet. His body is covered by what may be a depiction of an articulated anime breastplate, though, equally likely, this may simply be the decoration on his saye. Like many of the gens d'armes depicted in T&P he carries a coutelas rather than an espee as a sidearm. An extant partial suit of armour attributed to the prince is also shown. It is polished metal with gilt decorative bands. The helmet is again a burgonet, this time with a baviere to protect the face.

---

1 Armamentarium Heroicum, *The British Museum*, <https://www.britishmuseum.org/collection/object/P_1871-0812-469>, accessed 31 May 2020.
2 Bendict, *Tortorel et Perrissin*, p.32.

Montmorency, Condé and Henry IV

Henry IV

The King is depicted in numerous contemporary images wearing full cuirassier armour typical of the last Wars, albeit of significantly better quality than most.[3] He wears a white scarf over his right shoulder and around his neck hangs the blue ribbon and cross of the Ordre du Sainct-Esprit (and therefore dates the picture to after his re-conversion to Catholicism). This was the senior order of French knighthood, though only founded by Henry III in 1578. It was made up of eight churchmen, four officers and 100 knights. Henry popularised the wide-brimmed hat that dominated the proceeding century, but his helmet is also depicted. This is a burgonet with a tall, fluted crown. It may be of a type referred to as 'Hungarian'. Both hat and crown carry his trademark white plumes. His boots have heels. These were not common at the start of the wars, being only gradually introduced into Europe from Asia via Venice. They had not yet attained any significant height.

Guards

Cent Suysses

This figure is taken from a T&P print depicting the Colloquy of Poissy in 1561.[4] Several members of this guard unit are shown in identical uniforms, which are distinct from those of the French troops present. Their dress reflects that of their homeland, being similar to that of the German landsknecht mercenaries also employed by France. He wears 'pluderhosen':

---

3   This derived from the painting by Frans Pourbus the Younger dated to c. 1610. The original is in the Louvre, Paris. The hat has been added from other illustrations.

4   Benedict, *Tortorel et Perrissin*, p.9

The Maison du Roy.

baggy silk leggings contained by strips of cloth. This version is much less voluminous than those worn by the landsknechts. The T&P image is uncoloured, though the Funckens have a similar figure in a mi-parti livery (white with black beneath on the right side and black with white beneath on the left).[5] A sixteenth-century painting based on the T&P print has them in yellow with blue and white beneath and blue and white hose.[6] They have red caps. A contemporary oil painting depicting the Sainct-Barthélemy's Day Massacre shows several figures that may be members of this unit.[7] Except for the addition of breastplates and morions, they are dressed in a very similar fashion, but not uniformed. One has yellow slashed pink on his right side and dark blue-white-red-white striped on his left. The other has red slashed black on his right and yellow slashed black on his left. He carries a very functional-looking halberd and a typical Swiss longsword.

5   Funcken, Liliane and Fred, *Arms and Uniforms – The Age of Chivalry* (London: Ward Lock, 1981). Part 2, p.81.
6   'The Colloquy of Poissy, 1561 c. 1560–99', *Royal Collection Trust*, <https://www.rct.uk/collection/402691/the-colloquy-of-poissy-1561>, accessed 8 January 2021.
7   'Le massacre de la Saint-Barthélemy', *Musée cantonal des Beaux-Arts*, <https://www.mcba.ch/en/collection/the-saint-bartholomews-day-massacre/>, accessed 11 October 2020.

Gardes du Corps du Roy

This figure is taken from the same source as the last. It depicts a member of one of the other guard units, either French or Scots. These units typically wore the livery badges of the reigning monarch. Therefore, the Crown symbol is presumably that of Charles IX. The other images show the tunic of the Garde Ecosse under the reign of Henry II (crown, 'H' and crescent) and of the same unit in the reign of Henry III. His three crowns relate to those of France, Poland and Heaven and reflect the accompanying motto: 'Manet Ultima Coelo' (the best still in heaven). The Funckens depict the former as white with gold lace and devices and the latter as ermine with gold crowns and letters.[8] The coloured copy of the T&P print has the guards in yellow with green tunics laced in silver. A painting of the Sainct-Barthélemy's Day Massacre shows members of Charles IX's guards in white tunics laced in gold. Their pleated elbow-length sleeves and skirts are striped white-buff-green. Under Henry IV these guardsmen wore a tunic with a club of Hercules, wrapped in a streamer bearing the motto 'Haec Quoque Cognita Monstra' (they also will be recognised), though a print showing the baptism of the Dauphin, Louis (XIII), has the motto alone on a scroll.[9] This guardsman wears an 'Albanian' hat that was popular for a time. He carries a halberd like that carried by his Swiss colleagues, an espee and a dagger carried in the manner typical for the time.

Cavalry

Gens d'Armes

The first of these figures depicts the armour and equipment specified in the ordonnances, the second is taken from the very many T&P engravings showing these chevaliers in action. Only a small minority of the T&P figures wear greves, long boots being much more common. Genoüillieres can normally be seen above the top of the boot. While both figures carry the long espee d'armes, the shorter, curved coutelas or badelaire was a common alternative. The lance remained the homme d'armes' primary weapon, however. These were up to five and a half metres in length, though there are few extant examples and contemporary illustrations usually depict them shorter. Accounts of the Battle of Dreux highlights that after their initial charges, the Huguenot cavalry had broken their lances and had to rely on other weapons for the remainder of the battle, significantly reducing their effectiveness. This is clearly shown in the T&P series of engravings: they wield coutelas, hammers and maces.[10] The war hammer shown is from a surviving French example. It has a wooden haft. The spiked mace is Italian, and the shaft is iron like the head. It closely matches the appearance of the weapons shown by T&P, rather than the flange-headed maces more typical of the period. The second figure has tied the long, hanging

8   Funcken, *The Age of Chivalry*, Part 2, p.67.

9   'Représentation des Cérémonies et de l'Ordre de Garde', *Paris Musées* <https://www.parismuseescollections.paris.fr/fr/petit-palais/oeuvres/representation-des-ceremonies-et-de-l-ordre-de-garde> accessed 7 June 2020.

10   Benedict, *Tortorel et Perrissin*, p.21.

Gens d'Armes.

false sleeves of his casaque together to keep them out of the way. While the casaque eventually gave way to the scarf as a means of battlefield identification it continued to be used in some quarters, Ligueur gens d'armes still wearing them in the early 1590s, for example.

Chevaux Leger

This figure again depicts the sort of equipment expected of such horsemen in the ordonnances. His armour is much less complete than that of a homme d'armes, and he wears an open-faced burgonet. He carries a short spear known as an épieu. These originated as weapons used for hunting boar but were adopted for military use. Like the previous two figures he carries an espee d'armes. This term had been applied to the blades carried by knights since the fourteenth century, but this weapon is longer and narrower than weapons of that era. It increasingly resembles the espee rapier: a term originating in the late fifteenth century to describe lighter swords worn with normal clothing rather than armour. In addition to these weapons, he is likely to have carried a pistol or two on his saddle.

Light Cavalry.

Pistolier

This figure is based on La Noue's disparaging remarks on the state of the gendarmerie and other descriptions of poorly equipped cavalry. In general, he does not differ a great deal from the chevaux leger shown previously and could easily be a member of such a unit. The rear rank of gens d'armes compagnies, that is those designated as archers, are likely to have consisted of men equipped in a similar fashion. Ideally these would have carried a demi-lance, lighter and often shorter than the full lance, but many did not. The regular compagnies of the Royalist army (and those that defected) would, presumably, have maintained a better standard of equipment, at least in the earlier wars. This figure wears a burgonet with a rather mismatched baviere, cuirass, tassettes, spalières, mougnons and gauntlets. He wears a casaque split up the front, which became an increasingly popular fashion. This example is also rather short, making it look rather like the mandille. He carries a long pistol. These weapons varied considerably in length. Most were wheellocks. Initially, the aristocratic gens d'armes treated these weapons with disdain:

> It may be replied (by those claiming the lancer superior to the reiter), that the gens d'armes also carries one pistol which he uses when his lance is broken. It is soon said, but rarely practised: for the most of them scarcely bother to load their own pistols, but delegate this to their men, who make no greater use of it than themselves, and when they come to fight half of them fail to fire, as has been demonstrated often

enough, or else through poor loading do no hurt. He that will have any use of these weapons, must be as careful of them as of a horse: whereto it is hard to bring other nations (other than Germans), who consider this a base and servile occupation.[11]

Cuirassier

This figure is taken from an engraving of Henry IV's entry into Paris in 1593.[12] The King is depicted mounted, but he is surrounded by a dismounted escort of cuirassiers. They wear functional armour with closed armet helmets. Several of the figures depicted in the engraving wear additional perforated protection beneath their raised visors, as shown. He wears tassettes, but others would have adopted the 'lobster' cuissots, as shown in the previous illustration of Henry IV. Some of the figures have much simpler arrangements for armour around the elbow, with only a rondel covering this area. None wear casaques, having adopted the scarf as a means of recognition instead. These would have been white, regardless of religious confession. This figure's boots have their tops turned down to reveal the long stockings worn underneath. These are, in turn, held up by a button attached to his breeches. Others have garters.

Argoulets

The first figure is taken from a coloured print in the *Album Amicorum* dated to 1595 and labelled 'Ung Argoulet Francais'.[13] In the print, he has a light blue doublet and hanging sleeves, while his normal sleeves, upper and nether hose are scarlet. The plumes on his gilded helmet are also scarlet and blue. The helmet is of a comparatively rare type now referred to as a cabasset-burgonet as it combines features of both. He is shown mounted in the print; he does not carry any pistols on his saddle. The second figure is derived, with the addition of a morion, from a coloured print that was once thought to represent Jean de Poltrot,[14] the man who assassinated François de Guise in 1563. He has a turquoise mandille with gold lace and red lining. His trousers are also red and his shirt is white. The decorated morion secured with a ribbon is from another mid-sixteenth century print showing two arquebusiers à cheval. Both figures shown here carry short, matchlock arquebuses variously known as carbins or petronels. These varied in length, but generally had a barrel of between 60 and 90 centimetres. La Noue, describing the execution of several arquebusiers à cheval for looting in 1562, mentions them wearing casaques.[15] In T&P prints, argoulets are depicted wearing morion helmets but doublets (or conceivably cuirasses) rather than casaques, Like the infantry, a few of these have hanging sleeves. They are clearly wearing spurs, and presumably long boots.

---

11 La Noue, *Discours politiques et militaires*, pp.313–314.

12 'Anonyme, graveur', *Paris Musées*, <https://www.parismuseescollections.paris.fr/fr/musee-carnavalet/oeuvres/comme-le-roy-alla-incontinent-a-l-eglise-de-notre-dame-rendre-graces#infos-principales>, accessed 31 May 2020.

13 'Album Amicorum of a German Soldier', *Los Angeles County Museum of Art*, <https://collections.lacma.org/node/172051>, accessed 31 May 2020.

14 'Foot Soldier [*sic*] holding an Arquebus (formerly identified as Jean Poltrot de Meray)', *Ashmolean Museum* <https://collections.ashmolean.org/collection/browse-9148/per_page/100/offset/500/sort_by/random/category/drawings/start/1500/end/1599/object/49402>, accessed 31 May 2020.

15 La Noue, *Discours politiques et militaires*, p.576.

Argoulets and Trumpeter.

Trumpeter

Each compagnie of gens d'armes had two trumpeters.[16] They are frequently shown in the T&P prints of battle scenes accompanying their armoured colleagues into action. They themselves seem to be wearing little or no armour and carry only a sword for self-defence. They typically wear casaques like those of the rest of the company, with the same false, hanging sleeves. This figure also wears an 'Albanian' hat. The trumpets themselves are decorated with banners. These are usually decorated with heraldic or monogram motifs that do not necessarily have any relationship to the flags carried by the gens d'armes, although the anchor device of Coligny is shown on both. Of the remainder, one shows the chain device of Navarre from a decorated chimney place in the Louvre and another carries the fleur-de-lys of France.

Horses

Courier or Roussin

The courier or coursier was the heaviest and most expensive horse normally used in war. They were ridden, in theory, by all gens d'armes, but in practice probably only by the minority who could afford them. They were probably about 15 hands in height.[17] The roussin was slightly smaller and lighter and probably ridden by the majority, even in the regular compagnies. It was known for its easy gait while walking. The largest and most expensive horses, destriers, were not normally brought onto the battlefield, being reserved for tournaments and displays. Horses were imported into France from Spain, North Africa, Anatolia, Denmark and Eastern Europe.

---

16   Duparcq, *L'art militaire pendant les guerres de religion*, p.40.
17   Phillips, 'Of Nimble Service', pp.77–80.

Repeated ordonnances call for gens d'armes to furnish their horses with barding. This example is of boiled leather (cuir bouilli), though the head piece (chamfrain) is of steel. This type of armour originated in Italy during the fifteenth century and was probably always more common than the all-steel varieties, though naturally far fewer examples survive. This is taken from one partial set in the Metropolitan Museum of Art,[18] which closely matches those in mid-sixteenth century illustrations. The barding was painted in colours matching the sayes of the riders. The front face of the heavy saddle could also be armoured with steel plates. Note the support for the rear of the rider's thigh that can been seen in many illustrations.

War Horses.

Cavaline

The cavaline was a lighter and livelier mount than the courier. The ordonnances specify it for use by the archers of the gendarmerie compagnies and for chevaux legers. The courtaut or courtaud was smaller still and relegated to use by argoulets and as a beast of burden, though a 'double-courtaut' (presumably one of superior quality) was considered an acceptable mount for a chevaux leger as well.

The elegant hanging strapping around the animal's rear quarters (breeching) are typical of the middle of the century and persist toward its end, though gradually replaced by simpler styles. The straps could be significantly longer and the patterns much more complex than the design depicted here. They are shown in a wide variety of colours including black, tan, red, brown, yellow and blue. Two pistol holsters are fastened to the front of the saddle in what became a typical arrangement.

---

18 'Peytral and Crupper Plates, early 16th century', <https://www.metmuseum.org/art/collection/search/684253>, accessed 2 June 2020.

Artillery

Gunner

Gunners are generally depicted as entirely unarmed and wearing normal civilian dress, though occasionally they sport swords and morion helmets. This gunner carries a quadrant. This device was invented by the Venetian engineer, Niccolò Tartaglia, around 1545. The instrument looked like a set square, with a quarter-circle connecting the two sides. From the angle of the square dangled a weighted line. The gunner sighted one side of the quadrant along the barrel of the gun, and the line against the graduated quarter-circle showed the gun's angle of elevation. Gunners then used tables to calculate the range of a shot based upon the elevation of the barrel.

Pionnier

This figure has cast off his doublet and rolled down his nether hose (stockings) to work more comfortably. These were sometimes attached to the upper hose (trunks or breeches) or, as here, separate garments. His simple shirt is gathered around the neck with a drawstring. The illustration also shows a reconstruction of the green livery jackets with white crosses worn by the pionniers raised in Berne for service in 1573.

Coulverine

This image is taken from an oil painting showing the Huguenot sack of Lion in 1562.[19] The carriage is shown ochre-coloured and may, therefore, represent unpainted wood. The wheel rims, reinforcing bands and chain all appear to be made of iron, whereas the gun barrel itself is bronze. The wheels as well as the cheeks and trail of the carriage are far more heavily built than the canon of succeeding centuries. Next to the gun itself is a linstock (boutefeu), in this case, a simple wooden shaft with a metal head through which is threaded a length of match.

Gun Barrels

The illustration shows the relative dimensions of the standardised gun calibres introduced under Henry II, specifically: the cannon, grande-coulverine, bastard-coulverine, coulevrine-moyenne, faucon and fauconneau. Although standardisation of the bore width and barrel length had been achieved, the guns themselves varied considerably in appearance. These are rather plain examples, but some were highly decorated. An extant example of a bastard-coulverine dated to 1548 has an octagonal external profile and is not only decorated with Henry II's crowned 'H', but also the crescent moon devices of his mistress, Diane de Poictiers.

---

19 Le Sac de Lyon par les Calvinistes en 1562', *Gadagne Musées*, http://www.gadagne.musees. lyon.fr/index.php/histoire_fr/Histoire/Explorer-le-musee/Les-collections/Oeuvres-choisies/ Peinture, accessed 11 October 2020.

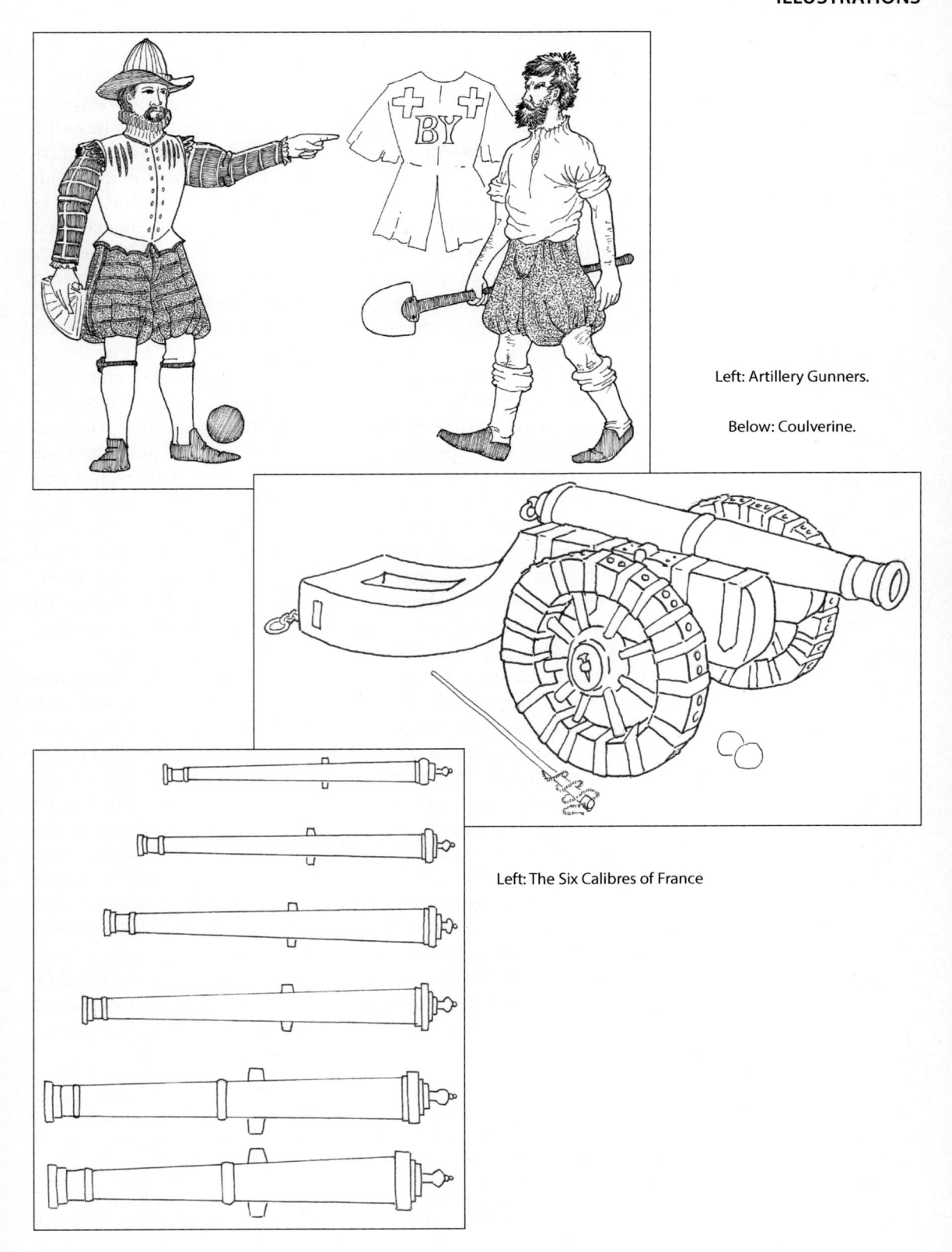

Left: Artillery Gunners.

Below: Coulverine.

Left: The Six Calibres of France

Infantry

Unlike their mounted brethren, the infantry who fought in the wars were not generally uniformed. A few exceptions to this general rule may be noted. Firstly, units, either whole regiments or, more likely, individual compagnies, might be issued with clothing or cloth at the same time. This might result in an almost accidental degree of uniformity for a short period. This is likely to have occurred only when units were campaigning for an extended period and the troops lacked the wherewithal to buy clothing for themselves. Secondly, units may have received clothing when they took part in a special event. Illustrations showing Henry II's triumphal entry into Rouen show small bodies of foot in near identical garb.[20] One group has black doublets with red sleeves and hose. Another has white doublets with yellow sleeves and hose. And yet another, red doublets with grey sleeves and white hose. Finally, infantry might wear a specific colour as a sign of their allegiance. At Moncontour, the entire Protestant army, including their German mercenaries, is reported to have worn white: 'The French cavalry with their normal white casaques, the reiters and all the infantry, both French and foreign, wearing their white shirts' (that is, over their armour and doublets).[21] This was a common enough tactic of the era, designed to help identify friend from foe. Hence it was widely used in night-attacks, to such an extent that such actions were known as camisades (from the Spanish camisa, or shirt). Many also wore a yellow and black scarf in honour of the recently deceased Zweibrücken. In contrast, The royal army wore red scarves in honour of their ally, the King of Spain, an act considered scandalous in some quarters.

Coloured illustrations showing French infantry invariably show them wearing a wide variety of individual colours. These were generally colourful and show little difference between the various factions. It is sometime suggested that the Huguenots adopted a more sober appearance than their Catholic opponents. Certainly, their preachers continually stressed the importance of doing so. Judging by contemporary images, there is little evidence this was complied with. An oil painting depicting the sack of Lion by Huguenots in 1562 depicts their troops in clothing little different from another painting showing Catholic troops participating in the Sainct-Barthélemy's Day Massacre.[22] An English commentator in 1596 was critical of foreign habits picked up by soldiers returning from overseas, including those of 'Frenchmen so garish and light in apparel'.[23] These English troops had, of course, been fighting for Henry IV. The only instance of such a difference mentioned by commentators occurred at the Battle of Coutras, where the gorgeously arrayed but inexperienced Royalists were defeated by Navarre's scruffy but veteran

---

20 'Relation de l'entrée de Henri II, roi de France, à Rouen, le 1er octobre 1550', *Rouen Nouvelles Bibliothèques* <https://rnbi.rouen.fr/en/notice/relation-de-lentr%C3%A9e-de-henri-ii-roi-de-france-%C3%A0-rouen-le-1er-octobre-1550-32>, accessed 11 October 2020.
21 La Popelinière, *La vraye et entière histoire des troubles*, p.311.
22 'Le Sac de Lyon par les Calvinistes en 1562' and 'Le massacre de la Saint-Barthélemy'.
23 Quoted in Conyers Read, *William Lambarde and Local Government* (Ithica, NY: Cornell University Press, 1966), p.129.

troops. This seems to be a comment specifically relating to the nature of these two forces, rather than any confessional differences, however.

Colours worn by infantrymen run the whole gamut of the spectrum: red, scarlet, pink, pale yellow, beige, white, grey, mauve, green and blue. On the whole, brown seems to have been avoided and black reserved for gentlemen. The upper and lower parts of the hose could either be the same or different colours, as could the body and sleeves of the doublet. Shoes were dark brown or black and hats were typically black, brown or grey.

Officers

Officers above the rank of serjeant are usually depicted either carrying an esponton or a sword and shield. The first figure comes from a print showing Huguenots fighting Native Americans during their ill-fated colonisation attempt.[24] He wears a cabasset and gilded peasecod cuirass over fashionably 'pinked' breaches and doublet. The pinking process involved punching small holes in the outer layer of the garment to reveal the lining beneath. He also has a sturdy round shield strapped to his arm for additional protection. Shields were also carried by troops, including gens d'armes, when assaulting breaches. They were often shot-proof, at least in theory. His upper hose are longer and narrower than in many other images, resembling seventeenth-century breeches. They became increasingly popular towards the end of the wars, but never entirely eclipsed the shorter, more voluminous alternatives.

The second figure, from a T&P engraving illustrating the peace talks near Orleans in 1563,[25] depicts an officer who has set aside his helmet in favour of a fashionable hat, complete with ribbon and plumes. His upper hose are both slashed and pinked, in this case with little z-shaped holes. The doublet has padded and slashed shoulder-rolls. His esponton is studded with decorative nails and is adorned with two tassels.

The steel shield was a heavy object, between six and 10 kg in weight. Officers frequently employed boys to carry them, even on the battlefield. This boy is also wearing the officer's morion-cabbaset helmet and carrying his coutelas. He is a composite figure derived from the T&P engraving of the peace talks in 1563 and oil paintings showing the clerical processions in Paris.[26] The boy's clothing does not differ significantly from that of an adult male. Those carrying shields at the head of the clerical procession are all dressed in white. The front surfaces of shields were often engraved or otherwise highly decorated. Some were gilded or silvered. Spiked bosses were also a common feature. This example, like many, has a thick material fringe. During the Siege of Rouen in 1562 the commander of the Sainct Caterine fort, Captain Monneins, was recognisable to the besiegers when walking the battlements by the green velvet fringe of his shield.[27]

---

24 'La Floride Française: Scènes de la vie Indiennes, peintes en 1564', Rare Book and Special Collections Division, Library of Congress <https://www.loc.gov/exhibits/1492/eurocla.html>, accessed 19 October 2020.

25 Benedict, *Tortorel et Perrissin*, p.25.

26 Benedict, *Tortorel et Perrissin*, p.25.

27 Duparcq, *L'art militaire pendant les guerres de religion*, p.36.

Infantry Officers.

Serjeant

This figure, taken from a T&P illustration of the killing of Seigneur de la Motte Gondrin,[28] wears a hat with a large brim. This style became increasingly common as the century progressed. Other serjeants are shown in helmets instead.

Mail was still used during the second half of the sixteenth century, though much less frequently than the preceding era. Gentlemen sometimes wore mail beneath their doublets if they feared assassination or brawls. The ordonnances specify mail as an acceptable form of armour for lighter cavalry. When depicted being worn by infantry, it is normally only shown as officers' sleeves, as in this instance, though it may extend beneath the doublet.

The two tassels on the serjeant's halberd are reproduced here as drawn in the original, with both the body or mould of the tassel and the fringe hanging down. A more common arrangement seems to have been to form both around the shaft of the weapon. France had, incidentally, a virtual monopoly on the production of 'passements' (trimmings of this nature) during the sixteenth century, due to the quality of workmanship and volumes produced. Many of these skilled passementiers were Huguenots.

---

28 Benedict, *Tortorel et Perrissin*, p.13.

Serjent, Drummer and Enseigne.

Drummer

This figure is derived from the T&P print of the peace talks near Orleans in 1563.[29] His hat is of a type frequently shown being worn by gentlemen, though this example lacks the plumes often sported by the wealthy elite. His clothing does suggest a certain amount of finery, however. He has a high collar to his doublet, again a feature associated with richer clothing. His shirt protrudes above, its folds resembling an informal ruff. Apart from its large size, the drum resembles the military side drums of the following centuries. It is suspended by a decorated strap.

Each company had one or two musicians. These could be fifers as well as drummers.

Enseigne

This illustration is taken from a T&P engraving showing the assault on Montbrison.[30] As an officer, this enseigne wears fashionable clothing and richly decorated armour: a cuirass, gorget and burgonet. His only weapon is a sword. The flag itself was typically square, six feet or more in depth and length. It was carried on a relatively short pole. Only a foot or so of the haft was available to grip beneath the flag. These flags are normally depicted being held in one hand only, often at shoulder height, so they cannot have been too heavy. They would normally have been constructed from a light material such as silk.

Arquebusiers

The first figure is typical of the arquebusiers shown by T&P. He is taken from the scene depicting the death of Seigneur de la Motte Gondrin.[31] T&P invariably

---

29 Benedict, *Tortorel et Perrissin*, p.25.
30 Benedict, *Tortorel et Perrissin*, p.15.
31 Benedict, *Tortorel et Perrissin*, p.13.

Arquebusiers.

depict arquebusiers with morions when they wear helmets, and the vast majority of their figures do so. These often sport a significant amount of decorative engraving, as do the few extant examples. He carries his tasselled powder horn on a cord across his body and a simple sword at his waist. Over his lower hose he wears stockings held up by garters around the knee. The more detailed figures in T&P prints normally wear clothing with a significant amount of decoration and no differentiation between Catholics and Huguenots.

The second figure, from the same source as the first shows a back view of an arquebusier in generally similar dress. His tight doublet sleeves are puffed and slashed at the elbows, probably to allow greater freedom of movement. The match for his arquebus is wound round his left wrist.

The third arquebusier is taken from the painting of the sack of Lion.[32] Unlike all T&P figures, he wears a burgonet. In addition to this he wears a padded jacque. Presumably, this is leather, as all the examples in the painting are coloured either brown or tan. His lower hose have been rolled down for the sake of comfort, a common occurrence in hot weather or on the march.

The final arquebusier, from the same source as the first and second, wears a hat in place of a morion. This is a broad-brimmed example that was common throughout the period of the wars, becoming more so towards the end. Two later forms of headgear are also shown. Both are common in the 1580s and 1590s. One resembles a bowler hat with a taller crown and more exaggerated curves to the brim. The other continued to be widely worn in the opening decades of the seventeenth century, as typified by pilgrims, puritans and witchfinders in popular imagination. The upturned brim of this example carries a badge showing allegiance to the House of Guise and the Ligue. He

---

32 'Le Sac de Lyon par les Calvinistes en 1562'.

Arquebusier and Caliverman.

also wears a mandille over his doublet, with the sleeves left unfastened as was normally the case. Although more often associated with cavalrymen, this garment was worn by infantry as well.

Caliverman

This figure also comes from the print of Huguenots in North America, though the arquebus he carries in the original has been replaced by a longer caliver and a forked rest.[33] This weapon still has a significantly curved stock. As the century progressed, this grew straighter and was nestled into the shoulder for firing 'in the Spanish manner'. He wears a ruff rather than a plain falling collar. This, and his fashionably 'pinked' clothing suggests a man of some wealth.

Armed Cleric

This figure is taken from the various paintings showing the ecclesiastical processions in Paris during 1590 in support of the Ligue. The participants are shown in their clerical garb: the grey, brown, black and white habits of the various monastic orders and the black robes of priests. To these have been added, rather incongruously, various items of military equipment. This figure carries a caliver, has a powder flask hanging round his neck and wears a simple sword. Others add a morion helmet and their officers, body armour. The latter either carry shields or short pole arms, as would have been normal in any body of footmen. No pikes can be seen in these paintings, but a woodblock print showing the same event does include these weapons. The figure shown here does not appear to be very confident in the handling of his firearm. The stock is much straighter than in previous examples, though he makes little use of this improvement. His hat displays a white or red double cross of Lorraine, indicating his allegiance to the house of Guise. These ecclesiastical units did not take part in any battles of the era but may have manned the walls of the capital during Henry IV's various forays against the city.

---

33 *La Floride Française: Scènes de la vie Indiennes, peintes en 1564.*

Pikemen.

Pikemen

The first figure, from the beginning of the wars, shows a fully equipped pikeman. He is derived from a T&P print depicting the assault on Montbrison in 1562.[34] The pikes are foreshortened in this print for artistic purposes, but they are clearly not intended to represent officer's espontons because of the grips on the shafts. The T&P prints invariably show pikemen wearing the burgonet. Full armour for the arms would have probably been restricted to only the best-equipped units. A cuirass, tassettes and spalières would have been more normal for the 'corseleted' pikemen.

The second figure depicts an unarmoured or 'seiche' pikeman. T&P prints tend to show all pikemen as armoured but muster rolls include a proportion number without such protection. Given the parlous state of Huguenot finances, the few pikemen found in their regional forces were probably equipped in this manner. The figure is actually taken from painted tiles dated to 1586 or 87, showing Spanish infantry celebrating the defeat of the English at the Azores. However, the clothing is very similar to that worn by their French neighbours. He wears a leather jacque and an Albanian hat in lieu of a helmet.

The final figure shows a pikeman from the last period of the wars. He is taken from an engraving dated 1606 depicting the expulsion of the Spanish garrison from Paris.[35] He wears a simple peasecod cuirass with gorget and tassets. The narrowness of the former between the shoulders suggests it may have been designed to be worn with spalières. His helmet is a cabasset, with articulated cheek guards.

34 Benedict, *Tortorel et Perrissin*, p.15.

35 'Départ des espagnols de Paris le 22 mars 1594', *Wikimedia Commons* <https://commons.wikimedia.org/wiki/File:D%C3%A9part_des_espagnols_de_Paris_le_22_mars_1594_Mus%C3%A9e_Carnavalet.jpg> accessed 19 October 2020. The original is in the Hôtel Carnavalet, Cabinet Des Arts Graphiques, Paris.

Royalist and Catholic Flags

Royalist and Catholic troops are normally depicted carrying flags bearing the white Cross of St. Denys. This had been worn by French armies since the middle ages as a national identifier, much as English armies wore the red Cross of St. George. It appeared on both flags and livery coats before and during the Italian Wars. Most Royalist flags depicted during the Wars of Religion continued this tradition.

The Catholic Ligue also adopted a cross as its most frequently used device, but in this case normally a cross with each arm ending in a perpendicular bar, known as a cross potent in heraldry. Sometimes the arms ended in a fleurs-de-lys, becoming a cross fleury. Green was the livery colour of the Guisard faction, and appeared on the flags of their followers, alongside the double cross of Lorraine. After the assassination of Henry de Guise in 1588, his followers adopted black flags as a sign of mourning.

Each commander of any importance with the army normally displayed his own standard. These were carried by their escort or their own company of gens d'armes. Henry III's banner was striped yellow–purple–green with a white scroll on the purple stripe bearing the motto MANET VLTIMA COELO in gold lettering. [36]

Royal Banner
I. A large blue banner, presumably bearing the gold fleurs-de-lys device of France was flown when the king or the lieutenant-general de royaume was present in the field. This example has a gold fringe and tassels.[37]

Army Banner
II. This depicts another large flag, probably that of the army commander. It comes from a print depicting the Siege of La Rochelle.[38] The colours are unknown, but the cross is most likely to have been white. It is about half again as deep and twice as long as the cavalry pennons shown in the same print. The shield probably carries the fleurs-de-lys of France, as can just about be seen in a similar flag shown by T&P.[39]

Ligue Religious Banner
III. This flag was carried by clerical adherents of the Ligue during the procession through Paris in 1593.[40] It is shown in several different sources, though a little differently in each case. The example depicted has a dark green

---

36 Funcken, *The Age of Chivalry*, Part 3, p.79 shows the banners of Charles IX, Henry II and Henry IV.
37 'Relation de l'entrée de Henri II, roi de France, à Rouen, le 1er octobre 1550' for the style of the flag, though this does not carry the fleurs-de-lys.
38 'Siege of La Rochelle 1572–1573', *Wikimedia Commons* <https://commons.wikimedia.org/wiki/File:Siege_of_La_Rochelle_1572_1573.jpg>, accessed 25 October 2020.
39 Benedict, *Tortorel et Perrissin*, p.25.
40 'Première grande procession de la Ligue pour maintenir le moral des assiégés', *Carnavalet, Histoire de Paris* <https://www.carnavalet.paris.fr/en/premiere-grande-procession-de-la-ligue-pour-maintenir-le-moral-des-assieges>, accessed 25 October 2020.

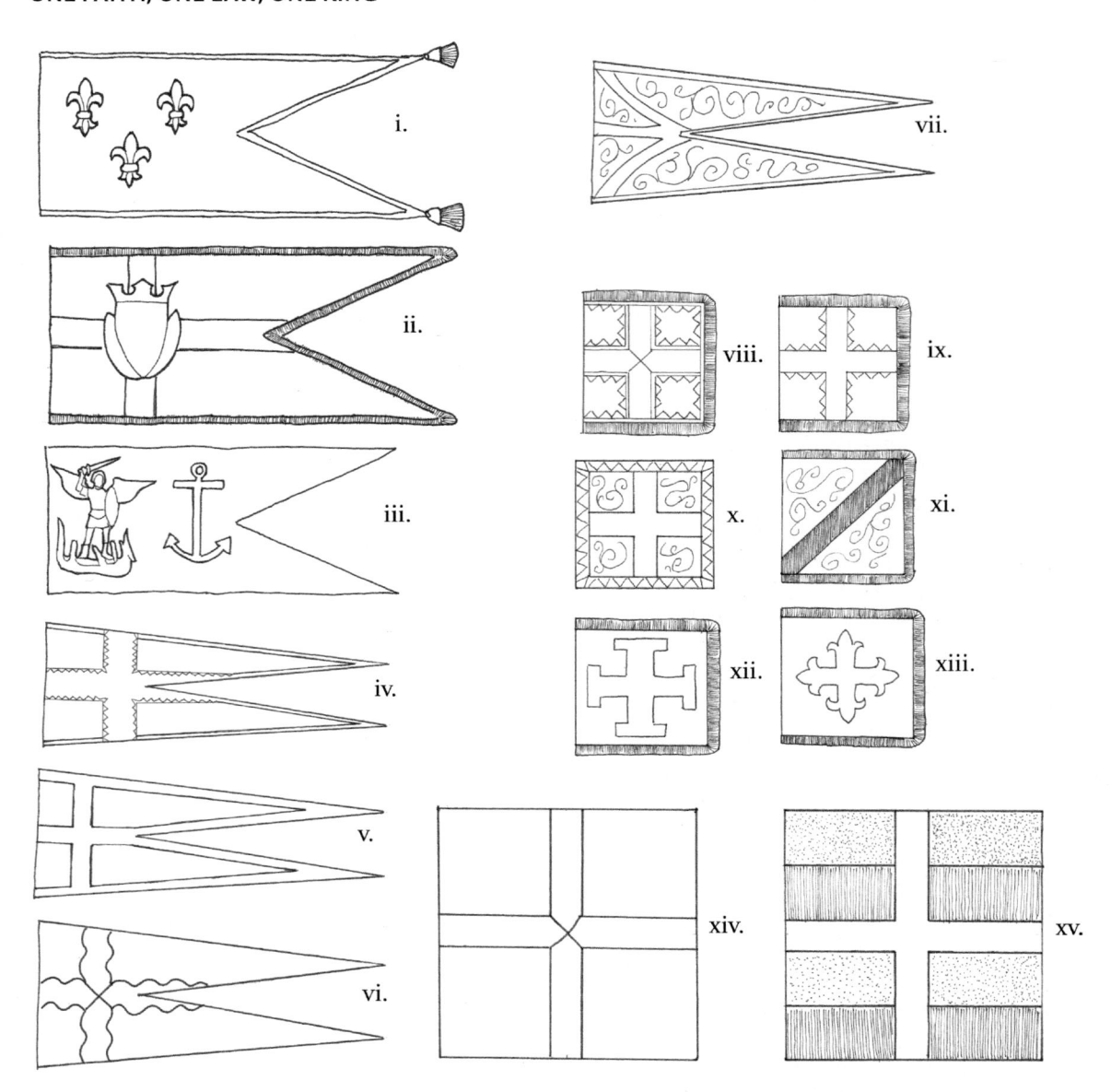

Royalist and Catholic Flags.

background. The angel, presumably Michael, is white with grey armour. The dragon he stands upon is red with a yellow belly. The anchor is silver or grey. In three other illustrations, a cross is positioned between the angel and anchor. In one of these versions, the field is white, the dragon green, the cross gold, the anchor silver and the angel silver with a golden shield and armour. In another the flag is pale green, both the cross and anchor are silver, the dragon in dark green and the angel is white with grey armour and a gold skirt. The final version has a red field. The angel is gold with silver armour and shield. The cross is also gold, as is the cross bar of the anchor, the remainder of which is black. The dragon is red and gold.

Royalist Cavalry Cornettes

Cavalry flags (of both sides) were generally swallow-tailed or square. Judging by pictorial evidence, the former seem to be most common in the early wars, giving way to square flags later in the era, though both are frequently shown together. The square standards seem to be about 60 cm deep and long. The swallow-tailed versions were of similar or slightly less depth but typically about two to three times as long. Both versions were carried by all types of cavalry.

Cavalry flags are normally shown being carried in the centre of bodies of horsemen, sometime a little ahead of the main line. A gens d'armes compagnie contained two officers associated with flags: the enseigne and the guidon. It is, therefore, likely that each company carried two flags. Whether they were the same or different is unknown, but some of the cornettes dating from the reign of Henry II and captured at Sainct Quentin and Gravelines (see below) show marked similarities to each other and could have been taken from a single company.

IV. This flag conforms to the normal arrangement of Royalist cornettes, with the added variation of a dagged edge to the cross itself.[41]

V. This flag is typical of the many shown being carried by Royalist cavalry in T&P, though there are many variations in the presence and thickness of the border. The few coloured illustrations almost always depict the cross in white, though the Jarnac tapestry has gold/yellow crosses on white fields as well.[42] Other field colours depicted include red, blue and yellow.

VI. This is an unusual variation in the shape of the cross itself. It is shown by T&P being carried alongside flags VII and X, below, at Jarnac.[43]

VII. This flag is one of the few clearly illustrated by T&P that does not bear a cross. The devices on others are indistinct, but not crosses. The decoration on the field probably represents the diapered patterns in the cloth itself This is likely to have been a widespread feature of such standards, but not often depicted in the small scale normally used by T&P. This is shown being carried at Jarnac.[44]

VIII. This design is shown twice by T&P, at both Cognac and Jarnac.[45] The simple cross design has been embellished by borders and edging.

IX. This design has similarities with the previous flag. It is shown being carried at Dreux by T&P.[46]

---

41   Benedict, *Tortorel et Perrissin*, p.29.
42   One of a set of three tapestries now in the Musee National de la Renaissance at Ecouen representing the battles of St Denis and Jarnac. Possibly commissioned by Michel d'Asterac Seigneur de Fontrailles. Each is closely based on a corresponding T&P engraving.
43   Benedict, *Tortorel et Perrissin*, p.32.
44   Benedict, *Tortorel et Perrissin*, p.32.
45   Benedict, *Tortorel et Perrissin*, p.29 and p.32.
46   Benedict, *Tortorel et Perrissin*, p.22.

X. This flag also has diapered patterns on the field. It is shown by T&P being carried at Jarnac.[47] Unlike most square cavalry flags shown in these engravings, this example lacks a fringe, though it does have a decorative border.

XI. This flag is interesting because its main device is not a cross, but a 'bend' or diagonal stripe. This was widely used by the Royalist's Huguenot opponents. The bend is occasionally seen on French flags in the reign of Henry II prior to the outbreak of the wars (see below). Three flags bearing this device are shown by T&P at the battle of Moncontour.[48] They are clearly being carried by the Royalist side and do not appear to be trophies. In two cases the bend is shown going from the top of the hoist to the bottom of the fly rather than as shown here.

Ligue Cavalry Cornettes

XII. This is the cross potent widely used by forces of the Ligue. It is shown on both a cavalry cornette and infantry enseignes in a print showing the Battle of Ivry.[49] It is used to clearly distinguish the Ligue forces from Henry IV's Royalists carrying the Cross of Sainct Denys.

XIII. This shows another variation of the cross used by Ligue forces, the cross fleury, from the same source as the last. This was a device used on flags during the reign of Henry II and during the Wars of Religion as well. It is shown by T&P being carried at Moncontour.[50]

Royalist Infantry Enseignes

Royalist infantry flags are almost invariably shown with a large cross overall. The field is either plain or divided into vertical or horizontal stripes. The flags of infantry units are depicted strung out along the width of a unit of foot when in battle. Normally this means in the middle of a block of pikemen, but they are also shown in units consisting only of arquebusiers. When on the march, they are sometimes shown at the head of a column. Enfans perdus are not generally shown carrying flags. Each compagnie would have its own enseigne, carried by the officer of the same name.

XIV. T&P show many Royalist banners, nearly all of which are simple crosses on plain backgrounds. A few examples have a modicum of decoration, as in this case, taken from the engraving of the Combat at Cognat.[51] Colours unknown.

XV. In a few cases the field of the flag is sub-divided into four to eight horizontal or vertical stripes, as in this example. In some examples the stripes are wavy. Colours unknown.

---

47   Benedict, *Tortorel et Perrissin*, p.32.
48   Benedict, *Tortorel et Perrissin*, p.35.
49   Anon.,'Bataille d'Ivry', *BNF Gallica Digital Library* < https://gallica.bnf.fr/ark:/12148/btv1b8400936s.item>, accessed 2 May 2020.
50   Benedict, *Tortorel et Perrissin*, p.35.
51   Benedict, *Tortorel et Perrissin*, p.29.

Huguenot Flags

The main Huguenot symbol carried on their flags was a heraldic device known as a 'bend': a stripe running diagonally from the top of the hoist to the bottom edge of the fly. Normally this was white, but on pale coloured banners, it could be a dark colour instead. This symbol was meant to represent the white scarf, worn from shoulder to hip, by Huguenot officers (and after Henry IV's accession by all French officers until the Revolution). The colour white, like the casaques of the gens d'armes, was chosen as a symbol of both purity and the lack of allegiance to any noble faction.

Many of the illustrations reproduced here are derived from the engravings of Tortorel and Perrissen (T&P). These two men, and their publisher Jacques le Challeux, were all Huguenots and produced their work in Geneva. Their informants were also likely to be have been mainly drawn from the Protestant community. T&P show a much greater variety of designs for the flags carried by Huguenot cavalry than those of their Catholic opponents. If this reflects reality, then it could be explained by the more irregular nature of the compagnies they raised. Alternatively, it may be that at least some of the Huguenot flags they depict were based on specific originals rather than simply generic images (as the Catholic flags seem to be). So, for example, Admiral Coligny's position is repeatedly indicated by both a swallow-tailed flag carrying an anchor motif and a fringed, square banner with three wavy bars in a darker colour.

Twelve of the Huguenot flags captured at the Battle of Jarnac were recorded by an unknown Spaniard.[52] This record consists of ink and watercolour images and some brief notes that identify the banners with specific individuals. They all appear to be cavalry cornettes, though the shape of some of the flags and orientation of some of the designs are highly unusual and may represent errors by the artist.

XVI. Henry IV's banner is striped, from the top, red-white-blue-red-white-blue.[53] The monogram, sceptre, swords, crown and edging of the scroll are gold. The scroll itself is red with black lettering. The six clubs are ermine: white with black tufts. The motto is given as either DUO PREATENDIT UNUS or DUO PROTEGIT UNUS (One Protects the Two), referring to the sword and sceptres.

Huguenot Cavalry Cornettes
XVII. This is one of three similar plain flags shown being carried by a body of cavalry commanded by the Prince de Condé at Jarnac in both the T&P prints depicting the battle.[54] Other versions are square or have a double rounded fly. They all have ornate edging but no device. An identical flag is shown in the

---

52 Alfonso de Ceballos-Escalera y Gila, 'Los estandartes de los caudillos hugonotes en la batalia de Jarnac, el 13 de marzo de 1569' in *Comunicaciones del XI Congreso Internacional de Vexilología* (Madrid: Sociedad Española de Vexilología,1985), pp.298–301.
53 Widely reproduced, but this also from Funcken, *The Age of Chivalry*, Part 3, p.79.
54 Benedict, *Tortorel et Perrissin*, pp.31–32.

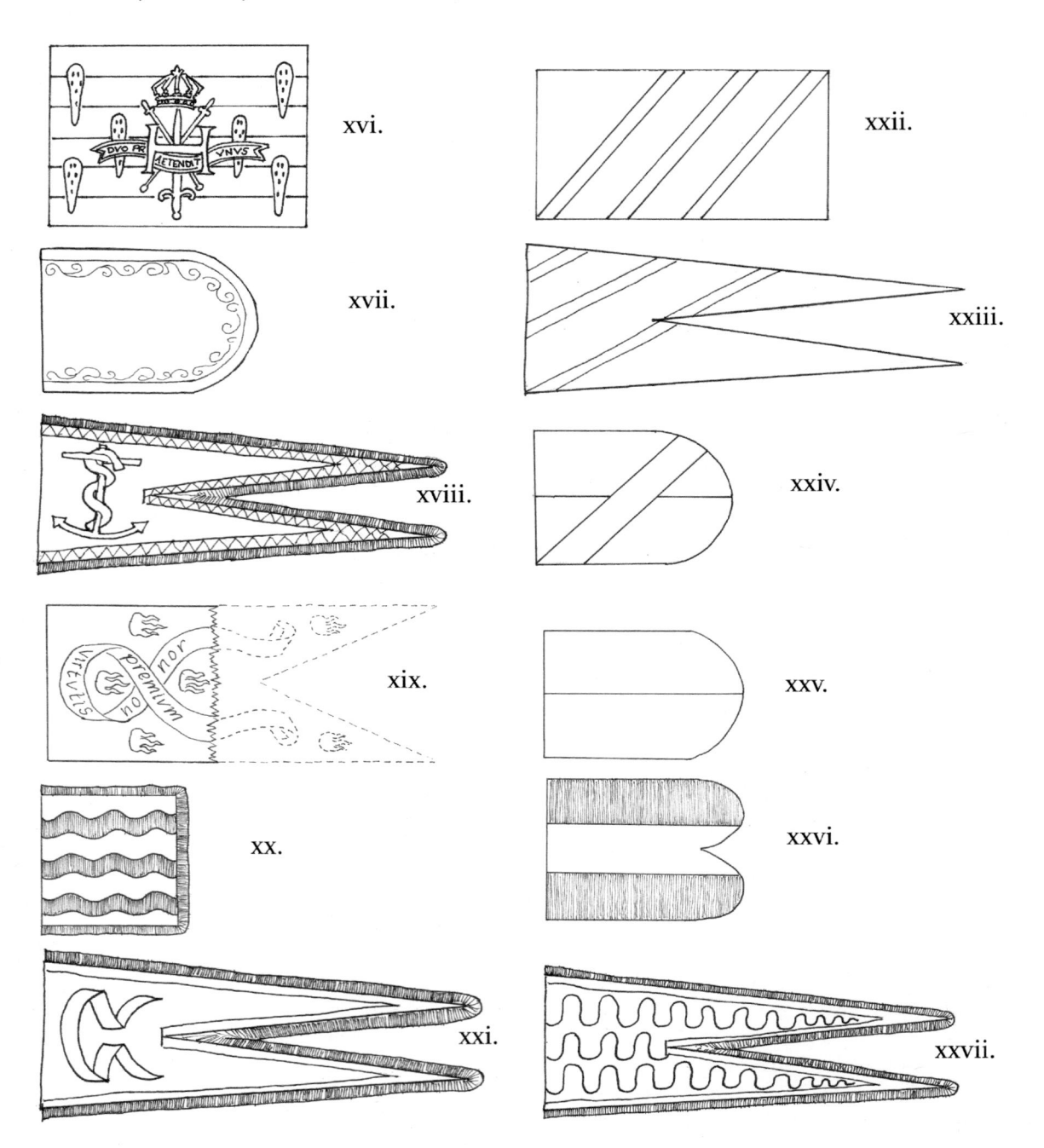

Huguenot Flags 1.

first print being carried by the squadron of Henry de Navarre. Two of the flags captured in the battle are ascribed to these two prominent Huguenot leaders. Both are plain white. That of the Condé is shown twice as deep as long, which would be highly unusual. It is likely it is depicted incorrectly and the dimensions should be reversed. Navarre's flag is square. White, or very pale yellow, was the livery colour of the house of Bourbon, to which both princes belonged. The Jarnac tapestry depicts it as a plain white flag with light blue or grey border (which might represent a silver fringe).

XVIII. This is undoubtedly the personal banner of Admiral Coligny or that of his gens d'armes company, it appears in the T&P prints of the battles of Jarnac, La Roche l'Abielle and Moncontour.[55] It is often associated with Flag XX, below. The Jarnac tapestry shows a similar banner with a white field and a dark coloured anchor and fringe.

XIX. A cornette belonging to the Admiral was amongst those captured at Jarnac and sent to the Pope as trophies. It is torn, but the remaining portion is red, with four yellow flame devices and a white scroll. The latter bears the motto PREMIUM VIRTUTIS HONOR (Honour is the Reward of Virtue). It is possible the flag originally had tails, and this illustration is a possible reconstruction. None of the 12 captured flags are depicted with fringes. This may be due to a simplified depiction, as most shown in other sources are.

XX. From the T&P prints showing the Battle of Jarnac.[56] It is associated with Flag XVIII, above, the Admiral's banner, in both prints. The Jarnac tapestry shows the flag as white with dark wavy bands.

XXI. Shown being carried by Andelot's escort of gens d'armes from the Orleans garrison at the peace talks in March 1563 in a T&P print.[57] Colours unknown. The scroll device bears some similarities to Flag XIX, above.

XXII. This cornette is ascribed to Andelot in the record of the banners captured at Jarnac. It is white with three bends that are reversed, or 'sinister' (from the upper fly to the lower hoist rather than the other way round) in blue.

XXIII. A very similar flag to Flag XXII, above, is shown in the T&P engravings being carried by gens d'armes retreating from the Battle of Dreux.[58] While this has a swallow-tail, it is tempting to believe they are two different renderings of the same object. Colours unknown.

XXIV. Yet another flag showing the bend sinister, this from the banners captured at Jarnac. It is brown or tawny above and blue below. The bend is

55 Benedict, *Tortorel et Perrissin*, pp.31, 32, 33 and 35.
56 Benedict, *Tortorel et Perrissin*, pp.31–32.
57 Benedict, *Tortorel et Perrissin*, p,25.
58 Benedict, *Tortorel et Perrissin*, p.22.

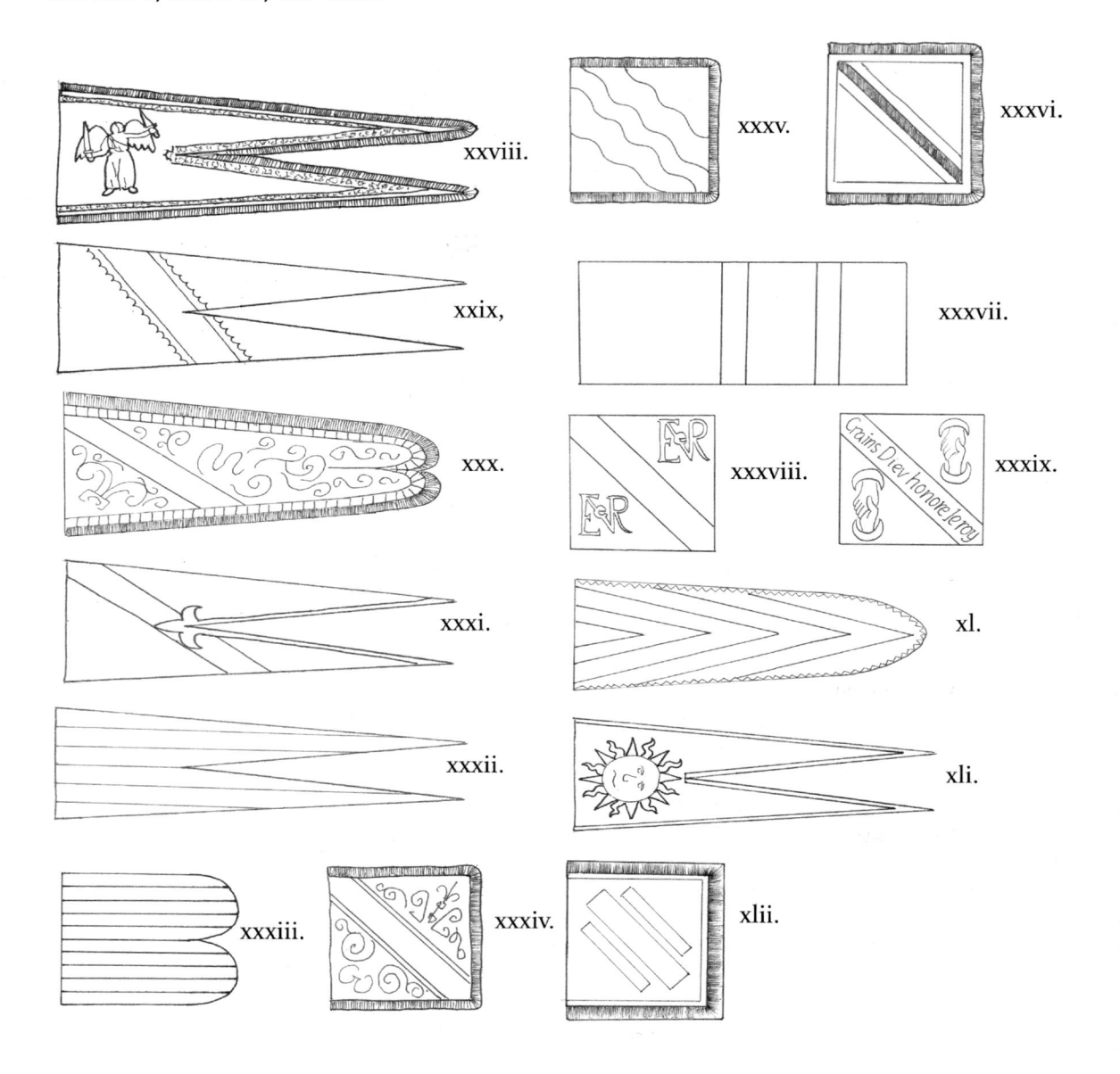

Huguenot Flags 2.

white. The document describes the flag as belonging to 'de Pouts de Bretaña'. Pouts is a village in the Principality of Bearn, so the unknown individual may have served in one of the compagnies raised by its ruler, Jeanne de Navarre. If so, the connection with Bretaigne (or even Britain) is unclear.

XXV. This captured Jarnac banner is described as belonging to François de Rochefoucauld. It is of a commonly encountered shape. The upper half is white and the lower described as dark brown, almost black. The watercolour from which it is taken may well have been originally black but faded over time.

XXVI. Another of the captured Jarnac banners, this time belonging to Montgomery. It is brown with a central horizontal stripe of white. A similar banner to this, though with only a single rounded tail, and from the same source, is white with a narrower band of blue. It is noted as belonging to 'Sancte Mesme', presumably Isaac de Culant Seigneur de Sainct Mesme (Saint-Même-les-Carrières).

XXVII. Shown carried by gens d'armes at Moncontour in a T&P print.[59] It is carried in the same squadron as Flags XVIII and XX, above. Acier's company also formed part of this squadron, so it may be associated with him. Colours unknown.

XXVIII. This standard is unusual for an army that espoused iconoclastic tendencies. It depicts an angel carrying two swords. It is shown being carried at the Combat of Cognat (La Fère) in 1568 by a group of gens d'armes led by the Jacques de Bousé Sieur de Ponsenat (who was killed in the fight) by T&P.[60] Colours unknown.

XXIX. Shown carried by gens d'armes at the Battle of Dreux in one of the T&P prints.[61] Colours unknown. A tapestry, from the same set as the Jarnac tapestry, depicting the Battle of Sainct Denys shows simple flags of this type that are yellow with a white bend, light blue with a white bend and white with a black bend. A coloured print of Moncontour shows a standard that is yellow with a dark blue bend.

XXX. Shown being carried by gens d'armes at Bourges in 1569 by T&P.[62] The shape of the flag is unusual, but not unique. The field is diapered. Colours unknown.

XXXI. This standard from one of the T&P prints depicting the Battle of Druex is carried by gens d'armes and combines the Huguenot bend with a fleur-de-lys device.[63] Colours unknown, though the field is a dark colour.

XXXII. From the T&P print of the Battle of Moncontour, shown being carried by gens d'armes commanded by the Comte de Choisy.[64] Colours unknown. A similar flag, but with a single rounded tail is shown being carried at Jarnac.

XXXIII. This another striped cornette, one of those captured at Jarnac. The colours are, from the top, brown–cream–white–brown–cream–white–brown–cream–white–brown. It is possible the cream is faded yellow and the brown, black. The flag is described as 'carried by Castellier' (Castellier Portant). This may refer to Jacques de Brevedent, Sieur de Castellier.

---

59 Benedict, *Tortorel et Perrissin*, p.35.
60 Benedict, *Tortorel et Perrissin*, p.29.
61 Benedict, *Tortorel et Perrissin*, p.22.
62 Benedict, *Tortorel et Perrissin*, p.39.
63 Benedict, *Tortorel et Perrissin*, p.20.
64 Benedict, *Tortorel et Perrissin*, p.35.

XXXIV. From the T&P print of the assault on Monbrison by the forces of Baron de Adrets.[65] A similar banner is shown alongside Flag XI, above, at La Fère. Again, the diapered background is shown in this detailed image. Colours unknown.

XXXV. From the T&P print of Moncontour.[66] Colours unknown.

XXXVI. This is from the T&P print of the Battle of Moncontour.[67] Another similar banner has a scalloped rather than plain border. Colours unknown.

XXXVII. This is one of the captured Jarnac flags. It is roughly twice as long as deep, with a dark blue field and two narrow white stripes on either side of a red stripe. Although shown as a simple rectangle, it is possible the original had a rounded fly or tails. The flag is identified as belonging to 'Clermo d'Amboise', presumably Antoine de Clermont d'Amboise, Marquis de Resnel, who fought at Jarnac and Moncontour. He was later murdered by his cousin, the Mignon Louis Bussy d'Amboise during the 1572 Massacre.

XXXVIII. Another of the Jarnac trophies. This is shown mounted on its side, so the bend is sinister, but this is undoubtedly an error as the monograms would be on their sides. The upper right field is red and the lower left is green. The bend is white and the monograms gold. The flag's notation is 'Le Jenuc Fernach'. The meaning is unknown, but the monogram should possibly be read as FERN.

XXXIX. This Jarnac trophy is ascribed to the famous La Noue. It is shown upside down in the original watercolour. The field is red, with white bend and hand/crescent moon devices and black motto reading CRAINS DIEV HONORE LE ROY (Fear God, Honour the King).

XL. This is shown in the T&P prints of Jarnac in the cavalry commanded by Admiral Coligny and his brother Andelot.[68] A long, single-tailed pennon is carried by François de Briquemont's command at Jarnac. This also has chevrons, but pointing along the flag rather than upwards. It has a scalloped border. No colours are known for either of these flags.

XLI. This is from the T&P print of the Battle of Moncontour.[69] It is carried by the gens d'armes under the command of Soubise. Colours unknown.

XLII. This is shown in the T&P prints of both Jarnac and Moncontour.[70] In the former it is carried by Soubise's gens d'armes, the latter by those commanded by Choisy. Colours unknown.

---

65 Benedict, *Tortorel et Perrissin*, p.15.
66 Benedict, *Tortorel et Perrissin*, p.35.
67 Benedict, *Tortorel et Perrissin*, p.35.
68 Benedict, *Tortorel et Perrissin*, p.31 and p.35.
69 Benedict, *Tortorel et Perrissin*, p.35
70 Benedict, *Tortorel et Perrissin*, p.31 and p.35.

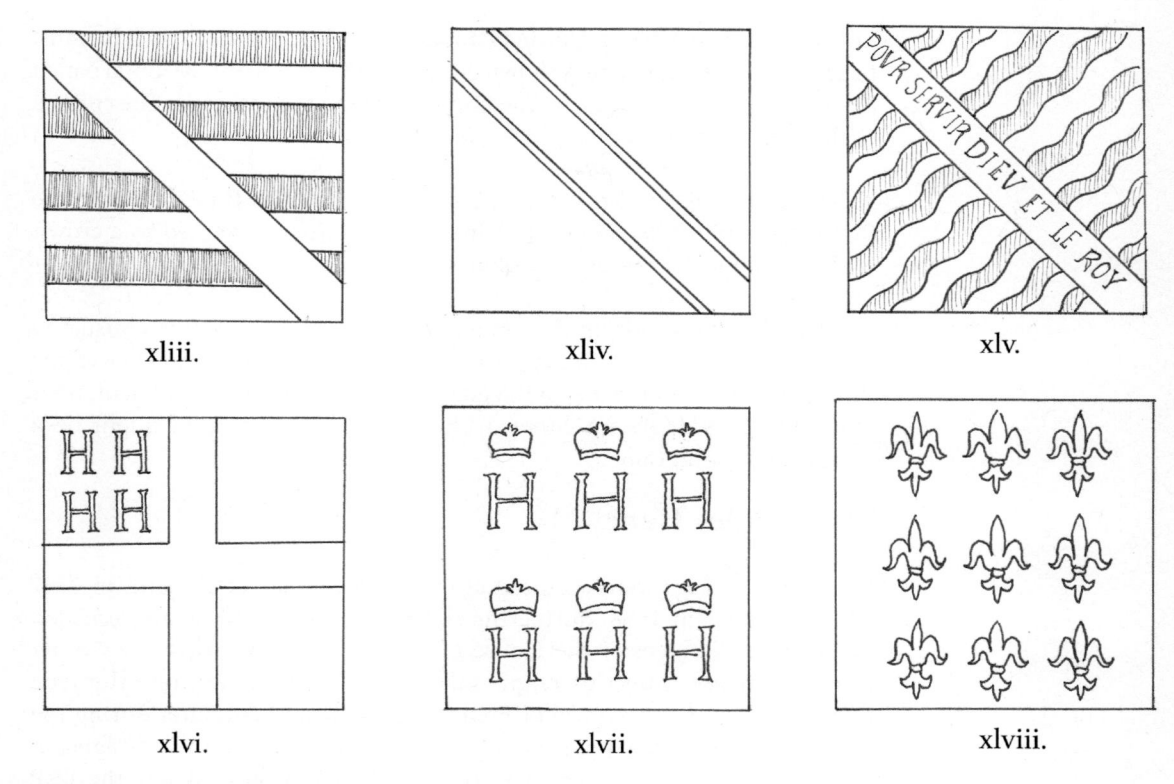

xliii.

xliv.

xlv.

xlvi.

xlvii.

xlviii.

Huguenot Infantry Enseignes

Most illustrations show little variation in Huguenot infantry enseignes. They typically have a bend on a plain field. A few variations are shown below.

XLIII. Occasionally the field of infantry flags is striped. The number of stripes varies from four to eight. They may be of more than two colours, but most illustrations are uncoloured so it is not possible to be precise.

XLIV. The bend on infantry flags might have a border. The version illustrated here is simple, but they could be scalloped instead. The bend could also be wavy.

XLV. This flag is shown being carried by the Huguenot troops sacking Lion in 1562.[71] It has a white field and bend with gold wavy bends sinister and motto POVR SERVIR DIEV ET LE ROY (For the Service of God and the King). This flag shows that there was more variation in the design of infantry flags than other illustrations may suggest.

XLVI. This flag is from a Hogenberg print showing Turenne defeating

---

71 'Le Sac de Lyon par les Calvinistes en 1562'.

Lorrainer force in Champagne in October 1592.[72] Most of the French Royalist flags depicted by Hogenberg shown either a simple cross or horizontal bands. Another shows a cross with a crown in each of the four cantons. The colours of these are unknown.

XLVII. This is also taken from a Hogenberg print, this time depicting the Royalist camp in 1591. Henry IV's initial, this time surmounted by a crown, is also prominently displayed. Colours unknown.

XLVIII. This is taken from the same source as the previous. It is unusual in showing the fleurs-de-lys on infantry colours. Given their use in later reigns, this could represent the flag of the guard regiment. The image is uncoloured, but gold fleurs-de-lys on either a blue or white background might be a reasonable assumption.

Flags under Henry II

Many French flags were captured at the Battles of Sainct Quentin in 1557 and Gravelines in 1558, during the reign of Henry II. These are recorded in the State Archives of the House of Savoy.[73] There are also a few other pictorial images from this reign. Taken together, they illustrate the type and colours probably typical of French enseignes and cornettes during the Wars of Religion a few years later. Given the complexity of their designs, in particular the cavalry cornettes, it seems likely that those shown in the T&P and Hogenberg prints have been greatly simplified. This is understandable, given the printing technologies available. Alternatively, it is possible that it was harder to tell friend from foe in a period of civil wars, necessitating the adoption of simpler, clearer symbols to identify the particular allegiance of the unit.

Cavalry Cornettes
The following are all long, swallow-tailed standards:

- Brown, white cross and a brown and white border
- Red, semé (scattering of small devices) of gold flames and bearing the Virgin and Child. Blue and white border
- Blue and white in four horizontal stripes, white cross overall, blue and white border
- Black, semé of cross of Jerusalem and double 'C's in gold. Near staff armoured arm holding a sword surrounded by a scroll of gold with the

---

72 Frans Hogenberg, 'Album met 345 prenten van Hogenberg', *Rijksmuseum Amsterdam*, <https://www.rijksmuseum.nl/en/rijksstudio>, accessed 22 March 2021.

73 Archives de l'État de Turin (Archivio di Stato di Torino), Enseignes prises à la bataille de Saint Quentin. Illustrations derived from Louis de Bouille, *Les drapeau francais de 507 à 1872* (Paris: Librarie Militaire de J. Dumaine, 1872) p.167 and Aldo Ziggioto and Andrea Rossi, 'Bandiere Francesi Tardo-Rinascimentali Insegne e Stendardi da una'antica raccolta piemontese', in *History & Uniforms* (Zanica: Soldiershop Publishing, 2016), Part 1 Issue Number 9 and Part 2 Issue Number 10.

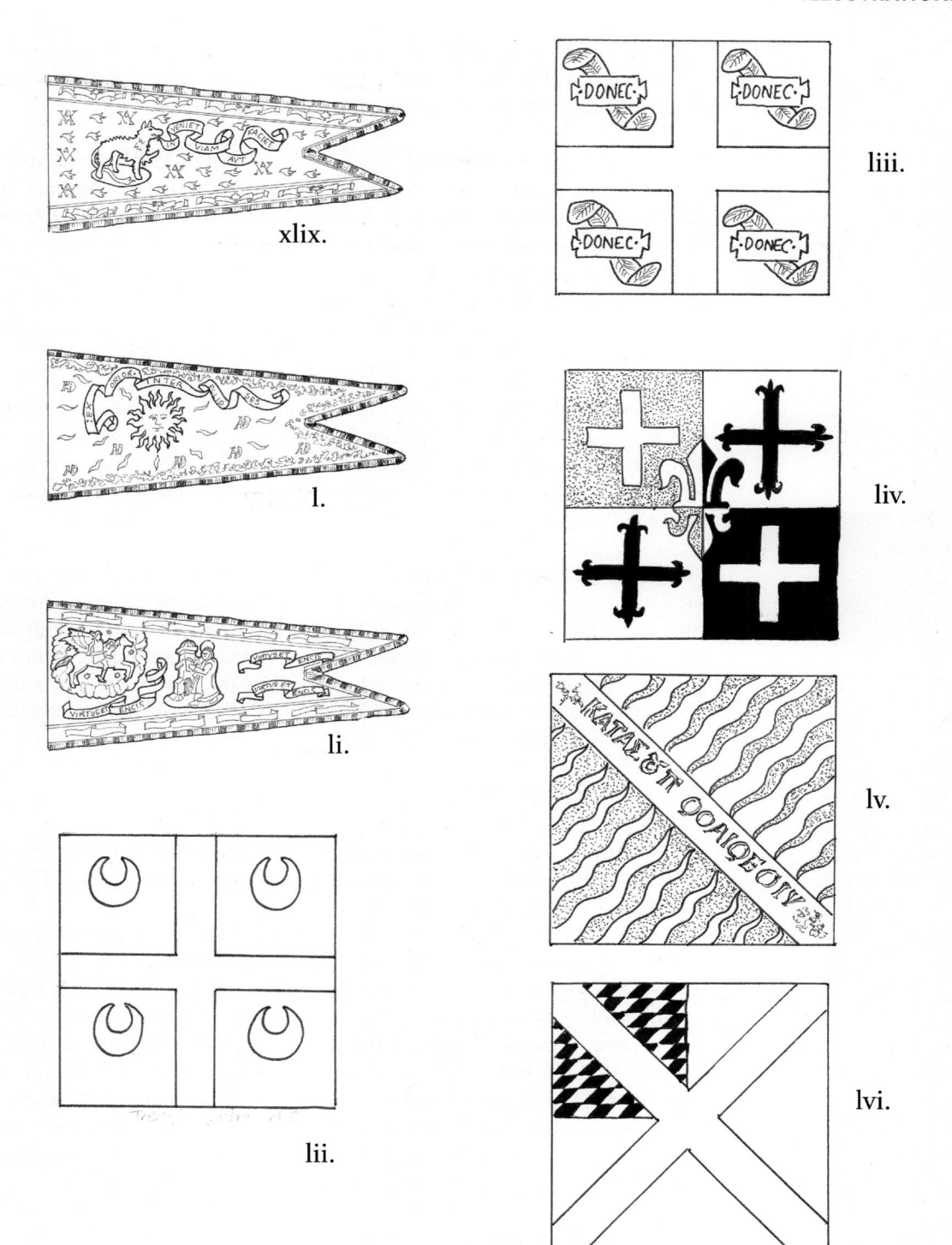

Flags under Henry II

motto FECIT POTENTIAM IN BRACCIO SUO (He Has Made Known the Power of His Arm). At the centre, the annunciation. Border red and yellow. This is the standard of Charles Duc de Lorraine.

XLIX. The standard of the company of Antoine Seigneur de la Roche Mabile et Vassé. A white field with a grey wolf on a light green patch of ground. The 'AV' initials, flames and scrolls are all gold. The scrolls in the border alternate. Those with palmate trees VICTO RIA HO NORATA (Victory Honours) and those with deciduous trees MOR TE CHA RA (Dear Death). The tree leaves are green and the letters black. The main motto is IN VENIET VIAM AVT FACIET (He Will Find a Way or Make One). The lining of the border is red. The fringe is white–red–blue.

L. The standard of the company of the Dauphin (Crown Prince), François (II) de Valois. The field is red. The foliate border, flames and sun rays are gold. The sun's face, monograms and scroll are white. The fringe is red and white. The motto in black letters reads EX ORIOR INTER ECLIPSES (Shine Between Eclipses).

LI. This is attributed to the company of Gaspard de Tavannes.[74] White field, scrolls, tower, clouds and Pegasus. Red lining to the border, Sainct Barbara's robe, Perseus' boots and Pegasus' wings. The sky is blue. Perseus' armour and shield and the saint's undergarment, halo and patch of ground are yellow or gold. Both figures have natural skin tones and the door of the tower is brown. The scroll letters are black and read VIRTUS TE ENCIS (Valour and Sword). The fringe is red and white.

The following are pointed, either with triangular or curved sides:

- Brown with brown and white border. Semé of gold flames. In the centre Sainct Barbara with two gold scrolls with the device VIRTUS EMICAT ARDENS (Valour Flashes Brilliantly).
- Another standard in white has the same borders, same charges and motto as above, but repeated on six instead of two scrolls.
- A third was brown with a brown and white border, bearing a gold cross and a gold scroll with the same motto as the previous two.
- Red, semé of gold crosses and gold scrolls bearing the words UT SORS VOLET, TAMEN STABO (Whatever Fate Wishes, I Will Stand). In the centre the Virgin holding the infant Jesus. Border blue, white and red. The motto is associated with the Mareschal Imbert de Bourdillon,[75] who was present at the battle, and so this is likely to be his personal banner or that of his compagnie of gens d'armes.

The final group are square:

---

74 Ferdinand de Liocourt, *La Mission de Jeanne D'Arc* (Paris: Latines, 1974) Vol. 1, p.221. Plate VII

75 Guy de Tervarent, *Attributes et symbols dans l'art profane: Dictionaire d'un language perdu* (1450–1600) (Geneva: Droz, 1997), p.181.

- Red with a gold cross dividing it into cantons. In each canton 'C' and 'T' intertwined, probably gold. Red and white border.
- Hoist red with six horizontal 'ragged' bands of white. Fly black with horizontal 'ragged' bands of white. Both divided by a vertical 'pale' (bar) in white.
- Red and white horizontal flames 'charged' (placed on top) with red and white stars. Overall a white bend. This shows that the use of the bend device on French flags predates the Wars of Religion.
- Brown with a red cross and, again, overall a white bend. Border red and white.

Infantry Enseignes

All the enseignes below have a white cross overall with coloured cantons (numbered one top hoist, two top fly, three bottom hoist and four bottom fly):

- Red (all cantons)
- Grey (all cantons)
- Sky Blue (all cantons)
- Light Green (all cantons)
- Red (all cantons), but in each canton the double cross of Lorraine
- Cantons one and four black, two and three yellow
- Cantons one and four violet, two and three white
- All cantons horizontally striped red, white, black, brown
- All cantons with vertical 'flames' (wavy triangles) of pink and blue
- All cantons with lozenges of red and white
- Cantons in three horizontal bands of red, blue, green, but in a different order in each canton
- Cantons one and four in horizontal stripes of violet and orange, two and four in wavy vertical bars of the same colour
- Cantons horizontally striped red, black, white with a black cross placed in the centre of the overall white cross
- Cantons two and three horizontally striped green and white; canton one white with green fleur-de-lys, canton four green with white fleur-de-lys
- Cantons in three horizontal stripes of 'dead-leaf' brown, white and blue, in canton two a crowned 'H' in red. Canton one and four blue, two and three blue with yellow bars.
- Cantons horizontally striped yellow, white, violet. On the cross the motto IN TE DOMINE SPERABO, NON CONFUNDAR IN ETERNUM (I Hope in You Lord, Never to Be Confounded).

LII. This flag is taken from the triumphal entry of Henry II into Rouen. It is black (all cantons) with white crescents in each canton.[76]

LIII. Red (all cantons) with a double-ended plume and cartouche carrying

---

76 'Relation de l'entrée de Henri II, roi de France, à Rouen, le 1er octobre 1550'

the motto DONEC (Until) in each canton. These devices were in white. This has been associated with Louis Duc de Montpensier, presumably because of the motto he adopted in honour of the King's mistress Diane of Poictiers: DONEC TOTUM IMPLEAD ORBEM (Until Her Orb Becomes Full). He was captured at the Battle of Sainct Quentin.

The following flags lack the white cross overall:

- Nine horizontal stripes of black and green. Overall, the double white cross of Lorraine.
- Horizontal stripes in white and black with the middle stripe red, carrying a small white cross with a white fleur-de-lys each side
- The same as above, but with two red stripes, so perhaps another company of the same regiment

LIV. Canton one red with a white cross, two and three white with black crosses fleury and four black with a white cross. Overall a fleur-de-lys, quartered white-black-red-white.

LV. Overall, a white bend. Lower hoist is red with white flames while the upper fly is white with red flames. The motto is in gold letters, which do not all seem to be Latin script. Its meaning is unknown. The leafy decoration on the bend is also gold. Overall, it has a similar look to the Huguenot enesigne, flag XLV, above.

LVI. Red field with the top hoist canton yellow and black lozenges. Overall, a white saltire cross. A square cavalry cornette depicted by T&P in their engraving of the Battle of Druex also shows a saltire cross.[77] It lies on the ground, so could have belonged to either side.

---

77 Benedict, *Tortorel et Perrissin*, p.19.

Glossary

Argoulet	A light cavalryman armed with a short arquebus. The term may derive from the Argolid, in Greece, suggesting a Balkan origin.
Armet	A close-visored helm.
Arquebuse	Harquebus; hackbut; a firearm used principally by infantry, normally some 1.4 metres long.
Avant-bras	Vambraces or lower cannons; armour covering the lower arm.
Avant-garde	Vanguard; normally one of the two major divisions of an army.
Banderolle	Pennon; a small flag flown from the end of a lance.
Bataille	Main battle; normally the largest sub-division of the army. Also referred to as the corps de bataille.
Baviere	Bevor or falling buffe; the term was used to describe both these types of guard for the chin and neck.
Bourguignotte	Burgonet; a peaked, open-face helmet.
Brassars	Rerebraces or upper cannons; armour covering the upper arm.
Caliver	A firearm longer than an arquebus but shorter than a musket.
Capitaine	Captain; commander of a company.
Carbin	Carbine; a short arquebus, about 90 cm long, but also the name given to cavalry that used these weapons.
Casaque	Cassock; a skirted coat worn over armour with false, hanging sleeves.
Cavaline	A type of light horse.
Chanfrain	Chamfron; armour covering the face of a horse.
Chevaux Leger	Light cavalry; horsemen slightly less well armoured and mounted than gens d'armes.
Compagnie	Company; an administrative unit of infantry or cavalry commanded by a capitaine.
Coronette	Cornet; a small, company sized, tactical body of cavalry, also the flag carried by such cavalry and occasionally the officer who carried it (otherwise the enseigne).
Courier	Courser; a warhorse, also called a Coursier.
Courtaut	A saddle horse, also Courtaud.
Coustilier	A servant of a homme d'armes, though originally an armed soldier.
Coutelas	Cutlass or Falchion; a curved, single-edged sword also known as a Badelaire.
Cuirasse	Breastplate.
Cuissots	Cuisses; armour covering the thigh.
Demi-Saye	Base; a heavily pleated skirt worn over full armour.

Enfans Perdus	Forlorne hope; small bodies of arquebusiers detached to act as skirmishers or to defend a particular location.
Enseigne	Ensign; third in charge of a company of gendarmerie, also a tactical company-sized unit of infantry or a flag.
Épieu	Boar spear; used for hunting but for military purposes as well.
Espee d'armes	Arming sword.
Esponton	Spontoon; a spear, often with an ornate head, carried by officers.
Estoc	Tuck; a long sword, normally carried from the saddle, used primarily to thrust between the joints of armour.
Flancars	Flanchards; armour covering the flanks of a horse.
Genoüillieres	Poleyns; knee guards.
Gens d'armes	Men-at-arms, whence gendarmerie, the body of armoured cavalry.
Greves	Greaves; armour for the lower leg or just the shin.
Guidon	A junior officer, fourth in command of a company of gendarmerie or a flag carried by cavalry.
Hautes pieces	Flanges raised from the spalière to protect the neck.
Hocqueton	Aketon; a coat worn over armour.
Homme d'armes	Man-at-arms; a fully armed and armoured cavalryman.
Jacque	Jack; a reinforced leather jerkin.
Mandille	Mandilion; a hip-length tunic open at the sides with sleeves generally worn unbuttoned and hanging loose.
Mareschal de camp	A senior officer charged with arranging the army's march and its deployment in battle.
Mareschal de logis	The most junior gendarmerie officer, as the name suggests, responsible for logistics, that is, the quartering of troops.
Mestre de camp	Commander of a regular French infantry regiment; as opposed to a provincial, volunteer, militia or foreign regiment.
Morion	An open helmet characteristic of arquebusiers.
Mougnon	Literally 'stump'; armour for the upper arm, between the brassar and spalière. These developed to cover the shoulder as well, replacing the spalière entirely.
Ordonnance	Ordinance; a statutory instrument issued by the king.
Petronel	A short arquebus or carbine, or a cavalryman armed with such a weapon.
Picorreur	Skirmisher or light infantryman.
Roussin	Roncin; a heavy horse 'of service' or 'service for war'.
Salade	Sallet; a helmet typical of the late fifteenth and early sixteenth centuries.
Saye	Surcoat, perhaps from the Middle French soye ('silk', in the same sense as a jockey's racing colours are called silks) a doublet with a heavy pleated skirt and, sometimes, short sleeves.
Scopette	A short firearm used by cavalry.
Serjent Major	An infantry officer responsible for drawing up individual units into their battlefield formations. The Serjent Major General performed this function for the army as a whole.
Spalière	Pauldron; armour covering the shoulder.
Tassettes	Tassets; articulated armour plates covering the hips.

Matters of Religion

In his preface to his historical novel centred around the Sainct-Barthélemy's Day Massacre,[1] G.A. Henty wrote in 1894, that: 'It is difficult, in these days of religious toleration, to understand why men should, three centuries ago, have flown at each other's throats in the name of the Almighty; still less how, in cold blood, they could have perpetrated hideous massacres of men, women, and children.' Sadly, recent history has provided too many examples of religious intolerance.

Many of the general histories of the French Wars of Religion were written in the nineteenth- or earlier part of the twentieth-centuries. At that time there was a general presumption that readers would be European or North American and that even those who had no particular religious inclination would have a general understanding of the main tenets of the Catholic and Protestant faiths and the differences between the two. As we now live in a global, multi-cultural and largely post-religious environment, a short explanatory note may be in order.

Despite the military focus of this book, the religious aspects are not irrelevant. It was the principal motivating factor of at least some, and perhaps many, of those combatants who took part (largely, it must be remembered, on a voluntary basis).[2] The relative importance of religion, as opposed to political, economic or social causes, has been widely debated. Even their contemporaries were subtle enough to distinguish between 'Huguenots of Religion' and 'Huguenots of State'. But if another distinction is drawn between religion on

---

1 George Alfred Henty, *Saint Bartholomew's Eve: A Tale of the Huguenot Wars* (London: Blackie & Son, 1894), p.V.

2 John H.M. Salmon (ed.), *The French Wars of Religion: How Important Were Religious Factors?* (Boston MA: D.C. Heath, 1967). Generally, the contributors tend to minimise the importance of religion. This is, in part, a reaction to the previous generation who were perhaps guilty of erring in the opposite direction. Carroll, *Noble Power During the French Wars of Religion*, p.2, suggests the pendulum of academic consensus has swung back the other way, commenting that 'Few historians would now challenge the central and autonomous role played by religion as a motivating force during the Wars of Religion.' Though his work focuses of the role of noble factions (or 'affinities' as he terms them) capitalising on this motivating force.

the one hand and faith on the other, and if religion is defined as essentially a political and social construct, then its importance must be deemed central.

The primary aspect of sixteenth-century religion in Europe that should be emphasised is that it was in no way a personal or private matter. Religion represented a set of public, social and cultural norms. Given that it was difficult to remain unobtrusive in early modern society, even in Paris, the only metropolis in France, if one did not attend regular corporate meetings (whether a Catholic Mass or a Calvinist Service) it was noticed and noted.

Equally important is to recognise that Catholicism was the state religion. It permeated every aspect of governance, as well as politics, education, economics and law. To stand against it was to stand against the state. It was an act of rebellion against the head of state, the king.

Protestantism sprang from the international challenge to the authority and supremacy of the Catholic hierarchy today known as the Reformation. It started as a call for internal reform of the Catholic Church, but, faced with opposition from vested interests and manipulated for political ends, it ended up creating a distinctive alternative. But Jean Calvin, indisputably the dominant figure in French Protestantism, did not champion freedom of conscience or the provision of an alternative to Catholicism in France; he sought to replace it. The Swiss city of Geneva, where he resided for the latter part of his life, became a virtual theocratic state under his influence and the religious structures he created dominated society no less completely than its rival in Paris, and possibly more so. He was also quite prepared to countenance armed resistance against monarchs who violently oppressed the common people: that is, resisted attempts to propagate the Protestant faith.

However, Calvinism was not synonymous with Protestantism. Large numbers of Protestants in the sixteenth century were Lutherans, following the teachings of the German ex-monk Martin Luther. They followed a less stringent and dogmatic approach. Initially, even in France, all Protestants were referred to as Lutherans. In England, the Anglican Protestant church was established, initially by Henry VIII and continuously after the reign of Queen Mary, as the state religion. It retained many of the outward trappings of the Catholic church whilst adopting most Protestant theology. It represented a compromise between different views on the matter of faith, and still does.

Calvinism, historically and currently, is strongly associated with short statements of faith known as the 'five points' or by the acronym TULIP:

- **Total depravity.** Humans are unable to gain salvation for themselves.
- **Unconditional election.** God choses those who will be saved.
- **Limited atonement.** Only the sins of the elect were atoned for by Jesus' death.
- **Irresistible grace.** It is not possible to resist God's salvation.
- **Perseverance of the saints.** Those whom God elects will remain in salvation until death.

In fact, these points were set out to define the Reformed Church's official dogma with respect to the competing Five Articles of Remonstrance published by the Protestant Arminian sect, rather than Catholicism. They were only formulated in the Netherlands at the Second Synod of Dordt in 1618, more than 50 years after Calvin's death. They do not necessarily represent the less codified views of the French Huguenots during the sixteenth century.[3] Nor were (or are) they a summary of the totality of Calvinist beliefs.

A further complication in the state of French religious affairs during this era was the strand of French Catholic thought dubbed 'Gallican'. Adherents held the view that the Papacy was not supreme when it came to determining the affairs of the Church in France (such as appointing archbishops), and that local affairs should be determined by them alone. The movement gained ground during the Great Italian Wars, during which Popes had been political and military opponents of French endeavours. Many of France's leading churchmen had Gallican leanings and were willing to consider some reform of the wider Catholic Church that would support a degree of local autonomy. Initially they were disposed to believe that Calvinism could be incorporated within their limited set of reforms. They would be disappointed.

Calvinists and Gallicans differed in the degree to which they challenged Papal authority. In the former case, this was total. They believed that the sole authority in matters of faith was the Bible itself, as divinely ordained scripture. In practice, this amounted to their particular interpretation of its meaning. In contrast, Catholics believed that the Church was the necessary and equally divinely ordained authority that mediated the relationship between God and his people. As such, it had the unchallengeable right to define what true faith looked like.

Another matter that divided these branches of Christianity included the degree to which good works were a necessary component of salvation. Calvinists argued that this was a freely given (though highly selective) gift of God and that there was nothing mankind could do to earn (or indeed, reject) this gift. The Catholic Church, partly no doubt with a view to encouraging crusaders or selling indulgences, was firmly of the view that faith required action if such salvation was to be assured or a lengthy spell of atonement in purgatory avoided.

Calvinists rejected the paraphernalia of saints, icons, holy days and most sacraments in favour of a more puritanical dogma of hard work, abstention and study. Many Huguenot aristocrats notably failed to exemplify these virtues, however. Calvinists also rejected the concept of a priesthood distinct from the body of believers, while simultaneously accepting that only those well-versed in theology should be allowed to preach or judge in matters of faith. As a result, they were hostile to religious communities such as monasteries and nunneries and often targeted these during civil unrest or military campaigns. To break down the distinction between clergy and laity, they used a Bible translated into French and other vernacular languages, rather than using the Latin of the Catholic Church. A printed French version of the New Testament section appeared in 1523, followed in 1530 by the whole text. This prompted Caterina de'Medici's quip, upon receiving the erroneous report of a Huguenot victory at Dreux, that they had all better get used to saying their prayers in French.

---

3   Geoffrey Parker, *The Dutch Revolt* (London, Penguin Books, 1985), traces the gradual suppression of the 'magnificent religious anarchy' (p.82), that existed in the early sixteenth century by the various church authorities in the context of the neighbouring Netherlands.

Colour Plate Commentaries

Plate A: Sack of Lion, 1562

These figures are taken from an oil painting by Antoine Caron,[1] a painter at the royal court, in 1565. It shows the sack of the city of Lion in 1562 by Calvinist troops.

Arquebusier
The vast majority of Huguenot soldiers shown in the painting are arquebusiers, though a few pikemen are clustered around a flag in the background and a pike lies on the floor in the foreground. The arquebusiers wear a mixture of morions and bourguignottes, some of which are gilded. About half of those in the foreground wear what appear to be padded jacques of buff- or brown-coloured leather. One has mail sleeves. In the background a figure carrying an arquebus wears a bourguignotte, cuirass and tassettes. If this is an accurate representation of such troops, it suggests that Huguenot soldiers equipped themselves with what they could acquire and bear to wear.

Serjent
This figure may actually be an arquebusier standing next to a serjent's halberd, as the other sergents in the painting have mail sleeves and a cuirass. Alternatively, the cuirass propped up against the cannon may be his.

Plate B: Sainct-Barthélemy's Day Massacre, Paris, 1572

These figures are taken from the only known surviving painting of the Calvinist artist François Dubois,[2] painted sometime between 1572 and 1584, showing the massacre in front of some of Paris' notable landmarks, including the Louvre. Although he had relatives in Paris, it is not thought that the artist witnessed the events first-hand. The painting shows both civilians and soldiers attacking Protestants. Several different contingents of soldiers are depicted. A group of Swiss, in their distinctive dress, are clustered about the

1   'Le Sac de Lyon par les Calvinistes en 1562'.
2   'Le massacre de la Saint-Barthélemy', *Musée cantonal des Beaux-Arts*, <https://www.mcba.ch/en/collection/the-saint-bartholomews-day-massacre/>, accessed 11 October 2020.

gates of the Louvre. A group of the The Maison du Roy, wearing tabards and carrying halberds, stand in another cluster. The remaining soldiers seem to be a well-equipped body of arquebusiers and pikemen. The latter have stacked their long weapons, obviously an encumbrance for the gruesome task in hand, against the wall of a building. It is likely that these troops belong to Strozzi's guard regiment, which was closely implicated in the massacre.

Arquebusier

Unusually, but not uniquely, as highlighted in the previous plate, many of the arquebusiers are depicted wearing cuirasses. The pikemen are similarly equipped. This figure, like most of his fellows, also wears a gilded morion helmet. He has a flask of powder typical of the period, but also a smaller one of a similar style. This contained more finely grained gunpowder and was used to prime the pan to increase the chance of a good ignition. The main flask seems to hang from the belt, rather than from a cord across the body as was normally the case.

Officer

A number of officers are depicted in the painting, carrying either espontons or swords and shields. Another gilded shield carried in the picture has a green and yellow fringe. The extant examples are circular, but many of those depicted, both here and in T&P prints, are decidedly oval. He has tied a strip of white cloth about his helmet. Other figures are shown with this tied to the upper arm or worn as a scarf. This was the field sign adopted by the Catholic forces (despite its similarity to the white scarf worn by the Huguenots) and is probably typical for this sort of insignia (for example, the yellow and black worn by the Protestant army at Moncontour).

Plate C: The Netherlands 1577–1583

These figures are taken from manuscript illustrations by Willem de Gorter compiled in 1610,[3] though painted a number of years earlier. They show French troops serving with the Dutch rebels against Spain.

Lancer

The first figure, along with two others similarly equipped, are labelled simply as French cavalry (Fransche Ruyters). They carry black-painted lances with triple-pointed red pennons. His blackened armour is of a distinctive Italian style often depicted in this period. A lance rest is mounted on the cuirass. His helmet is a bourguignotte with a baviere. The latter has bars that pierce the peak of the helmet. Towards the end of the century, cavalrymen carrying lances but incomplete armour were increasingly referred to simply as 'lancers' in both Dutch and French sources.

---

3   'Handschrift van Willem de Gortter, ms. 15662', *Royal Library of Belgium.*

Homme d'armes

The second figure is from an image depicting 'Fransche Ruyters van duc d'aleneson'. The three horsemen, all shown from the rear, are wearing decorated blue casaques with a white cross, though the detail on each differs slightly in arrangement. They carry unpainted lances with triple-pointed pennons divided horizontally blue–white–red. Given that they are wearing the white cross of France, the men may be members of Duc d'Alençon's regular compagnie of gens d'armes. The image is the only coloured example found showing the casaque in a reasonable amount of detail. In its general arrangement, the decoration resembles some of the casaques depicted in T&P prints. All three figures in the original watercolour wear narrow-brimmed hats and ruff collars. It is unclear whether their upper legs are armoured.

Plate D: Saincte Ligue Procession, Paris, 1590

There are multiple versions of this scene, executed both in oil paint and print, showing the procession by Paris' monastical and clerical orders in support of the 'Saincte Ligue'. The most notable being the painting attributed to François Bunel the Younger.[4] Amongst the clerics are shown several figures in more normal civilian/military garb. These may be members of the Paris city militia.

Drummer

This musician wears a distinctive suit of pale grey slashed and laced in red. Along with many other figures in the painting, he wears the double cross of Lorraine as a symbol of his allegiance to the Ligue. Although the ruff is still very much in evidence, this figure, like most of his fellows, has a falling collar instead. His tall hat with a conical crown and wide brim is the most common form of headgear.

Arquebusier

While many of the figures in the painting carry forked rests, none seem to be equipped with muskets. Their weapons appear to be arquebuses or calivers, though these have straighter butts than earlier examples. This figure's rich clothing suggests a man of some wealth. He probably depicts a well-to-do member of the civic militia. He carries his main and priming flasks hanging from his waistbelt alongside a coil of match. He also wears a red scarf, which was increasingly identified with the Ligue and its ally, Spain. This is fringed in gold.

---

4   François Bunel, *Procession de la Ligue dans l'Île de la Cité*, Musée Carnavalet.

Plate E: Royalist Flags

A. This is the cornette of Anne de Montmorency.[5] It its white, with an armoured arm emerging from a cloud holding a drawn sword, with the motto DEXTERA DEI VIRTUS MEA EST (Valour Is My Right). It was captured at the battle of Sainct Quentin, so technically belongs to slightly before the onset of the wars.

B. The personal standard of Charles IX.[6] It is a simple striped flag, but the colours are reminiscent of those used by Henry IV (see flag XVI, Chapter 5) and the banderoles of Alençon's gens d'armes (see Plate C). All predate France's adoption of the Tricolore, of course.

C. The standard of Sainct Andre.[7] The green field carries several motifs of an arm, emerging from a cloud and cutting a knot. The motto reads: NODOS VIRTU TE RESOLVO (Knot Loosened By Virtue). A similar cornette was captured at Sainct Quentin and also belonged to Sainct Andre. This had a green field and a white cross overall. In each canton there was an arm and knot device virtually identical to that depicted here.

D. This is a French infantry enseigne. The white cross on a red field is shown in numerous illustrations before, during and after the Wars of Religion. Incidentally, four of the senior French infantry regiments, the so-called Vieux Corps, had their origins in the Wars of Religion. Flags of this colour were carried by the Regiment de Picardie.

Plate F: Huguenot Flags

A. This is the cornette of Admiral Coligny.[8] It shows similarities to two flags shown in T&P prints. One has the anchor device (see flag XVIII, Chapter 5) and the other the wavy bars (see flag XX). Both are associated with Coligny in these prints. The motto on this flag reads AUDACE FORTUNAT JUVAT TIMIDO Q REPELET (Fortune Favours the Bold and Spurns the Coward).

B. A Huguenot infantry enseigne based on a design shown in a T&P print. The colours are conjectural, though a white bend (diagonal stripe) was typical and flags with black fields are depicted (for example, in tapestries).

C. The livery colour of the House of Bourbon was pale yellow or white. White banners seem to have been adopted by Louis Prince de Condé who was a member of that house (see flag XVII, Chapter 5). At the Battle of Jarnac,

---

5   Anon., *Les Drapeaux Français*, vol. 1, f.3 (Paris, Ministère de la Guerre, 1879). This rendition has the motto directly on the field of the flag rather than on a scroll, which would be unusual and unlikely.

6   Funcken, *The Age of Chivalry*, Part 3, p.79.

7   Anon., *Les Drapeaux Français*, vol. 1, f.63.

8   Anon., *Les Drapeaux Français*, vol. 1, f.25.

where he met his death, he carried a banner bearing the words 'Doux le péril pour Christ et la patrie' *or* 'Doux le péril pour Christ et son pays' or even the same motto in Latin, PRO CHRISTO ET PATRIA DULCE PERICULUM (Sweet Is the Danger for Christ and My Country).[9]

D. This is a reconstruction of the appearance of Andolet's standard. It is based on a watercolour of flags captured at Jarnac (see flag XXII, Chapter 5) and one shown in a T&P print (see flag XXIII). The more detailed illustrations of cavalry flags show them with a diapered (textured) background as shown here. This has been omitted from the other plates for the sake of clarity.

Plate G: Ligue Flags

A. This standard is shown being carried in a procession of clerical orders and civic militia in Paris in 1590.[10] The Virgin Mary standing on a crescent moon and illuminated by a sunburst was a common image in Catholic military iconography. The shape is unusual for an infantry flag, these being almost universally square or nearly so. It may reflect its ecclesiastical origins.

B. This is the cornette of Charles de Lorraine Duc de Mayenne's company of gens d'armes. It is described as a white enseigne sewn with black fleurs-de-lys. Although the banderoles of the gens d'armes were supposed to match the colour of their casaques, there appears to be no link between these and the colour of their cornettes. The casaques of Mayenne's gens d'armes were black velvet covered with silver crosses.

C. This flag is conjectural. Green was the livery colour associated with the Guise faction, although Mayenne's followers temporarily adopted black flags of mourning after the death of Henry de Guise. The cross of Lorraine was widely used as a device by the Ligue.

D. The cross potent was the most recognisable of the Ligue's devices. It is usually shown as red on a white field in coloured illustrations. Although technically not French, Lorrainer troops supported the Ligue on occasion. A Hogenberg print shows them carrying the arms of Lorraine on their flags: a yellow field with a red bend, three white eagles on the bend.[11]

---

9 Aubigné, *Histoire Universelle*, vol. 1, p.395.
10 'Première grande procession de la Ligue pour maintenir le moral des assiégés', *Carnavalet, Histoire de Paris*, <https://www.carnavalet.paris.fr/en/premiere-grande-procession-de-la-ligue-pour-maintenir-le-moral-des-assieges>, accessed 25 October 2020.
11 Frans Hogenberg, 'Album met 345 prenten van Hogenberg', Rijksmuseum Amsterdam, <https://www.rijksmuseum.nl/en/rijksstudio>, accessed 22 March 2021.

Plate H: Flags from the Reign of Henry II

Although dating from 1557, these flags were probably typical of those carried in the early years of the Wars of Religion.

A. It is not known which company or commander carried this standard.[12] It carries an image of John the Baptist and a motto repeated at the top and bottom. This reads: FATA VIAM INVENIENT IN MANIBUS TUIS SORTES ME (Fate Will Find a Way for Me Into Your Hands).

B. Again, it is not known who bore this cornette.[13] It is black with a gold dragon. Beneath the dargon's feet is a cartouche in red bordered in gold with the motto JE LE TIEDRAY (I Will Hold It). It also has a gold border and two gold flames.

C. This is a cornette belonging to François de la Tour, Vicomte de Turenne.[14] He was Anne de Montmorency's son-in-law. The motto reads, DIEU ET MA TOUR ET FORTERESSE (God Is My Tower and Fortress). This, of course, is a pun on the family name.

D. An infantry enseigne displaying both the white cross of Sainct Denys and the fleur-de-lys of France.[15]

---

12 Anon., *Les Drapeaux Français*, vol. 1, Folio 83.
13 Anon., *Les Drapeaux Français*, vol. 1, Folio 89.
14 Anon., *Les Drapeaux Français*, vol. 1, Folio 3.
15 Archivio di Stato di Torino.

Bibliography

Primary Sources, Memoires and Near Contemporary Histories
The sixteenth century saw an explosion of military memoirs and histories, many written by those who took part in the Wars of Religion (or those immediately preceding them).

Avila, Enrico Caterino d', *History of the Civil Wars in France* (London: Henry Herringman, 1678), translator Roger L'Estrange

Aubigné, Théadore-Agrippa d', *Histoire universelle du Sieur d'Aubigné* (Geneva: 2nd Edition 1626), 3 volumes

Brantôme, Pierre de Bourdeille, Seigneur de, *Discours sur les couronnels de l'infanterie de France* (Paris: Renouard, 1873)

Castelnau, Michel de, 'Mémoires de messire Michel de Castelnau: seigneur de Mauvissière at de Concressaut, baron de Jonville, comte de Beaumont, Le Roger etc.' in *Collection Complète des Mémoires relatives a la Histoire de France*, Volume 33 (Paris: Foucault, 1823)

Guicciardini, Francesco, *The History of Italy* (Princeton NJ: Princeton University Press, 1984), translator Sidney Alexander

Mergey, Jean de, 'Mémoires du Seigneur Jean de Mergey, gentilhomme champenois' in *Collection Complète des Mémoires relatives a la Histoire de France*, Volume 34 (Paris: Foucault, 1823)

Montluc, Blaise de Lasseran-Massencôme, Seigneur de, 'Commentaires de Messire Blaise de Montluc' in *Collection Universelle des Mémoires Particuliers Relatifs à l'Histoire de France*, Volume 24 (Paris: Roucher, 1786)

La Noue, François de, *Discours politiques et militaires du Seigneur de La Noue* (Basle: François Forest, 1587)

Rabutin, François de, 'Commentaires des dernières guerres en la Gaule belgique' in *Collection Complète des Mémoires relatives a la Histoire de France*, Volume 31 (Paris: Foucault, 1823)

La Popelinière, Henri de, *La vraye et entière histoire des troubles et choses memorables avenues tant en France qu'en Flandres, & pays circonuoisins, depuis l'an 1562* (Basle: Pierre Davantes, 1573)

Tavannes, Jean de Saulx, Vicomte de, 'Mémoires de très-noble et très illustre Gaspard de Saulx, seigneur de Tavanes, mareschal de France, admiral des mers de Levant, gouverneur de Provence, conseiller du Roy, et capitaine de cent hommes d'armes' in *Collection Complète des Mémoires relatives a la Histoire de France*, Volume 23 (Paris: Foucault, 1822)

Vitelli, Etienne, *Commentaires sur la guerre civile de France: de la surprise de Meaux à la Bataille de Saint Denis, 1567* (Paris: École de chartes, 2005) translator Anne Lombard-Jourdan.

Williams, Roger, *A Briefe Discourse of Warre* (London: Thomas Orwin, 1590)

A summary of military ordonnances is set out in the following work, which, despite its title, this covers the ordonnances and reglements issued from 1537, under François I, to those of Henry IV:

Ordonnances militaires tirées du code du Roy Henry III. Roy de France et de Pologne (Paris: Fougé, 1625)

This can be supplemented with:

Pierre Guenois, *La Conference des Ordonnances Royaux* (Paris: Boun, 1707)

Secondary Sources

There are many French works dealing with the political, social, cultural and local aspects of the Wars of Religion, but fewer recent offerings address its military aspects or the armies that took part.

Benedict, Philip, *Commentaire des gravures des Quarante tableaux de Tortorel et Perrissin source principale des commentaires* (Geneva: 2007)

Carroll, Stuart, *Noble Power During the French Wars of Religion* (Cambridge, Cambridge University Press, 1998)

Ceballos-Escalera y Gila, Alfonso de, 'Los estandartes de los caudillos hugonotes en la batalia de Jarnac, el 13 de marzo de 1569' in *Comunicaciones del XI Congreso Internacional de Vexilología* (Madrid: Sociedad Española de Vexilología,1985), pp. 298–301

Coudy, Julien (ed.), *The Huguenot Wars, an eyewitness account* (London: Chilton Book Company, 1969) translator Julie Kernan

Creveld, Martin Van, *Technology and War* (London: Macmillan, 1991)

Gustave Desjardins, *Recherches Sur Les Drapeaux Français* (Paris: A. Morel, 1874)

Duffy, Christopher, *Siege Warfare, The Fortress in the Early Modern World 1494–1660* (London: Routledge, 1979)

La Barre Duparcq, Édouard de, *L'art militaire pendant les guerres de religion* (Paris: Charles-Lavauzelle, 1864)

Coynart, Raymond de, *L'Année 1562 et là Bataille de Dreux* (Paris: Firmin-Didot, 1894)

Fuller, John F C, *Armament and History* (London: Eyre and Spottiswoode, 1946)

Funcken, Liliane and Fred, *Arms and Uniforms – The Age of Chivalry* Part 2 and Part 3 (London: Ward Lock, 1981 and 1982)

Gigon, Stéphan C, *La troisième guerre de religion. Jarnac-Moncontour (1568–1569)* (Paris: Charles Lavauzelle, 1911)

Harding, Vanessa, *The Dead and the Living in Paris and London, 1500–1670* (Cambridge: Cambridge University Press, 2002)

Hart, Marjolein 't, *The Dutch Wars of Independence, Warfare and Commerce in the Netherlands, 1570–1680* (London, Routledge, 2014)

Heap, William A, *Elizabeth's French Wars 1562–1598* (London: Unicorn Publishing, 2019)

Heath, Ian, *Armies of the Sixteenth Century* (Guernsey: Foundry Books, 1997)

Howard, Michael, *War in European History* (Oxford, Oxford University Press, 1976)

Jouanna, Arlette; Boucher, Jacqueline; Biloghi, Dominique; Le Thiec, Guy, *Histoire et Dictionnaire Des Guerres de Religion* (Paris: Laffont, 1998)

Knecht, Robert J., *The French Civil Wars, 1562–1598* (London: Routledge, 2000)

Lloyd, Howell A., *The Rouen Campaign 1590–1592* (Oxford: Clarendon Press, 1973)

Love, Ronald S., '"All the King's Horsemen": The Equestrian Army of Henri IV, 1585–1598', in *Sixteenth Century Journal: A Journal for Renaissance and Reformation Students and Scholars*, volume 22 (Kirksville, MO: Sixteenth Century Journal Publishers,1991), pp.345–53

Lynn, John A., 'Tactical Evolution in the French Army, 1560–1660', in *French Historical Studies*, volume 14 (Durham, NC: Duke University Press, 1985), pp.176–91

Noseworthy, Brent, *The Anatomy of Victory: Battle Tactics 1689–1763* (New York, NY: Hippocrene, 1992)

Oman, Charles., *A History of the Art of War in the Sixteenth Century* (London: Greenhill Books 1987)

Parker, Geoffrey, *The Army of Flanders and the Spanish Road 1567–1659* (Cambridge: Cambridge University Press, 1984)

Parker, Geoffrey, *The Dutch Revolt* (London, Penguin Books, 1985)

Phillips, Gervase, '"Of Nimble Service": Technology, Equestrianism and the Cavalry Arm of Early Modern Western European Armies', in Hammer, Paul E.J. (ed.) *Warfare in Early Modern Europe 1450–1660* (Farnham: Ashgate, 2007), pp.59–80

Potter, David, 'The French Protestant Nobility in 1562: "The Associacion de Monseigneur le Prince de Condé"' in *French History*, Volume 15, Issue 3 (Oxford: Oxford University Press, 2001), pp.307–328

Potter, David, *Renaissance France at War: Armies, Culture and Society, c. 1480–1560* (Woodbridge: The Boydell Press, 2008)

Read, Conyers, *William Lambarde and Local Government* (Ithica, NY: Cornell University Press, 1966)

Roberts, Michael, *The Military Revolution 1560–1660* (Belfast: Boyd, 1956)

Salmon, John H M ed., *The French Wars of Religion: How Important Were Religious Factors?* (Boston MA: D.C. Heath, 1967)

Susane, Louis, *Histoire de l'ancienne infanterie française* (Paris: Corréard, 1849) Volume 1

Thompson, James Westfall, *The Wars of Religion in France 1559–1576: The Huguenots, Catherine de Medici and Philip II* (London: Unwin, 1909)

Trim, David J.B., 'The Huguenots and the European Wars of Religion, c. 1560–1697: Soldering in a National and Transnational Context', in Trim, David

J.B. (ed.) *The Huguenots: History and Memory in Transnational Context: Essays in Honour and Memory of Walter C. Utt* (Boston, MA: Brill, 2011), pp.153–192

Trim, David J.B., 'Huguenot Soldiering c, 1560–1685, The Origins of a Tradition', in Glozier, Matthew and Onnekink, David (eds), *War, Religion and Service: Huguenot Soldiering, 1685–1713* (Farnham: Ashgate, 2007), pp.9–30

Turrel, Denise, *Le Blanc de France – La contruction des signes identitaires pendant les guerres de Religion 1562–1629* (Droz: Geneva, 2005)

Wood, James B., 'The Royal Army during the Early Wars of Religion, 1559–1576', in Mack P. Holt (ed.), *Society and Institutions in Early Modern France* (Athens, GA: University of Georgia Press, 1991), pp.1–35

Wood, James B., *The King's Army: warfare, soldiers and society during the Wars of Religion in France, 1562–1576* (Cambridge: Cambridge University Press, 1996)